The Principal's Leadership Counts!

Also available from ASQ Quality Press:

There Is Another Way! Launch a Baldrige-Based Quality Classroom
Margaret A. Byrnes with Jeanne C. Baxter

Charting Your Course: Lessons Learned During the Journey Toward Performance Excellence
John G. Conyers and Robert Ewy

Quality Across the Curriculum: Integrating Quality Tools and PDSA with Standards
Jay Marino and Ann Haggerty Raines

Permission to Forget: And Nine Other Root Causes of America's Frustration with Education
Lee Jenkins

Smart Teaching: Using Brain Research and Data to Continuously Improve Learning
Ronald J. Fitzgerald

Improving Student Learning: Applying Deming's Quality Principles in the Classroom, 2nd Edition
Lee Jenkins

Successful Applications of Quality Systems in K–12 Schools
The ASQ Quality Education Division

Futuring Tools for Strategic Quality Planning in Education
William F. Alexander and Richard W. Serfass

Insights to Performance Excellence 2006: An Inside Look at the 2006 Baldrige Award Criteria
Mark L. Blazey

Thinking Tools for Kids: An Activity Book for Classroom Learning
Barbara A. Cleary and Sally J. Duncan

From Baldrige to the Bottom Line: A Road Map for Organizational Change and Improvement
David W. Hutton

To request a complimentary catalog of ASQ Quality Press publications, call 800-248-1946, or visit our Web site at http://qualitypress.asq.org.

The Principal's Leadership Counts!

Launch a Baldrige-Based Quality School

Margaret A. Byrnes
with
Jeanne C. Baxter

ASQ Quality Press
Milwaukee, Wisconsin

American Society for Quality, Quality Press, Milwaukee 53203
© 2006 by Margaret A. Byrnes, Quality Education Associates
All rights reserved. Published 2006
Printed in the United States of America
12 11 10 09 08 07 06   5 4 3 2 1

Library of Congress Cataloging-in-Publication Data

Byrnes, Margaret A.
  The principal's leadership counts! : launch a Baldrige-based quality school / Margaret A. Byrnes with Jeanne C. Baxter.
      p. cm.
  Includes bibliographical references and index.
  ISBN 0-87389-679-3 (pbk. : alk. paper)
  1. School principals—United States. 2. Educational leadership—United States.
  3. School management and organization—United States. 4. Total quality management—
United States. I. Baxter, Jeanne, 1934–II. Title.
  LB2831.92.B97 2006
  371.2'012—dc22   2005036266

ISBN-10: 0-87389-679-3
ISBN-13: 978-0-87389-679-5

Publisher: William A. Tony
Acquisitions Editor: Annemieke Hytinen
Project Editor: Paul O'Mara
Production Administrator: Randall Benson

ASQ Mission: The American Society for Quality advances individual, organizational, and community excellence worldwide through learning, quality improvement, and knowledge exchange.

Attention Bookstores, Wholesalers, Schools, and Corporations: ASQ Quality Press books, videotapes, audiotapes, and software are available at quantity discounts with bulk purchases for business, educational, or instructional use. For information, please contact ASQ Quality Press at 800-248-1946, or write to ASQ Quality Press, P.O. Box 3005, Milwaukee, WI 53201-3005.

To place orders or to request a free copy of the ASQ Quality Press Publications Catalog, including ASQ membership information, call 800-248-1946. Visit our Web site at www.asq.org or http://qualitypress.asq.org.

∞ Printed on acid-free paper

Quality Press
600 N. Plankinton Avenue
Milwaukee, Wisconsin 53203
Call toll free 800-248-1946
Fax 414-272-1734
www.asq.org
http://qualitypress.asq.org
http://standardsgroup.asq.org
E-mail: authors@asq.org

ASQ
AMERICAN SOCIETY
FOR QUALITY™

To Sue, Donna, and Bill

We are better people because of our association with you.

"We can't solve problems by using the same kind of thinking
we used when we created them."

—Albert Einstein

Contents

Figures and Tables

Figures

Tables

Foreword

Principals shoulder the monumental task of leadership in a complex world. Although rarely compared to the duties of the CEO of some of our familiar corporations, the principal's role is often just as demanding and, some would argue, the stakes are just as high. Adding to high expectations are the pressure and dilemma of balancing leadership and managerial duties. As managers, they are concerned with organizing and directing; as leaders they must practice systems thinking and two-way communication and must build capacity for understanding while motivating the organization to achieve its vision. And principals are expected to accomplish all of this by modeling and demonstrating passion, spirit, and values.

This book is a leadership guide for principals who want to learn how to integrate the Baldrige criteria in the pursuit of performance excellence. It is the leadership companion piece to the first book by the authors, *There Is Another Way! Launch a Baldrige-Based Quality Classroom.* While the focus of this book is on leadership support and "how to lead," it leaves no doubt that leadership and management must be bridged. Unlike most midsize to large corporations, few schools have the luxury of employing one person as leader and others to manage. School principals are left with the task of balancing both, which is difficult at best and impossible for some. Unfortunately, leadership is the aspect that is most likely to suffer, especially in times of high-stakes testing and accountability. What is required is a paradigm shift with the realization that without visionary leadership, it is unlikely any school will reach performance excellence.

In 1987 the Malcolm Baldrige Award was established with seven criteria providing a framework for achieving excellence. In the 1990s, as schools and school districts began to explore continuous improvement through quality, the Baldrige office began to explore the feasibility of adding criteria for education and healthcare organizations, which were formally added in 1999. While the Baldrige Award is national in scope and recognizes organizations already at the excellence level, many states have initiated their own recognition system, modeled after the Baldrige, but more developmental in nature. Whether or not your state has a program, your school will achieve higher levels of success if quality is practiced within the Baldrige framework.

This book presents a straightforward way for principals to learn more about Baldrige-based quality, and how they can lead the necessary cultural shifts, and support classroom teachers in their efforts.

The principal is the key leader in this transformation, and therefore I highly recommend this book to all principals. As you absorb the content you will understand that the journey you begin is not for the faint-hearted, although the rewards are well worth the effort. You would not be in your current leadership role if courage and determination were not yours in large measure, so prepare to capitalize on this energy and become a role-model leader.

—Anthony S. Earl
Former Governor of Wisconsin

Preface

This is a book for principals, and it should also prove helpful to school leaders in the central office or at the building level. The authors hope that the readers sense the underlying admiration and esteem with which we view today's practicing principal. Common sense suggests that one leader cannot be asked to walk the tightrope of leadership, balancing the expectations of the visionary leadership with the managerial tasks of organizing and directing the many operations at the building level that should foremost include the learning needs of the students. Yet that is what we are asking the legions of principals across the country to accomplish every day! We wrote this book to build knowledge and give support to these principals because our experience shows that the Baldrige criteria, practiced with quality tools and continuous process improvement, does produce outstanding results. Add that to the fact that the criteria are based on solid research and, while they are nonprescriptive, provide a framework for organizational performance excellence.

Our hope is that this guide will help you learn more about the Baldrige framework and what it takes to reach schoolwide excellence, and gain the skills to start your school on the journey to performance excellence. The chapters in this book focus on the criteria aspects that we believe are necessary for everyone's journey, and therefore some details of the criteria may not be discussed in as much depth. However, at the ends of chapters 3–7 you will find a self-assessment checklist that does get into more criteria detail to use as a "yardstick" on your journey to performance excellence.

We would also recommend that you check out the Baldrige National Quality Program, www.baldrige.nist.gov, to obtain a free copy of the *Education Criteria for Performance Excellence* booklet. It is updated every other year and provides more detail about the Baldrige criteria.

This book is a companion to *There Is Another Way! Launch a Baldrige-Based Quality Classroom* (Byrnes and Baxter, ASQ Quality Press, 2005) and can be helpful as you work with teachers to support their Baldrige efforts.

The Baldrige framework implies giving up things you are currently doing only when they are no longer reaping the benefits you planned. The framework requires you to identify your strategic challenges and align everything (plans, resources, measurement system, materials, training, technology, and so forth) with your vision, mission, strategic goals, and objectives. It requires you, as a leader, to assist people in learning how to integrate all services and departments so that everyone is focused on reaching the strategic goals and objectives.

The organization of the book clarifies your role as a leader, not a boss manager. Baldrige is not an "add-on program" with a limited life span. Rather, *it is a journey* that becomes a way of life and doing business within your school or district. We have also included, "From the Trenches," a series of interviews with principals from CCSD-15 (Community Consolidated School District 15) in Palatine, Illinois. This diverse K–8 district of about 13,000 students was the 2003 Malcolm Baldrige National Quality Award Education Winner.

Wherever your school is now, it is not too late to start. The length of your journey will be never-ending, just as the drive for excellence is never-ending. However, you can predict better results when you follow the Baldrige path.

Acknowledgments

We owe a great deal of gratitude to the principals of Community Consolidated School District 15—Guy Hermann, Karen Hindman, and Jean Sophie, who agreed to be interviewed for this book. You demonstrate excellence each day and are role models for your peers. We appreciate your candor and your willingness to take time to speak with us in spite of very busy schedules. Your input will prove invaluable to our readers.

To the hundreds of principals we've been fortunate to work with over our careers, we thank you for sharing your insights, questions, and enthusiasm for our approach. You have inspired us to reflect repeatedly on our approaches, clarify our own thinking, and continually seek better ways to serve you.

We also want to thank Paul O'Mara, our editor at ASQ, for his patience, insights, expertise, and support. Amanda Hosey Dugan, our project editor at Thistle Hill Publishing Services, has once again been an invaluable asset. Her keen eye and abilities have made this a much better product. Thank you.

—Margaret A. Byrnes
—Jeanne C. Baxter

1

Why

Conversation with the Principal

We readily acknowledge the pull between manager and visionary leader that principals today experience, especially as you find yourself balancing the expectations of the board, central administration, teachers, and parents. At the same time, we recognize that your job is the most difficult and also the most important in leading any school to improvement. It is interesting to note that while school leaders hold the key to greater results and/or improved satisfaction among staff, students, and parents, few school districts provide support in the form of visionary leaders who act as skilled mentors. Perhaps this is because the availability of such leaders is lacking, or perhaps it is because the central administration and board of education don't see the value of such assistance. This book is intended to be a guide, not in lieu of a mentor, but a handy step-by-step document that can be referenced over and over along the journey.

We will begin by laying out the urgent case for change and share statistics about the high cost of non-quality. We believe you will agree with us there is no time to lose. School leaders must learn and model new skills based on systems thinking now if we are to give all students a chance at a successful future. Though accountability may be an impetus for change, it has thus far not been able to "carry the day" for systemic change as provided by the Baldrige framework for excellence. Yet, it is only through this approach that we can predict consistent, improved educational experiences of all our children and youth.

Driving Force of Change

Change is one of those odd things about life that happens even when we don't want it or think we need it. If you don't think your life has changed much, think about the past year or two. What is different now than it was before? Perhaps you've gained or lost family members or close friendships. Perhaps you've gained or lost some weight or hair or experienced other physical changes. You may have experienced a significant event such as buying or selling a house; made a major move to a new location; taken a new job or lost one; gotten married or divorced. Maybe you've learned something, such as a new hobby, or gone back to continue your formal studies. Maybe you have had to learn new things to survive. When you think about it, you quickly realize *nothing* stays the same. Change is inevitable, and the measure of a person is how he or she copes with it. This logic applies to changes in education as well as life changes. If you have been an educator long enough,

1

you have seen several cycles come and go, and probably you have ideas about whether we are better off because of the changes.

Most recently, the changes in education stem from accountability requirements at the federal and state levels. These resulted from increasing discontent from the corporate world, politicians, taxpayers, and others over the lack of basic skills and abilities students have when they leave our public educational system. Add to this the absolute necessity of an educated populace to support our democracy, and you can see why accountability is necessary.

Other issues that affect effectiveness and efficiency cannot be overlooked. These include the high cost of unfunded federal and state mandates, budget cuts, overcrowded classrooms, the teacher shortage, and buildings in disrepair. If we are to educate all children and be held accountable for high-stakes test results, any weak links in the educational chain can be disastrous. The need to be more efficient and effective has never been clearer, yet few understand the ultimate significance of even slight inefficiencies. Even one or two students who don't meet the grade-level requirements add up to enormous costs in opportunity loss and rework that zap the school of precious resources.

As evidenced by school violence leading to death or serious injury to students, faculty, and staff around the country, educators have problems with student satisfaction, persistence, civility, and respect for self and others. It is very troubling to hear about children or youth who endanger others by bringing weapons to school, worse when their random acts end in the deaths of innocent ones. Unfortunately, there seems to be a "disconnect" between understanding the root cause of such acts and the solutions adopted in response to zero-tolerance policies. If educators understood the cause of such deep-rooted hatred, anger, and rage, solutions might be found that would vastly improve the safety of everyone. This is clear evidence of a societal problem that has serious implications and has become an education system problem. Because of its seriousness, it requires schools to take steps to understand the causes and collaborate with local human service agencies and the community to find solutions.

For example, in both the Columbine (Colorado) and Red Lake (Minnesota) cases, the perpetrators were bullied by other students. Some say that "boys will be boys," or that "it is a rite of passage to haze younger student athletes." We don't know what caused those students to take lethal action against their classmates, but we are sure that all schools would benefit from a self-assessment process that would provide insights into system problems before they lead to a catastrophe. Adding more rules or imposing additional restraints without a complete and thorough understanding of the problem is another example of faulty thinking. Principals, however, have to respond to the public who naturally (during times of crisis) scream for immediate intervention. Wouldn't it be better to be proactive and work together so these problems never occur?

We are not advocating not responding immediately to instances in which student safety has been violated. Of course, protecting students and staff has to be a primary concern. We do, however, believe that the most effective approach after such incidents is to hold focus groups with students (being careful to randomly select students who represent all subgroups within the school, including ethnicity, academic ability, clubs, athletics, gender, special education (SPED), "floaters," and those who represent the counterculture), survey all students, and then collect and analyze the information and data. Based on a root-cause analysis, decisions can be made about strategies that will eliminate the problem. One of the worst things educators can do is change the rules for all when the perpetrators represent a very small percentage of the student body.

Principals, often caught in the crossfire between edicts from the board of education and central administration and the teachers, must understand the importance of *non-quality* and how it can "bring down any house" quickly. This chapter provides information about the high cost of non-quality that can be used to inform yourself, the board, central administration, teachers, and parents about the necessity for changing course and reforming (or, if the current system is too broken, reinventing) the building-level system.

When Basic Needs Aren't Met

As Dr. William Glasser (famed psychiatrist and father of reality therapy) notes, every human being has five basic needs: survival, love (respect), pride (in work and play), freedom (to choose what one does and pursue that which one enjoys), and fun. "Students who are hungry, sick, troubled or depressed cannot function well in the classroom, no matter how good the school," he wrote. Other experts have indicated a link between dropouts and students who are lacking in these needs. All in all, it is not a win-win situation for anyone.

In 2003, the Educational Testing Service (ETS) published a national report, *One-Third of a Nation: Rising Dropout Rates and Declining Opportunities* (see "Interesting Websites" to download a free copy). This report warns that little is being done to stem rising dropout rates and their economic costs. The following information shows certain groups of young people are more likely to drop out before graduation.

- Students in large cities are twice as likely to leave school before graduating than nonurban youth.

- More than one in four Hispanic youth drop out, and nearly half leave by the eighth grade.

- Hispanics are twice as likely as African Americans to drop out.

- More than half the students who drop out leave by the tenth grade, 20% quit by the eighth grade and 3% drop out by the fourth grade.

- More than 25% changed schools two or more times, with some changing for disciplinary reasons.

- Almost 20% were held back a grade, and almost half failed a course.

- Almost one-half missed at least 10 days of school, one-third cut class at least 10 times, and one-quarter were late at least 10 times.

- 8% spent time in a juvenile home or shelter.

- One-third were put on in-school suspension, suspended, or put on probation, and more than 15% were either expelled or told they couldn't return.

- 12% of dropouts ran away from home.

The gap between dropouts and more educated people is widening as opportunities increase for higher skilled workers and all but disappear for the less skilled. Even though in the last 20 years the earnings level of dropouts doubled, it nearly tripled for college graduates. Alarming trends on lifestyle and the future for dropouts are evident in the following statistics.

- Recent dropouts will earn $200,000 less than high school graduates, and $800,000 less than college graduates, in their lives.

- Dropouts make up nearly half the heads of households on welfare.

- Dropouts make up nearly half the prison population.

Additional findings from the study track dwindling high school completion rates throughout the 1990s, which persist today. The ETS researchers report that the national dropout rate has dropped to 69.9% in 2000, down from 77.1% in 1969. Even with this small improvement, high school completion rates have declined in all but seven states. In all but 10 states, it declined by 8 percentage points or more. In high school completion rates, the United States has slipped to 10th place in the world, making this a major national issue. It is especially disconcerting when we consider that Hispanics will become the majority ethnic group nationally before 2020, yet they have the lowest high school completion rates. While educators alone cannot resolve this crisis, the data most certainly points out the need for change, based on systematic analysis and problem solving.

Almost 45 years ago, James Conant, former president of Harvard University, called the dropout problem "social dynamite." The explosion has occurred, according to author Paul Barton: "At the same time that the dropout rate is increasing and out-of-school education and training opportunities are dwindling, the economic status of young dropouts has been in a free fall."

According to the ETS report, the reasons why youth drop out of school provide compelling information to educators, and they especially point to the need for systemic reform—not simply adding one or two more programs to further bandage the problem. Here are the reasons dropouts stated for leaving school:

- Didn't like school in general or the school they were attending

- Were failing, getting poor grades, or couldn't keep up with schoolwork

- Didn't get along with teachers and/or students

- Had disciplinary problems or were suspended or expelled

- Didn't feel safe in school

- Got a job, had a family to support, or had trouble managing both school and work

- Got married, got pregnant, or became a parent

- Had a drug or alcohol problem

When basic human needs are not met within the normal institutions of society, people seek other sources to have them met. Cults and gangs offer proof. Students who are not honor students, athletes, or active in clubs or the arts frequently become "lost" at school. If a student is average in a large school (we call these students "floaters") it is easy to overlook them and their needs. They become invisible. Some even drop out of school because, "none of my teachers know my name." (Translate that into "No one cares about me.") Others become more counterculture and join groups that share their views. Using their dress, make-up, tattoos, and body piercing, these students appear in "costume" to draw attention to themselves. They hang together and demonstrate their discontent with their more conventional peers.

Students out of the mainstream (usually based on skill levels or behavior) of school learn early that they will be treated differently by teachers, administrators, and fellow students. Many of these students, already feeling left behind, begin altering their behaviors and by the end of the third grade patterns have been set that are difficult to overcome. It is part of a downward spiral—the child can't read and feels the embarrassment and shame of not being like his peers. To compensate and out of frustration, acting-out behaviors (symptomatic of a deeper problem) start to appear. Teachers react to the acting-out behavior and isolate the child. Unless a successful intervention is achieved, this child is likely to begin dropping out of school in the early grades and therefore experience a loss of his or her future. It also spells the beginning of a huge loss to the community.

Calculate the Cost of Non-quality

Few people really seem to understand the high cost of non-quality and rework in education and the result it presents for communities. This formula was first developed by the author and published in *The Quality Teacher: Implementing Total Quality Management in the Classroom* (Byrnes et al., 1992). Initially, it was developed to draw attention to the faculty and staff from one small school district in the northeast about the urgency they faced when some of the teachers said, "Let's get rid of those kids [those failing two or more core subjects]. Let them drop out; it'll make our jobs easier." The formula and its results are as compelling today as they were in the early 1990s, and we present the updated research here. If your staff has a similar mentality as those from that rural district, you might plug in the numbers for your school or district and share the implications with them.

When Students Fail to Graduate

Nationally, the cost of students dropping out of school is extremely high and is, in itself, a powerful reason to change the way schools do business. To grasp the full impact we present these national data:

- Only 40% of 16–19-year-old dropouts are employed, and fewer than 60% of 20–24-year-old dropouts have jobs.

- Earnings for men ages 25–34 without a diploma dropped 34.7% (in 2002 constant dollars) from 1971 ($35,087) to 2002 ($22,903). Earnings for women in the same age group without a diploma went from $19,888 in 1971 to $17,114 in 2002.

In his article "Missing: Texas Youth—Cost of School Dropouts Escalates" for the *Intercultural Development Research Association IDRA Newsletter,* Roy Johnson writes, "The cumulative costs of students leaving public high school prior to graduation with a diploma are continuing to escalate. Between the 1985–86 and 2000–01 school years, the estimated cumulative costs of public school dropouts in the state of Texas were in excess of $441 billion."

An article in the *Journal of Quantitative Criminology* by Mark A. Cohen, "The Monetary Value of Saving a High-Risk Youth," reveals the following:

The typical career criminal causes $1.3–1.5 million in external costs; a heavy drug user, $370,000 to $970,000; and a high school dropout, $243,000 to $388,000. Eliminating duplication between crimes committed by individuals who are both heavy drug users and career criminals results in an overall estimate of the "monetary value of saving one high risk youth" of $1.7 to $2.3 million. That's just one student!

Each year's class of dropouts will, over their lifetime, cost the nation $260 billion in lost earnings and foregone taxes.

- In a lifetime, a male high school dropout will earn $200,000 less than a high school graduate and contribute $30,000 less in taxes (based on 2004 tax rates).

- In 2004, the United States spent more than $50.1 billion in cash assistance payments and food stamps (Temporary Assistance for Needy Families, or TANF) for individuals and families living below the poverty line. An additional $4.8 billion was spent on day care for mothers on welfare to work.

- 85% of juvenile offenders are illiterate.

- A year of Head Start preschool costs an average of $5,000 per child; a year in juvenile incarceration costs between $35,000 and $64,000.

- In 1999, nearly 104,250 teenagers between the ages of 14 and 18 were incarcerated for delinquency, up from 84,000 in 1995 (the most recent year for which data are available).

- Nearly 1.5 million teenagers not in school are unemployed. This is nearly twice the average unemployment rate.

- Dropout rates among children of migrant workers are estimated to be between 45% and 90%.

- One-third of public school students drop out nationally. The rate for some inner-city schools is 75%.

The Local Cost of Waste

Note: The following section is based on a Wisconsin school district in which 100 students did not return for the 1998–1999 school year. It provides an example of the potential costs to the district five years later.

Loss to the school district in state education funding:

- Lost state revenue per student = $8,000 (one year)

- Total lost revenue for 1999–2000 school year ($8,000 × 100 students) = $800,000

- Approximately 14.4 faculty positions lost because of the loss of $800,000 in state funding (In this district, new teachers are hired at $28,000, and the average teacher salary is $56,000. This formula calculates the average between the salaries of new teachers and other teachers, or 28,000 + 56,000 = $84,000.

Divide that in half, $42,000, to approximate the salary costs and add 32% fringe benefits. The calculated average cost per teacher is $55,440.)

Imagine an equal drop in enrollment each year over a five-year period. This district would have 500 fewer students than in 1998–1999. Even though enrollment may be rising, the cost to the district for the loss of potential revenues must be calculated. Assume that the amount of per pupil spending remained the same, at about $8,000 per year.

Over five years, therefore, the conservative estimate of the total loss of revenue to this Wisconsin school district is a staggering $4,000,000. This amount would equal a loss of about 72 faculty positions over a five-year period if no additional students came into the system.

Cost to Taxpayers in Lost Federal, State, and Local Taxes

Assume a high school graduate would earn (minimum wage $6.50/hour $\times$ 40 hours/week $\times$ 50 weeks/year) approximately $13,000 per year.

- The approximate loss of local, state, and federal revenue (based on 2004 tax rates) is $1,596 per year per individual or $159,600 per year for our 100 dropouts.

- Over five years, the amount of lost federal taxes is $798,000.

This does not even attempt to calculate the lost revenue from state income tax, sales tax, or property taxes. While dropouts may find temporary employment, and a fraction of the entrepreneurs may even become wealthy, the overwhelming majority end up with dismal futures.

Cost to Taxpayers in Public Assistance Programs

The federal government has passed sweeping welfare law reform since the early 1990s. Mostly, these reforms have focused on putting people to work and placing a cap on the lifetime of benefits. Currently, most states still allow single parents to get an education and count it as "work," but this may soon change. With this scenario looming, it is even more urgent for schools to adopt a systemic approach to reform and reduce the number of dropouts, especially teen mothers.

Look at the problem from a taxpayer's perspective, and the high cost of schools not doing the job right in the first place. For the purposes of this example, we assume that half of the 100 students who drop out take advantage of some kind of public assistance. The following is the approximate cost to taxpayers in welfare benefits, including Foodshare (Wisconsin's food stamp program) and Wisconsin Works, known as the W2 program, which replaced the federal assistance program (AFDC) that ended several years ago. These calculations are based on Wisconsin amounts, and for the purposes of our example we assume that half the individuals receive Foodshare and W2 assistance and the other half simply received Foodshare.

Individuals with dependent children:

- Fifty receive W2 Program assistance: $638 $\times$ 12 months $\times$ 50 households = $382,800.

- Fifty receive food stamps (parent and 1 dependent child): $274 × 12 months
  × 50 households = $164,400.

Single individuals with no dependents:

- Fifty receive food stamps at $149 a month: $149 × 12 months × 50 people
  = $89,400.

Total benefits paid to these 100 individuals for one year is $636,600.

Assume there are no changes in the number of individuals or in the number of people in the households receiving government benefits. Simply multiplying the aforementioned number by five years equals $3,183,000 in government assistance to this group of 100 Wisconsin high school dropouts.

This is a conservative estimate because it doesn't calculate other costs such as:

- Women, Infants, and Children (WIC) payments

- Medicaid

- Legal assistance

- Cost of juvenile justice

  —Court costs

  —Incarceration ($35,000 to $64,000 per inmate per year)

  —Restitution

  —Victim expenses

- Adult literacy and GED costs

It is staggering to realize the high cost of waste in education, especially if you were to multiply these numbers across the total number of dropouts nationally. We hope this exercise has allowed you to understand, with no uncertainty, the problems that exist in education and the enormous and psychological costs that accompany them. This is one, if not the primary reason, why the No Child Left Behind law was enacted, and while it may be flawed and underfunded, it has brought accountability to the forefront of educators' minds.

If you lead a private or parochial school, you may not feel the stress of accountability that your public school peers do. Boards of most schools, however, do expect students to learn and be able to apply their learning to other tasks. It is a smart principal who brings data to demonstrate the effectiveness and efficiency of the school when making a presentation to the board and parents. These data, when trended, can prove to be strong selling points for student and faculty recruitment or as motivation for staff development funds to help teachers improve instruction.

If you lead a public elementary or middle school you may not think the aforementioned formula has much to do with what's happening at your school. On the contrary; the research is quite clear. It affects your school on two levels. First, students who fall two or more years behind in reading are on a fast track for dropping out or opting out of school. Unless targeted interventions are designed and delivered appropriately, there is little chance these students will be able to make up their learning deficiencies. Second, when students' needs and expectations are not met, they turn to more destructive ways to cope with life. These behaviors may be caused in part by bullying, relentless teasing, or the need to get attention. Frequently the acting-out behavior begins in the early grades and becomes magnified each year if appropriate interventions are not taken. Now, more than ever with an increase in non-English-speaking or limited-English-speaking immigrants, the challenges for every grade and level of school are magnified.

Stressors on a School

A part of the problem is that educators have not received adequate training and professional development in systems thinking and, because of that, aren't certain how to align and integrate their district or school to reach the goals. Add to that the lack of accountability over the years from accrediting institutions and from staffers in state departments of education who serve as inspectors. These same staffers might be service providers who lend assistance, provided they have the skills lacking at the local level.

We recognize poverty as one of the most critical issues, but it is not new. There are examples around the country where students attending schools in high-poverty areas have had impressive results. One such example is Charles R. Hadley Elementary School in Miami, Florida. There is the added stress on education systems from students who are non-English speakers or have limited English-speaking abilities, while too few teachers are bilingual or multilingual. As more immigrants come without literacy skills in their native language, the difficulties become staggering in some parts of the country. Frequently, immigrant children also live below the poverty line, complicating their problems.

Other major issues confronting educators include a breakdown of civility and too many children lacking adequate supervision from parents or guardians, who are working more hours to make ends meet. These students are used to doing what they want, often spending too many hours in front of television, playing video games, or listening to music with violent and explicit lyrics. The violence and lack of civility reported by the news media and portrayed by the entertainment industry also adversely contribute to students' school experience.

We also cannot ignore the issues associated with unprepared or underprepared teachers and those in schools lacking a visionary leader who understands systems and also the skills to inspire and motivate everyone to become part of the solution. Dr. Robert Marzano, a leading educational researcher, has studied the results of teacher effectiveness research over 35 years and summarized it in a must-read book, *What Works in Schools: Translating Research into Action* (ASCD, 2003). Table 1.1 shows his conclusions about the effects of student achievement compared with school and teacher effectiveness when students enter a school at the 50th percentile on previous normed tests (Marzano, 2003, pp. 74–75).

Further, Marzano (p. 10) concurs with the research literature "that the school (as opposed to the district) is the proper focus for reform. Indeed, this is a consistent conclusion in the research literature [Scheerens & Bosker, 1997; Reynolds & Teddlie, 2000; Wang, Haertel, & Walberg, 1993]."

Table 1.1 Marzano's research on the impact of school and teacher effectiveness and student scores on normed tests.

School and teacher scenario	Student percentile score after 2 years	Net gain (loss)
Average school—average teacher	50th percentile	No change
Least effective school and least effective teacher	3rd percentile	47 percentile-point loss
Most effective school and least effective teacher	37th percentile	13 percentile-point loss
Least effective school and most effective teacher	63rd percentile	13 percentile-point gain
Most effective school and most effective teacher	96th percentile	46 percentile-point gain
Most effective school and average teacher	78th percentile	28 percentile-point gain

Getting from Where You Are to Where You Want to Be

A case in point is CCSD-15, the 2003 Baldrige Education–winning K–8 district in the northwest suburbs of Chicago that began its Baldrige journey in the late 1990s after winning the Illinois State Lincoln Award. The superintendent, Dr. John Conyers, with board approval, set student performance targets: 90% of those attending school for one school year must meet or exceed grade-level expectations on the normed tests given at each grade level. Two things forced the district leaders to standardize their key learning processes. First, while their results were above the national average, it was clear (based on trend data) the current instructional process was not capable of yielding the desired results (for example, every teacher had his/her own process and there was no consistency among schools). Second, as the district's demographics began a more rapid change and more students with limited or no English-speaking skills enrolled, the administration and teachers realized the current interventions were not working.

In response to this, the district began to analyze the problem. It drilled down into the data and identified each student who did not meet the requirements. From an analysis of the data, the leadership decided to standardize the instructional process throughout the district. What you see in Figure 1.1 is the result of CCSD-15's newly designed, standardized instructional process. All teachers received training in the process. As a result of this approach, the schools improved the way instruction was delivered and more students met the targets.

To address the strategic objective of improved student learning results, the district designed an additional process for those identified in the academic warning or does not meet (DNM) category based on the previous year's results (Figure 1.2). Academic warning meant a student was so close to not meeting the standards that on any given day, she or he might not have been successful. Please note that for the at-risk students, teachers were expected to report monthly or weekly on the progress of each identified student. This in-process measurement system, along with leadership monitoring, made a huge difference in the end result. You'll learn more about process design and implementation in chapters 4 and 6.

Meanwhile, reading specialists from the Division of Curriculum and Instruction (C/I) researched and designed an early intervention approach for kindergarten and first- and second-graders identified in the "at risk of not meeting the targets" group. Training was

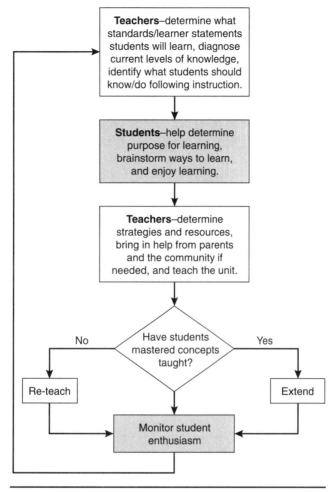

Figure 1.1 CCSD-15 instructional process flowchart.

provided to individuals responsible for implementing the intervention programs, and a measurement system was put into place allowing the Division of Curriculum and Instruction to monitor in-process results.

At the same time, CCSD-15 was improving its student support services, especially SPED services, and expanding the capacity of all employees through training on the Plan-Do-Study-Act improvement process. Teachers received training in the use of quality tools and began to use student feedback as a regular way to improve instruction and other classroom processes. In schools where student satisfaction survey results showed the students didn't think they respected one another, one of the School Improvement Plan goals was related to this issue. Schoolwide Plan-Do-Study-Act improvement cycles were undertaken (more on PDSA in chapters 3 and 7), and students began to treat one another with greater respect. The importance of balancing student satisfaction, enthusiasm for learning, and feeling safe at school with the focus on improved learning results cannot be understated.

Because every system has its challenges, it is important to identify them. Challenges are opportunities for improvement. They are not excuses. Brazosport Independent School District in Freeport, Texas, also standardized its instructional process to eliminate gaps between student subgroups with impressive results (refer to the Recommended Readings).

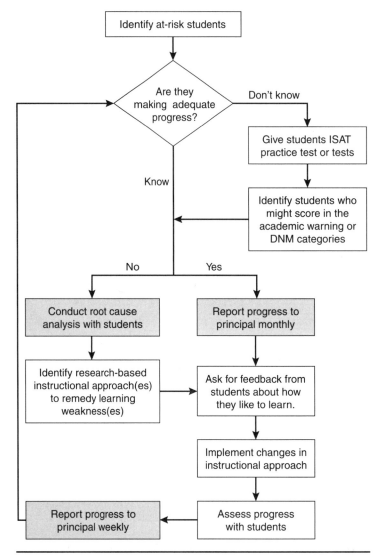

Figure 1.2   CCSD-15 at-risk process flowchart.

In the Chugach School District in Anchorage, Alaska (a 2001 Baldrige Education winner), all students are considered at-risk, and because the district is spread across 22,000 square miles the administration instituted Individual Education Plans (IEPs) and individualized competency-based computer instruction for all students. The increase in student learning results were phenomenal and primarily caused by improvements in the learning-centered processes. Pearl River School District in New York, which had previously demonstrated above-average student learning results (a 2001 Baldrige Education winner), was faced with changes in state policy that required all students to graduate with a Regents diploma (much more rigorous requirements related to passing the Regents Exams). This significantly raised the bar on expectations of students. By mapping the curriculum, altering the instructional process, and using in-process measures this school district was able to meet the challenge.

No matter what your circumstances, the Baldrige framework can help guide your school to performance excellence. While the Baldrige approach requires you to identify your key challenges, it also helps you understand how to align and integrate the system to adequately address them. The results provide you with a picture of how well your plans addressed the challenges.

The Goal Is Effectiveness and Efficiency

The goal of every school and school district remains the same: Improve effectiveness (achieve the vision, mission specificity, and strategic goals) and efficiency (faster, eliminate problems, and with fewer resources). Figures 1.3 and 1.4 provide a graphic representation of this concept.

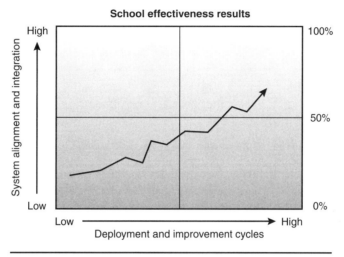

Figure 1.3 Effectiveness increases with deployment and cycles of improvement.

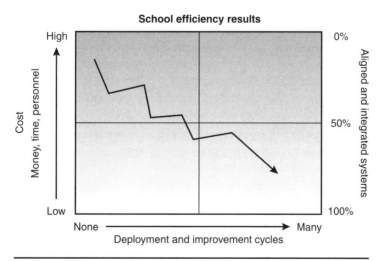

Figure 1.4 Efficiency improves with deployment and cycles of improvement.

Effectiveness measures include such things as student learning results; student, parent, staff, and stakeholder satisfaction; value-added comparing per pupil expenditure and achievement increases; professional development training and improved learning results; hiring practices yielding improved diversity among faculty and staff; graduation rates; attendance; and so forth.

Examples of efficiency measures include decrease in cycle time for students to meet IEP goals and removal from SPED services, turnaround time for maintenance or technology equipment repairs, on-time bus rates, a decrease in number of students reading two or more grade levels behind peers, a decrease in cycle time for changes in course offerings, and so forth.

The Baldrige criteria use a self-assessment approach to identify the gaps in efficiency and effectiveness. Then the criteria become a guide to teach you to align and integrate all aspects of your system to improve all results.

Why a School Can't Fix Itself

Dr. W. Edwards Deming (the father of modern quality upon whose theory the Baldrige framework is based) believed that it is almost impossible to turn a system around without help from the outside. The reason is simple—those on the inside have a one-dimensional view of the system and its problems and opportunities. It doesn't mean a leader is incapable; it simply indicates that competent outsiders can see things that may not be evident to you in the system. The right coach can provide guidance and become a trusted mentor along the way to a better future.

The most significant thing to be learned from using the Baldrige criteria as a self-assessment instrument is where the gaps exist in key processes that lead directly to the results. *If you are not happy with the results you are getting, learning about your system using the Baldrige framework will be invaluable and save you and the organization valuable, often nonrenewable resources.* We can say that with confidence because so many schools and school districts have tried one thing or another, paying lots of money to purchase new curricula, textbooks, software, and other programs, only to discover that the problems are not solved. If you knew where to start your improvement efforts, based on information gleaned from a self-assessment, wouldn't it be helpful? If you had a self-assessment instrument that asked critical, research-based questions that require you really to evaluate *what you do, how you do it, how often, and how "lessons learned" are used to improve,* would it be helpful?

You may be thinking, "I don't have time to do this. I am swamped and overworked already. We are not meeting the requirements for student learning, and I've got to put all my energy into that. This (the Baldrige framework) is just more work for me and for my staff, who are already overworked, burned out, and threatening to quit." If so, you have just stated the compelling reasons for learning about and using the Baldrige approach.

This book offers hope for school leaders by providing a systematic process, using the Baldrige framework, for achieving a different end result. Our children and youth, families, communities and the nation—indeed, our democracy—hinges on decisions you will make today and in the future. There is no more time to think about it. It is time to act.

Summary

Now that you've learned about the high cost of non-quality, we think you'll agree with us that we can no longer afford the current situation. The time to begin is now, and it is the authors' intent that you use this book as your guide and coach as you learn to engage your staff in achieving performance excellence.

In the following six chapters, you will find the knowledge base and support needed to lead a Baldrige-based quality school. You will learn about the Baldrige framework and the glue that holds it together—the core values—and how to link the Baldrige criteria and quality tools to your school's vision, strategic planning and instructional practices. Most important, you will learn how to make data-driven decisions, to measure and monitor key learning processes, and to get results. This is what we call practicing visionary leadership. You are the cheerleader who inspires and draws the organization together in support of the vision. Although you need a basic knowledge of the managing side of data-driven decision making, there are parts that you will want to delegate. Through it all, you will build a team that supports one another, acknowledging that all are important players contributing to performance excellence.

It has been our experience in working with and listening to Baldrige-based, quality-practicing principals that once you begin, you will never go back.

2
Systems and the Baldrige Framework

Conversation with the Principal

This chapter makes the case for systems thinking and how vital it is to understand it within the school context. If you have been practicing quality, you will immediately see the connection with the Baldrige criteria. You will also learn how the Baldrige core values are embedded and how the seven criteria categories relate to school improvement. If you are new to both quality and Baldrige, however, take more time to think about what you are reading and how your circumstances might "fit." Systems thinking is not a lofty business idea; it can and must be understood and practiced by everyone in the school. As principal, you are positioned to be the "lead learner" and the leader who sets the direction. We understand that taking the first steps take courage, so swallow hard and get going!

An Introduction to Systems Thinking

Systems thinking is essential for moving your school from where it is to a position of excellence. Deming, in his book *The New Economics for Industry, Government, Education,* states:

> A system is a network of interdependent components that work together to try to accomplish the aim of the system. A system must have an aim. Without an aim, there is no system. The aim of the system must be clear to everyone in the system. The aim must include plans for the future. The aim is a value judgment. (p. 50)

Deming goes on to say:

> It is management's job to direct the efforts of all components toward the aim of the system. The first step is clarification: everyone in the organization must understand the aim of the system and how to direct his efforts toward it. Everyone must understand the danger and loss to the whole organization from a team that seeks to become a selfish, independent, profit centre. (p. 50)

Although the reference to profit centers is not applicable to public schools, the message Dr. Deming is trying to get across is clear: When one department or one group within a school believes it is the most important, the whole school ultimately loses. For example, at a high school you might have advanced placement (AP) teachers claiming that more resources ought to be devoted to their classes because "it is imperative that the students pass the AP test." Or, you might hear parents and the athletic director wanting to change the requirements for graduation so that the most gifted athletes are given relief from academic requirements and that all athletes receive academic credit for varsity athletics. Another example would be cutting class size for K–1 down to 16 per class, necessitating an increase in class size for grades 2–5 to 32 or 35. While arguments might be made for any of these situations, Dr. Deming's point would be that everyone needs to understand the impact of each decision on the whole system and work together to accomplish the aim of the organization.

In the latter example, while ABC School can brag about how advanced its early learners are when they leave first grade, a look at how well students do in grades K–5 is the true test of an elementary school. It might be that students leave the first grade with all the skills needed to be successful in second grade, but large class sizes might result in a reduction of learned skills and lower normed test results when students are not able to receive the attention needed all through the elementary years.

A School System

A system is a series of processes linked together to achieve the aim of the organization. A school may be a subsystem of a school district, or it may be a system of its own. Charter schools, private schools, independent schools, and some parochial schools are examples of the latter. Figure 2.1 shows a high-level view of a school district–level system and a school-level system. If your school is part of a larger district, this is how you fit into the larger system. In such a situation, alignment at the school level with the district's aim, mission, and goals and integration of all services is vital. If you are a stand-alone school, alignment and integration is essential of all departments, services, and classrooms to achieve excellence.

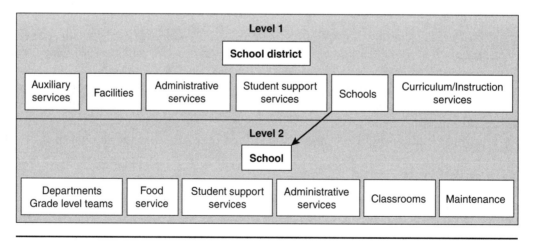

Figure 2.1 High-altitude look: Levels of district subsystems.

Figure 2 .2 gives details about a school-level system. Specifically, it is important that the school leader understand how changing one part of the system automatically affects every other part of the system. Failure to recognize this often leads to tinkering with the system. The result might be that new problems occur in areas where previously there were none, or minor problems suddenly become large problems. Neither of these is desired, so to avoid

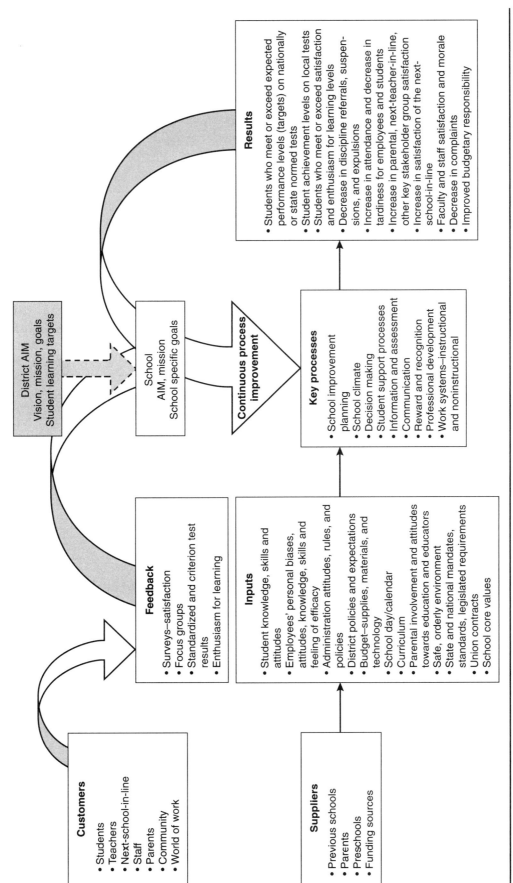

Customers
- Students
- Teachers
- Next-school-in-line
- Staff
- Parents
- Community
- World of work

Suppliers
- Previous schools
- Parents
- Preschools
- Funding sources

Feedback
- Surveys–satisfaction
- Focus groups
- Standardized and criterion test results
- Enthusiasm for learning

Inputs
- Student knowledge, skills and attitudes
- Employees' personal biases, attitudes, knowledge, skills and feeling of efficacy
- Administration attitudes, rules, and policies
- District policies and expectations
- Budget–supplies, materials, and technology
- School day/calendar
- Curriculum
- Parental involvement and attitudes towards education and educators
- Safe, orderly environment
- State and national mandates, standards, legislated requirements
- Union contracts
- School core values

District AIM
Vision, mission, goals
Student learning targets

School
AIM, mission
School specific goals

Continuous process improvement

Key processes
- School improvement planning
- School climate
- Decision making
- Student support processes
- Information and assessment
- Communication
- Reward and recognition
- Professional development
- Work systems–instructional and noninstructional

Results
- Students who meet or exceed expected performance levels (targets) on nationally or state normed tests
- Student achievement levels on local tests
- Students who meet or exceed satisfaction and enthusiasm for learning levels
- Decrease in discipline referrals, suspensions, and expulsions
- Increase in attendance and decrease in tardiness for employees and students
- Increase in parental, next-teacher-in-line, other key stakeholder group satisfaction
- Increase in satisfaction of the next-school-in-line
- Faculty and staff satisfaction and morale
- Decrease in complaints
- Improved budgetary responsibility

Figure 2.2 Detailed school-level system diagram.

such issues the school leader must understand the whole system and how each part contributes to the results, and be able to articulate it to all employees and other stakeholders.

In his book *The New Economics,* Dr. Deming speaks eloquently about destruction of any system because leaders don't understand systems thinking and how to put processes into place to address issues systemically. Dr. Russell Ackoff, a systems expert, described the situation using this analogy. If you were able to take only the "best" parts of any car and put them together, you would not have a working automobile. Why? It is because the individual parts would not form a system. They would not be compatible with the other individual parts, and therefore would not work together.

There is a lesson for school leaders in this analogy. School leaders must understand each component of the school (building-level) system, the interactions with every other component, and seek ways to improve the whole system. Anything short of that leads to tampering with the system, which usually makes things worse. As an example, review the issue of smaller class size for kindergarten and first grade. Although it is a great idea to optimize the effectiveness of such an approach, changes to other parts of the system would have to be put into place as well. The overall cost must be considered, especially when there are limited dollars. In a site-base managed school, therefore, the leader must consider all the ramifications to the rest of the system because of decisions to improve one aspect. If you "copycat" another school's system without considering the unique elements of your own, you may not make the gains you counted on.

Another example is paying large sums to buy and implement a one-on-one reading program to improve reading abilities for all students. Such reading programs work naturally, because they give special attention to a very few people, but at the same time they are very expensive (high labor, training, and materials costs). We would expect them to work wonders, but at what expense? How many other students are left behind because the resource allocation went so heavily in favor of a one-on-one program? A wise leader would seek alternatives that yield positive results for many more students, leaving more resources available for the greater good and therefore system improvement.

Malcolm Baldrige National Quality Award Program

Historical Perspective

When President Ronald Reagan signed the Baldrige National Quality Program into law on August 20, 1987, he did so because of a need to recognize manufacturing and business for performance excellence. Award winners were considered role model organizations with processes leading to excellence in the products or services delivered. The hope was that other organizations would learn from Baldrige Award winners and that performance excellence would improve America's economy during the 1990s. The Baldrige program has expanded and now includes criteria for small business, healthcare, education, government, and nonprofits.

A Common Language

Figure 2.3 shows the Baldrige framework for education. Not only do the criteria provide a common language for business, manufacturing, healthcare, education, and nonprofits, but the requirements are also nonprescriptive and adaptable to each organization. Minor language changes to the criteria suit the unique cultures of education and healthcare. For example, Category 3 in the Education criteria is Student, Stakeholder, and Market Focus; in Healthcare, Category 3 is Focus on Patients, Other Customers, and Markets; and in Business, Category 3 is Customer and Market Focus. The only other criteria category that is a little different is Category 5. In Education, its title is Faculty and Staff Focus; in Healthcare, it is Staff Focus; and in Business it is Human Resource Focus. Otherwise, all categories of criteria are the same as shown in Figure 2.3.

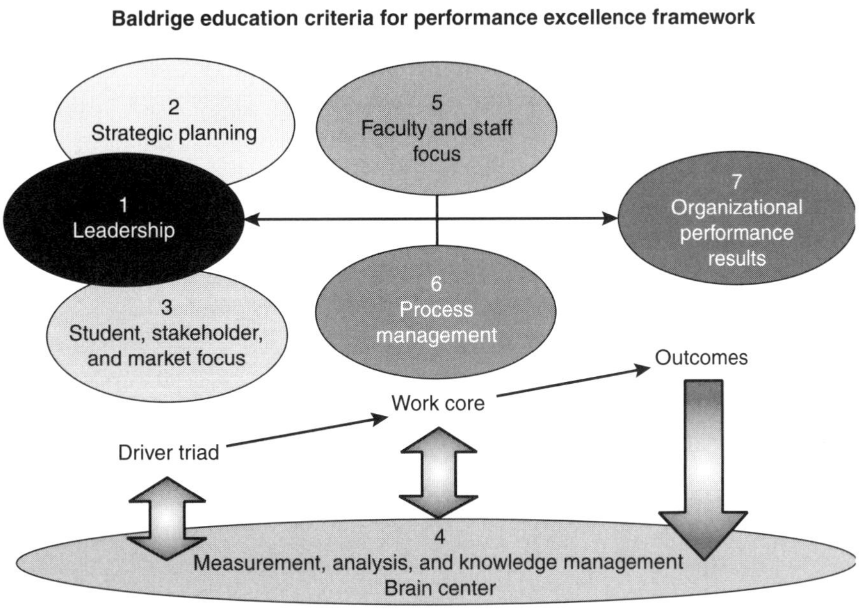

Baldrige education criteria for performance excellence framework

Figure 2.3 Education framework.

A school leader might question the importance of a common language with business and healthcare. You may even be thinking, "We don't produce widgets and we aren't concerned with the bottom line, so what could we possibly have in common?" This is a good question. While the *product of education* is not something you sell, it is *the sum total of all knowledge, skills, abilities, and wisdom students have when they leave your school.* Does what the students know and are able to do have any relationship to the world of work? Absolutely! And, even if you are the leader of an elementary school, the foundation skills students learn and their ability to communicate, take leadership roles, and make good decisions all start in kindergarten. Therefore, every educator and every school leader has the challenge of producing results that are wanted and needed by the community and business. Now, with increased accountability, the consequences of not achieving such results can lead to loss of jobs. This potential is precisely the challenge business leaders face every day.

We implore you to realize that the loss of jobs is *not* why you would pursue a Baldrige approach. Likewise, healthcare institutions should not be focused on the loss of jobs should they lose accreditation and have to close. When healthcare providers make mistakes, people can die. When educators make mistakes, children are deprived of a future that allows them to become productive and successful citizens. This is why you would pursue a Baldrige approach.

When you seek grants or wish to collaborate with businesses and healthcare organizations, the benefit of the Baldrige language is invaluable. In spite of the fact that the aim of education is different, you can learn a lot from role model businesses and healthcare organizations. You might be getting a little skeptical now, but think about it. The process of seeking customer satisfaction, complaint management processes, reducing cycle time for training programs, on the job mentoring, data collection and analysis, ways to share lessons learned, and development of an intranet are but a few of the opportunities to learn from others outside education. The scope of possibilities is far-reaching, and there are many sources available. For example, you can log onto American Productivity and Quality Center (APQC), at www.apqc.org for many free resources, or sign up for a free newsletter at the Benchmarking Network at www.benchmarkingnetwork.com. Other websites are listed in the Helpful Websites at the end of this book.

The desire to improve must rest with your passion to assure that children and youth gain the skills they need. Remember Deming's haunting words: *Your system is yielding exactly the results for which you planned.* The Baldrige framework for performance excellence guides you directly through the self-assessment process by asking key questions that have proven to be critical to understand where the gaps between results, planning, and process exist.

Baldrige Core Values

Underpinnings of the Framework

The core values of the Baldrige criteria are:

- Visionary leadership

- Learning-centered education

- Organizational and personal learning

- Valuing faculty, staff, and partners

- Agility

- Focus on the future

- Managing for innovation

- Management by fact

- Social responsibility

- Focus on results and creating value

- Systems perspective

When you read the criteria requirements, it will become evident how the criteria language is tied to the core values. That is one of the notable differences between the Baldrige framework and an accreditation process. The standards or audit procedures are not readily associated with a set of core values. The Baldrige framework not only references these core values, but the criteria also draw linkages between items within the categories to provide evidence to organizations of the necessity of embedding the core values deeply.

Indeed, one has to do only a quick review to see that core values are not evident in some districts or schools. Or, just as likely, an organization might select core values but not have them guide the organization with every decision that is made. As we look at the Baldrige core values, for example, you can see that if your leadership style is not comfortable with *agility* (rapid response, rapid change to meet current and/or future needs), then your results will demonstrate that. You will lag behind others in ways you value and support faculty, staff, and partners to take risks and rarely implement innovative approaches that might improve results. It is less likely that you will evaluate your core instructional and support processes regularly to ensure that they meet customer expectations. This one thing alone can spell mediocrity, or even disaster, when looking at your results. Furthermore, if you don't have a systems perspective, you may well misinterpret the current results, and make decisions based on what you *think* rather than what you *know,* which is antithetical to a management-by-fact approach.

Remember the Baldrige core values have proven to be the bedrock of the criteria. These are tested values that, if not adhered to as a whole, will not lead to performance excellence. We cannot overstate how important these values are to the school's future success. You would do well to spend time and reflect on your deepest thoughts and feelings about each one and how your own past actions have supported or negated each of the core values. Now, attempt to recall specific incidents where you've demonstrated a commitment (or not), to each core value. Reflect on the consequences of those actions. Once you have come to a deeper level of understanding of the significance of the core values, you are in a position to educate your staff and parents about them. Make it clear: These values are what will guide our decisions!

Whatever core values are adopted by the school or school district, your role as leader is to ensure that every decision, every process, and every action lines up with the values. Don't let the core values sit on a shelf somewhere, or be printed on a document or hung in the halls if actions don't follow words. If the latter describes your situation, there is a need to revisit the core values *now,* because clearly the core values do not guide your school.

The Education Criteria Categories

As shown in Figure 2.3 (on p. 21), the Baldrige framework is composed of seven categories. Here is a summary of each.

Leadership

Leadership sets the tone and vision, brings passion, care, and concern for all stakeholders, is a key participant in strategic planning, and creates a measurement system with a balanced scorecard and in-process targets. Leaders make certain action plans are aligned with the strategic objectives that are derived from strategic challenges, and assures that resources are aligned to carry out the action plans.

Leaders then regularly and consistently monitor progress and ensure that midcourse corrections are made.

A primary leadership function is to seek information about needs and expectations of students and stakeholders, and barriers to student success. This is accomplished through strategic planning, process design, and management. Leaders are also responsible for being role models for ethical and legal behavior and demonstrate through policy, actions, and a compliance measurement system, their dedication to the highest standards. It is significant to note that in a Baldrige-based school, leaders identify and actively support and strengthen key communities. (See page 38 for more information on key communities.)

We have devoted Chapter 3 to a more in-depth and broader discussion of visionary leadership including collaborative leadership that inspires, builds capacity, and models caring qualities as the culture of the school is established.

Strategic Planning

Strategic planning is a systematic and regular process in which leaders review vision, mission, core values, and use an environmental scan and review of previous results to identify strategic challenges. Strategic goals are derived from the challenges; key success factors are identified, and an aligned measurement system is determined. Focus on three or four primary goals that are key drivers of success and develop action plans specifically aligned with each goal. Employee capability is assessed and human relations (HR) plans are developed to provide education/training, identify needed skills for hiring purposes, and so forth.

As part of the strategic planning process, a measurement system is developed at the time strategic goals and objectives are identified. This measurement system includes targets to address action plans for improvement. The purpose of a measurement system is to monitor progress and create an environment for improvement in order to meet the strategic objectives, innovative efforts, and measure organizational agility. Creating a measurement system is detailed in Chapter 3.

At the school level, the strategic planning process would generally be considered the annual School Improvement Plan (SIP), with marking periods or the semester as the shorter-term plans. However, a school might want to develop a three-year plan and view the SIP as a short-term plan, covering only one year. For public schools, this probably needs to be negotiated with the district; however, for charter, private, or parochial schools without the bureaucracy of a district, a full-blown strategic planning process is the best way to work.

Student, Stakeholder, and Market Focus

The student, stakeholder, and market focus category is the subject of an annual needs and expectations assessment performed with current and future students and key stakeholders. An assessment includes satisfaction survey results; parental, governmental, community, district, and the next-school-in-line expectations, research on future employability skills, and so forth. Use a variety of listening and learning posts and maintain two-way communication channels. Evaluate the effectiveness of comparable schools and other competitors—for example, public, parochial, or private schools—to ascertain your uniqueness and/or theirs and how this affects your enrollment. The results of the annual assessment are fed into the strategic planning process. Relationship management and satisfaction among students, parents and other stakeholders is part of this category also. Identify, as part of a measurement plan, how you will determine satisfaction and dissatisfaction with your services.

Measurement, Analysis, and Knowledge Management

This category relates to how data are aligned, collected, and analyzed for tracking day-to-day operations and overall organizational performance levels relative to the strategic goals and action plans to support organizational decision making. Who has access to the information and how quickly information is made available to people for midcourse corrections are key factors in success. Included in this category is how information and knowledge, including "best practices," are shared throughout the organization to improve overall performance. Data accuracy, integrity, and reliability, timeliness, and security and confidentiality issues are part of this category.

Faculty and Staff Focus

The faculty and staff focus category has to do with how people are organized to do their work, how work is organized, how performance is managed and evaluated, and how the work system is improved to meet the strategic objectives. Also of concern is how employees are motivated and participate in their own education and development to carry out the action plans and for career progression. Last, the question of how leadership takes care of faculty and staff health, safety, and well-being and how it understands the key drivers of satisfaction or dissatisfaction are addressed. Areas to consider include how you seek to understand key motivators and drivers of satisfaction within a diverse workforce (for example, different jobs, educational levels, age/stage of life, ethnicity, religion, and so forth).

Process Management

The process management category addresses both the learning-centered and support processes. Identify the key learning-centered processes (for example, instruction, curriculum, assessment, and special education) and support processes (for example, custodial, transportation, food services, and administrative services). Assess the capability of each key process to produce the desired results to meet the strategic objectives. Process designs must meet all key requirements and include a measurement plan and training and implementation plans. How are these key processes monitored and how are they improved? Annually review the process used to design and manage key processes. Is it adequate, or does the basic approach to process management need to be improved?

Organizational Performance Results

What are the results of the system? Results always tell the story of the effectiveness and efficiency of key processes. They provide information about the effectiveness of action plans developed to address strategic goals and objectives. Results inform the leadership about gaps that exist in any of the prior categories. Results are reported for:

1. Student learning

2. Student–stakeholder-focused feedback, such as satisfaction, dissatisfaction, perceived value, persistence, and positive referrals

3. Budgetary, financial, and market (including cost containment, and measures of market performance such as increase in enrollment)

4. Faculty and staff, such as work system performance and effectiveness, education and training, well-being, satisfaction/dissatisfaction

5. Organizational effectiveness (performance of learning-centered processes —capacity to improve student performance, responsiveness to students and stakeholder needs, school climate and support processes—cycle time, supplier and partner performance, and other measures of effectiveness and efficiency)

6. Leadership and social responsibility (accomplishment of organizational strategy and action plans, ethical behavior, stakeholder trust, fiscal accountability, regulatory, safety, accreditation, and legal compliance, and organizational citizenship)

Levels and trends are sought for each of these results, as well as comparative and competitive data. The significance of this is to give you a clear picture of how well the school is doing over time, and how well you are doing compared to similar schools (in size, demographics of student body, grades, and services provided) and other schools in your area, state, and nationwide.

This snapshot of the seven Baldrige categories gives you an idea of how different the approach is to an accreditation process. Throughout this book you will learn more about each category and how each is integrated with others to achieve performance excellence. However, we have captured the heart of each category within this book, rather than details. For more information, you can download a copy of the criteria for free from the Baldrige website, www.baldrige.nist.gov. Multiple copies of the criteria can be ordered from the American Society for Quality, www.asq.org.

The Framework Is Unique and Powerful

While the Baldrige criteria are evaluated on a rotating basis by the Baldrige office and members of the Board of Judges and Examiners, the basic framework remains the same. This is because it has been proven over the years and across all sectors to be a model for excellence. That is, if an organization follows the framework and addresses each aspect of the criteria, results will improve. What follows are what separates the Baldrige framework from other approaches to system excellence.

Regular Revisions Keep Criteria Current

Although the basic framework has not changed, the Baldrige office recognizes that the criteria requirements must remain current with the needs of customers and stakeholders. Therefore, every year, after the Baldrige award cycle, the Baldrige office holds an "Improvement Day" on which the Board of Examiners and other hands-on practitioners discuss criteria requirements that lead to performance excellence. Current issues putting pressure on leaders are discussed and reviewed against the criteria to ascertain whether changes need to be made. Recent examples of changes include the No Child Left Behind accountability expectations and the emphasis on ethics that stemmed from cheating and other scandals. For this reason we recommend you order a free copy of the criteria and use it, along with this book, to guide your journey.

Recognize Your Uniqueness: The Profile

The Baldrige program recognizes that each organization is unique. Though the central purpose may be similar, each school has unique characteristics such as the community demographics, the budget, types and number of students and families served, setting, school facilities, special programs, and so forth. The Organizational Profile allows the leadership to set the stage for external review. Also, by responding to the questions about (1) organizational environment, (2) organizational relationships, (3) competitive environment, (4) strategic challenges, and the (5) performance improvement system, the initial self-assessment begins. Topics will surface and potential gaps or conflicts in key information will begin to emerge. Gaps may emerge between process requirements and performance results, making it clear to leadership that a closer look must be taken. The closer look is done as the self-assessment is completed and improvement plans are identified. Complete the abbreviated profile (modified from the Baldrige criteria booklet) at the end of this chapter.

Criteria Are Nonprescriptive and Adaptable

The criteria are nonprescriptive and no judgments are made about the approach(es) taken or structure that any organization uses to achieve its aim. However, the criteria are focused on results, so when a process does not yield the desired results or if the results are weak or mixed, leaders must look at the design and management of key processes, how often they are evaluated and improved, and whether faculty and staff have the capability to implement action plans to reach the desired results.

Criteria Integrate Key Educational Themes

Themes of educational excellence are evident in the criteria. The primary focus of the education criteria is on teaching and learning. Remember the core value, learning-centered education? The criteria recognize students as primary customers of educational organizations, but other stakeholders as well. Excellence is defined in the 2005 Baldrige education criteria book: "1) a well-conceived and well-executed assessment strategy; 2) year-to-year improvement in key measures and indicators of performance, especially student learning; and 3) demonstrated leadership in performance and performance improvement, relative to comparable organizations and to appropriate benchmarks" (2005 *Education Criteria for Performance Excellence*, p. 7).

Uses a Systems Perspective to Maintain Organizational Goal Attainment

Alignment with every aspect of the system is required for reaching excellence and is achieved when measures are connected with key processes and strategies. Measures focus the activity of the organization and serve as a major communication tool throughout the organization. Linking the criteria categories and items together ensures that there is integration and cycles of learning to reach the goals.

Provides Goal-Based Diagnosis

Results fully address key student, stakeholder, market, process, and action plan requirements. Because the results cover 19 requirements, the net gain for an organization is an in-depth understanding of strengths and opportunities for improvement. By knowing what the results are, the goals each are "hooked to," and the processes responsible for the results, the leadership has a clear sense of the sources of the gaps.

To demonstrate performance excellence, your results are expected to show the following:

Trends—Depending on the cycle time of any process and the number of data points, at least five data points are required to show a trend. For standardized tests (SAT, ITBS, state standards test, and so on), three years of data demonstrate the beginnings of a trend, but it takes five years of data to show a statistically significant trend. Other processes may yield daily, weekly, or monthly data, and therefore the cycle time for a trend to develop is significantly shorter.

Performance levels—Current results show good levels of performance in all areas of importance to the school.

Comparisons—Performance levels are measured against comparable schools (demographics, student body, region, state, and so on), which gives significance to your results by putting them into perspective.

Competitive—Performance levels are measured against competitor schools (charter schools, private, or parochial schools and other public schools) in your market area. Along with comparative data, measuring your results with results from competitive schools provides you with important information that may not otherwise be evident.

Benchmark—Compare your results to "best practice" schools such as previous Baldrige winners, Blue Ribbon schools, or other schools recognized for excellence by an external review process. You can also benchmark other key processes from organizations outside education. For example, the Ritz-Carlton hotels have been noted for their customer service, and this process has been benchmarked by school districts, manufacturing, healthcare, and other businesses. (See the Recommended Reading and Websites at the back of the book for ways to find benchmarking opportunities.)

Sprinkled throughout this book are school report cards demonstrating where a leader might look to assess the effectiveness and efficiency of certain key processes. If you are not happy with the results, look at the process that is responsible.

The first six criteria categories seek information about your key processes. Organizations that aspire to performance excellence realize how each of the following factors is required:

Approach—Describe the methods, the appropriateness, effectiveness, and replication of the methods used by the school to achieve its goals. What do you do and how do you do it?

Deployment—How often do individuals or departments use the aforementioned approaches; how many use them, and how consistently are they used?

Learning—Describe how the approach is evaluated and refined (Plan-Do-Study-Act); whether breakthrough learning is required (benchmarking); and how lessons learned are shared throughout the school.

Integration—To what extent are your methods aligned with the strategic challenges? Describe how measures and information systems are complementary across all departments of the schools. An integrated systems approach assumes that you understand the effect of each decision on the rest of the organization and that all plans, processes, analyses, and actions are harmonized across work units to support your school goals.

Alignment and Integration

Alignment begins with the vision and mission. Strategic goals address the most pressing organizational challenges that are required to meet the vision and mission. A measurement system, action plans, education and training of employees, and key learning-centered and support processes are all designed and determined with the end in mind. Every decision the leadership makes, including resource allocation, is integral to meeting the vision, mission, and goals. There is no wasted time, resources, or energy. Everyone is focused on the same thing, and this message is sent via leadership to every employee, student, and stakeholder.

Alignment also means that the school selects, collects, and integrates data and information and manages it so those who need it to make decisions have it in a timely fashion. Learning is both personal and organizational as leadership regularly reviews operational progress and Plan-Do-Study-Act improvement processes are instituted when measures drop below a specific trigger point. There is transparency (open communications) throughout the school. Historical logs of PDSAs are housed on an intranet or in an easily accessible place, if technology is not available. This alerts everyone to lessons learned and provides a valuable history of the improvements made at the school. As leaders embark on annual strategic planning, part of preplanning includes a review of results from the lens of pre/post improvements.

Integration means that all plans are harmonious and bring together the collective efforts of all employees working together and that all departments or grade-level teams are working with all other departments or grade levels. Everyone understands how his or her job supports the vision, mission, and strategic goals of the school. As an example, payroll clerks who deliver checks late or who make errors in calculating sick leave lower the morale of faculty and staff. If morale is low, energy is lost as people complain and lose focus on their purpose. Likewise, if the kindergarten teacher has philosophical differences of opinion about how children learn or what they are capable of learning, he or she may be working contrary to the focus of the school. A final example is food service workers who insist that students eat one of two breakfasts and refuse to give food to those who do not want that particular meal. Consequently, students go to class without breakfast and are not ready to learn. (These are all real examples, by the way.) We'll discuss integration in more detail later.

Baldrige and Accreditation

A natural question for educators might be "What difference is there between the Baldrige framework and an accreditation process?" The Baldrige criteria ask a series of key questions about your processes and require you to look at them relative to results. It also asks how the organization learns and makes decisions for improvement. The Baldrige framework integrates six criteria categories that produce results (the seventh criteria category). Central to the Baldrige framework is the requirement of a fact-based (data-driven) decision-making process both in-process and at year's end. Data analysis provides leadership with information about gaps in the system (inefficient, ineffective, or missing processes) that cause the results. Organizational and personal learning is accomplished through two-way communication practiced by leadership and the leadership team to share lessons learned and through continuous or breakthrough improvements throughout the organization. The Baldrige criteria are widely used as a self-assessment and improvement tool by many organizations in this country.

On the other hand, accreditation has traditionally served more as an audit process, although recent changes and accountability demands have required accrediting agencies to become more rigorous in needs assessments, data collection and analysis, and evaluation. In some states, departments of education have allowed schools to provide a Baldrige self-assessment in lieu of traditional school improvement process (SIP) plans and/or accreditation self-assessments, in the belief that Baldrige provides a more thorough assessment. The fact that accrediting organizations are beginning to align their requirements toward the Baldrige framework is testimony to its effectiveness.

Table 2.1   Abbreviated profile.

Your School Profile	
School environment	
Describe the main educational programs, offerings, and services and how you deliver them to students.	
Describe the school's purpose, vision, mission, and values.	
Who works for you? Describe the faculty and staff—education levels, gender, diversity, numbers, etc.	
Do you have bargaining units? Describe these and other special health or safety requirements.	
Describe your facility; what major technology and equipment are used?	
Who regulates the school and what constraints do you work under in terms of regulatory and policy-making bodies?	
What are the school's attendance and service boundaries?	
School relationships	
What is the governance and reporting system?	
Who does the principal report to?	
Who are your key student segments, stakeholder groups, and market segments?	
Describe the needs and requirements for each segmented group listed above.	
Describe the role suppliers and/or partners play in your learning-centered processes.	
What requirements do you have of key suppliers?	
How do you communicate with suppliers, partners, students, and stakeholders to build and maintain relationships?	
Competitive environment	
Describe the size and growth of the school in relation to others in your service area.	
Who are the school's key competitors?	
What are the most important success factors that distinguish your school from the competitors?	
What changes are taking place that may affect your competitive situation?	
Where do you get comparative and competitive data from within and outside the academic community?	
Strategic challenges	
What are the key education and learning, operational, human resource, and community-related strategic challenges you face?	
Performance improvement system	
How do you approach organizational performance improvement and use it to guide systematic evaluation and improvement of key processes?	
What approach do you use for organizational learning?	

Today, the Baldrige National Quality Program and the Baldrige Award recipients are imitated and admired worldwide. More than 40 states and many countries, including Japan, have programs modeled after Baldrige.

—2005 Baldrige National Quality Award Criteria

Baldrige Recognizes Your Uniqueness

Each organization is unique. Each has its own culture, based on its history, its location, the services it offers, and the environment within which it is located. To begin the Baldrige process, complete a school profile that will set everything you do and everything you are in context. Table 2.1 is an abbreviated profile based on the Baldrige criteria.

See the latest edition of the Baldrige Education Criteria booklet (at www.baldrige.nist.gov) for a detailed profile description.

Summary

This is a chapter you may want to reread as you begin to put systems thinking into practice. The criteria provide a powerful guide, and as system language becomes the norm in your school, you will surely notice a "change in climate." As we noted in this chapter, however, it is the principal's commitment to quality and the Baldrige framework and criteria that must be explained to teachers and staff in order to enlist their enthusiastic commitment. Is this easy? Most likely, it is not going to be a smooth, easy task as in any organization; there are those who are "from Missouri" (the "Show Me" state) and those with a jaded view having lived through many previous management "flavors of the month"! Is there a cookie-cutter template that you can use? No. If you know of other schools that are already on their journey using quality and the Baldrige framework, you might want to contact your principal colleagues for lessons learned in getting started. Just remember that learning with your staff is not an abdication of your leadership role. And, yes, we guarantee some fun along the way.

3
Visionary Leadership
The Driver of Excellence

Conversation with the Principal

We have devoted an entire chapter to the principal's leadership because, in addition to what all the research concludes, the Baldrige criteria clearly suggest how leaders need to function in order to achieve extraordinary results. As we provide more detail and examples of the responsibilities, skills, and attitudes that combine to achieve performance excellence, we can picture you wondering aloud, "What human being can possibly embrace all of this?" Once again, we make the point that leading a Baldrige-based quality school is a journey. Be patient with yourself and never underestimate your ability to exercise continuous improvement.

The Scope of Leadership

Excellent organizations have visionary leaders at the helm. These are individuals with passion and a deep commitment to the aim of the organization. They inspire, encourage, and allow everyone to contribute to a brighter future. A visionary leader is someone who is capable of balancing the needs of all stakeholders, including teachers, current and future students, parents, the central administration, the board, and other policy makers, as well as the next-school-in-line or the world of work. A visionary leader seeks to know his or her customers' needs and expectations and realizes that a systematic approach to relationship management is the way to achieve higher satisfaction. Satisfied customers (staff, students, parents, and so on) maintain higher levels of morale and are more willing to help achieve the aim.

The most effective leaders are those with low ego needs who do not need to be in the spotlight but eagerly allow others to share the glory. At the same time, these leaders faithfully practice fact-based analysis of the current reality by systematically monitoring organizational performance and forming continuous process improvement teams when targets are not met. A regularly informed leader is in a better position to know what processes need improving to achieve the strategic goals.

Summing it up, a Baldrige-based quality school system is one that requires leadership to interact with all phases of the organization, but knowledge is not enough. The leader must be dedicated to the use of data to inform the rest of the system about what needs to improve. Many school leaders have relied on intuition and made decisions based on what felt right rather than on what the data revealed. Consequently, schools do not always stay the course, which leads to failed or inconsistent results, lower morale, and many dissatisfied parents, students, and employees. The responsibility for putting together and leading a highly skilled, motivated, and passionate professional and non-certified staff who continuously learn and work together as a high-performing team belongs to the leader.

Research suggests the principal's job is the most difficult in the school, and even in the school district. One reason is that as middle managers, principals have to be agile and respond to many crises, often daily. They feel the heat from parents and teachers as well as from the superintendent and the central administration. Sadly, too often those in the central administration fail to understand their role as service providers to the principals. When this happens, supportive services become replaced with micromanagement and an inspection mentality, further hampering a principal's ability to lead.

Principals are often caught between teachers and parents too. It frequently happens that teachers feel that unless a principal backs his or her decisions all the time, they report that the "administration is not supportive." These individuals become disenchanted and sometimes sabotage the efforts required for excellence. In reality, not all decisions teachers make should be supported. Likewise, not all parental requests are appropriate, and when a principal does not honor these, parents sometimes do take their grievances to the superintendent or board level.

To minimize these issues, a principal leading in a Baldrige-based school would, in the words of the 2005 criteria:

> set directions and create a student-focused, learning-oriented climate; [with] clear and visible values; and high expectations. The directions, values, and expectations should balance the needs of all stakeholders. . . . Senior leaders should inspire and motivate . . . [the] entire workforce and should encourage all faculty and staff to contribute, to develop and learn, to be innovative, and to be creative. . . . Senior leaders should serve as role models through their ethical behavior and their personal involvement in planning, communications, coaching, development of future leaders, review of organizational performance, and faculty and staff recognition. (p. 1)

We continue to hear from principals of low performing schools that there is not enough time to 'take on one more thing' and that the Baldrige would just be too much. These principals are good people who are working as hard as they can to keep up morale, get the resources, and encourage teachers to employ new tactics to meet the district and/or state requirements.

While we empathize with their plight, the words of Pooh Bear articulate more clearly than we how this mentality manifests.

> *Here is Edward Bear, coming downstairs now, bump, bump, bump, on the back of his head, behind Christopher Robin. It is, as far as he knows, the only way of coming downstairs, but sometimes, he feels that there really is another way. . . if only he could stop bumping for a moment and think of it.*
>
> —*A.A. Milne*
> The Complete Tales of Winnie-the-Pooh

Other principals of schools with low-performing students spend their time searching for new programs, curricula, textbooks, technology, or other nonsystemic approaches that will (guaranteed) turn the school around and in many cases become disappointed with the bang for the buck. In reality, it is just like anything else—*to improve, you must work on the system. You must have the right people working for you; those who are totally dedicated—as you must be—to the end goal: performance excellence.* After you analyze the system and determine the capability of current processes, it is likely that new programs, technology, and curricula may be required. But unless you understand how the system works holistically, with all the components aligned and integrated, the "magic" of new programs or any of the other aforementioned approaches will not yield the desired results. As painful as it may be, we must remember the words of Dr. Deming: "Your system is yielding exactly the results for which you planned."

In some cases, the principals are hampered by teachers union contracts that specify to the minute the length of faculty meetings and how much time principals are allowed to keep teachers after school during a semester or school year. If this is your situation, we suggest you engage the union leadership from your school in a partnership based on the necessity of improving student achievement and morale among faculty. If for no other reason, they may agree because every employee will be vested in keeping his or her job. In the current accountability requirements of No Child Left Behind, this is definitely not a guarantee, especially if the school drops into restructuring. Visionary school leaders set the tone and direction of the school, and they must find a way to engage union representatives, informal teacher leaders, and other key stakeholders in getting on board. Collaborative, creative thinking about the reward and recognition system with union leaders might be a helpful way to start, based on student learning results, of course.

We believe every problem has a solution. However, not every solution is feasible or workable all the time. The key is a visionary leader who can help sort through various alternatives and lead everyone to a win-win result. Problems often begin with poor communications that, if not improved, lead to rumors, resistance, and often hard feelings. We would say that good, open, and two-way communication is one vital step a leader must take with the entire workforce and all key stakeholders. This is not to say that a principal must give in to any stakeholder request. We have found that those who maintain a clear focus on the aim and desired results work ethically, communicate expectations clearly and consistently, are able to achieve better relationships and buy-in. When your processes are in place for organizational improvement, you can resolve nearly all problems without discord. See Chapter 6 for more details on listening and learning (communication) posts.

> *Perfection is not attainable, but if we chase perfection we can catch excellence.*
>
> —*Vince Lombardi*

To test your current mind-set about leadership, here are four actual examples we've seen. Think about how you, as a school leader, might have dealt with each situation. Speculate on the ramifications of such an approach. How does your thinking reflect what you've learned about visionary leadership?

Example A. A high school in the northeast realized student performance results were terrible. The school operated on a 50-minute class period. The teachers had heard about block schedules and how they could help students learn more, but they were skeptical about how it would work. The principal asked for volunteers to become a team to research different school schedules and make a recommendation. The volunteers spent about a year researching, visiting other schools, and discussing different approaches with teachers and students from other schools. They reviewed the student achievement results from schools with block schedules. The committee presented its findings at a faculty meeting and received overwhelming support to change to a block schedule. The principal never took the recommendation to the superintendent for approval. Instead, this school kept its original schedule. No explanations were given, and student learning results stayed about the same.

Example B. One middle school, in a large district in the South, lagged behind all other middle schools in the district in terms of student achievement. Trend data showed that this pattern held for many years. This occurred in spite of the fact that the demographics at this particular school showed relatively few students on free or reduced lunch, few immigrant students, and most students coming from homes of professional parents. The school did not ascribe to a traditional middle school model (with students grouped in "families" with a team of teachers), but instead used the old junior high model of individual classes and no teaming among teachers. Other middle schools in the same district had a much more diverse student population with many on free or reduced lunch, yet these students consistently scored better on the same nationally normed tests. The staff at the more traditional school were not impressed by the results of the comparable school, nor deterred by results of their students, and decided to stay their course.

Example C. An elementary principal in a southwestern state decided to take this approach for school improvement. Every two months, students in each classroom took the last 15 minutes of the afternoon to reflect on the school, thinking about the good things and the things that could be better. Their suggestions were shared with the student council, a committee of teachers and other staff members, and the principal. Ideas were prioritized and a group of students and staff were given the task to collect data and come up with improvement suggestions for one of the high prioritized ideas. Everyone in the school was, over the course of two years, engaged in one or more improvement projects.

Example D. A foreign-language teacher from a very diverse large school district in the West asked the principal if the students could help assess textbooks under consideration for adoption. Though this request was unusual, the principal agreed. The teacher invited the principal to a session where the class agreed on the criteria a textbook should have to help them learn. The teacher made certain that students received all the sample textbooks being considered by the district. Students carefully followed the evaluation criteria and made recommendations for purchase, which the teacher shared with the district's textbook adoption committee. Later, the superintendent called, criticizing the principal's decision to engage students in the process.

Leadership Team and System

Your leadership team may or may not be dictated by the central administration. Typically, except for the smallest schools, there is at least one assistant principal and a guidance counselor. This may be considered the leadership team. Other schools include department chairs, grade-level chairs, special education (SPED) and English for speakers of other languages (ESOL) coordinators, and even the nurse on the leadership team. Site-based managed schools frequently consider parent representatives as part of the leadership team. The way the school is organized generally gives a clear picture of membership on the leadership team. If, however, students are not learning at their peak capacity you might consider reflecting on the leadership system and how it can be changed to lend effectiveness and efficiency to the school. We all know of organizations that are so laden with administrators—or "administrative groupies"—that they muddy the water and frequently cause more bureaucratic problems.

If you are able, fill your leadership team with people with passion (like yours), high energy, and great communication skills and who are big-picture thinkers and willing learners. Make certain the representation includes key personnel (for example, grade-level representatives or department chairs) and not just your "cronies." Otherwise, you run the risk of alienating staff. One of the major responsibilities of the leadership team is regular, systematic review of organizational performance. This means that everyone helps analyze data and prioritize improvement efforts. This group is also a major player during strategic planning. Most importantly, members of the leadership team must commit themselves to the values, vision, mission, and expectations outlined by you.

Once you get the right team on board, take a close look at your leadership system and how it functions. What communication channels are open so others can listen and learn? How often does the group meet? What data are reviewed regularly? How are decisions made? Is support provided to others? How are resource allocations determined? These are just some of the critical responsibilities of the leadership team. Of course, you'll want to create a process to regularly evaluate the effectiveness of the leadership system. Figure 3.1 shows what results would give you clues about the effectiveness and efficiency of your leadership system.

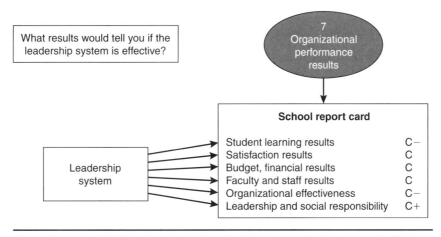

Figure 3.1   Results that demonstrate leadership system effectiveness and efficiency.

Governance and Ethics

A significant responsibility leaders have is to be role models for employee and public trust by exhibiting ethical behavior. Governance ought to be as transparent as possible (personnel matters being the exception), with meeting minutes, fiscal accountability (audit results), and results of health, safety, and other regulatory bodies made available to all. Not only are leaders expected to be role models of ethical behavior, but there also is an expectation that education and training in ethical behavior and diversity will be provided to all employees and that there are measures to monitor the behavior of everyone connected with the school. Ethical behavior is expected of students too, especially in terms of Internet usage, cheating, and plagiarism. Senior leaders monitor ethical behavior as one part of the balanced scorecard. See Appendix C for an example of a balanced scorecard process.

Leaders who demonstrate a willingness to be held accountable for their own actions set the tone and expectation for everyone. Being held to the high standards expected of others adds to the public trust and makes a big difference when seeking budget increases, or positive referrals. Therefore, it's important to give employees a means to evaluate you, the senior leader, and the leadership system. Some schools use a 360-degree evaluation process, in which senior leaders select one or two others to evaluate them and share feedback. We think it is important for all staff (or a representative, random sample) to evaluate the leaders without fear of reprisal. While this may be uncomfortable, it also provides enormous amounts of information that cannot be discounted. Seeking feedback regularly and systematically from your key customers and sharing the results with staff is expected in a Baldrige-based school in order to inform you about the effectiveness of your own leadership and that of the leadership system.

We caution you not to ask, however, if you don't want to know employees' perceptions. Unless you are prepared to share the results and inform people of ways you plan to improve, you will lose the trust it takes so long to build. On the other hand, you become handicapped and less able to lead the organization to excellence if you don't have a process for personal and leadership system improvement. The choice is yours!

Leadership and Social Responsibility

Another role of a Baldrige-based principal is to encourage good citizenship and social responsibility; to be a role model and recognize the efforts of teachers, staff, and students as all work to improve the community. It makes sense for senior leaders (after the environmental scan during the strategic planning process, for instance) to annually review or identify key communities that are integral to your school and achievement of the goals and that would benefit from school support. Examples might include students who live below the poverty line, a group of new immigrant families, or students whose families are homeless. Once the key communities have been identified, senior leaders take the lead in learning about opportunities to help and in identifying ways the school can support and strengthen them. As the year progresses, contributions made by students, entire classes, teachers, staff, and the leadership team are evaluated. How the leaders choose to empower and recognize support efforts contributes to pride and to a sense of efficacy and teamwork. It is part of community building in the largest sense.

Leaders' Role with the Work Core

By virtue of your title, you already know that how well that you work with faculty and staff plays a significant role in overall success. The Baldrige framework helps you understand all the alignment and integration issues that can help you lead the group to excellence. Look at Figure 3.2 to see how a school leader would begin to work with faculty and staff.

The first thing for you to notice is that Category 4, Measurement, Analysis, and Knowledge Management, is the brain center. Aside from data collection and analysis, you'll want to provide a way for everyone to share information and knowledge gained as well as the best practice. Results of each Plan-Do-Study-Act (PDSA) improvement proj-

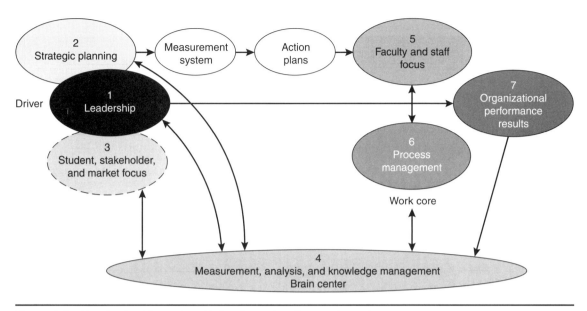

Figure 3.2 How leadership works with faculty and staff to reach results.

ect undertaken by any team within the school are magnified when lessons learned are shared throughout the organization. Leaders can take great advantage of this, even in a school with few technology resources, by maintaining a school improvement library. This might consist of a series of notebooks by grade level, department, and whole school that contain the details of each improvement project and PDSA results. Make these available for all staff to review. As problems crop up, the first requirement would be to go back into the record and see if it is a recurring issue. If it is, the previous PDSA provides teams with a great starting point for analyzing the problem. Of course, if technology is available, developing an intranet site that every employee can access is useful.

You see from the arrows on Figure 3.2 that everything is integrated with data. The next awareness step is how faculty and staff get their direction from action plans derived from the strategic plan. These action plans address key strategic challenges uncovered from student and stakeholder needs and expectations as well as the constraints within which your school operates. Also note that organizational performance reviews are based on the measurement system of the strategic plan with leading and lagging indicators as shown in Table 4.6 in Chapter 4.

The work core, Categories 5 and 6, basically are how work gets done in the organization. The arrow running through indicates leadership support. As you can see, it is impossible to imagine how any organization could reach performance excellence with good to excellent trended results and the efficiency factors of cycle time, financial, and reduction of errors or rework without using a structured problem-solving approach (PDSA). (The PDSA reflects the core value of organization and personal learning.) Likewise, it is impossible to imagine how organizations can reach the highest levels of performance excellence without an understanding of systems and a framework to evaluate the degree to which each aspect of the system is aligned and integrated for optimal performance.

The Driver Triad

Let's look at how categories one (Leadership), two (Strategic Planning) and three (Student, Stakeholder, and Market Focus) are aligned and integrated to form the Driver Triad as indicated by Mark Blazey, author of *Insights to Performance Excellence in Education.*

(See the Recommended Reading for more information about Blazey's book.) Figure 3.3 shows Blazey's organization of these categories. As the leader, you set direction, tone, and expectations of employees. You play a pivotal role in strategic planning based on student and stakeholder needs and expectations and in determining the reward and recognition system for employees. Consequently, you and your leadership team are responsible for the results. Results are directly related to planning, process design, and management. Therefore, *whatever you've planned for is reflected in the results,* as Dr. Deming wrote. If you are not happy, the question for you becomes, "*What* is the source of the problem?"

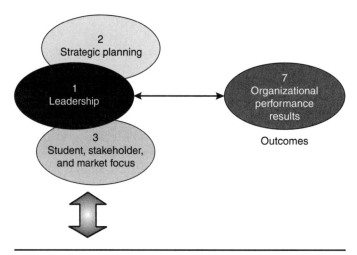

Figure 3.3   Driver triad.

Waiting until the year is over to discover problems is too late to ensure that goals and objectives will be met for that year. Worse, there is no way to make midcourse corrections to improve the chances of meeting the goals. It is the leader's responsibility to ensure that processes are in place to establish regular and systematic accountability throughout the school year. There is more on this in Chapter 4, Strategic Planning. Leaders have to be informed about all aspects of the system in order to lead for excellence. If you've ever worked in an organization that does not reward open and honest communication, but kills the messenger, you know that is a surefire approach to mediocrity, or at least keeps an organization from reaching its potential.

You must also understand that every school *does* have competitors, as there are reasons why parents choose to send their children elsewhere. Key competitors of public schools include private, parochial, charter, and home schools. In states where students are allowed to attend school outside their local district, other districts may also be considered competition. And, just as in other businesses, it is important to know your competition and any special niche your school has. This is why the Baldrige framework requires data from comparative (schools like yours in demographics, size, and focus) and competitive schools. It does matter because it gives you insights into the actual or perceived strengths and weaknesses of your school.

After you've been on this journey for several years, you'll want and need to collect data and compare your results with the "best in class" schools. These are schools that have been recognized by external groups (for example, Baldrige) for excellence. It all begins with the naked truth: an open-eyed self-assessment document that is based wholly on fact.

How to Begin the Baldrige Self-Assessment Process in Your School

When you've taken the time to reflect on your situation and you have decided to commit to performance excellence, it makes sense to implement a process to jumpstart the effort. Here are four steps that we believe will help you begin (and continue on) your journey:

1. **Familiarize yourself with the Baldrige education criteria.** Lay out your idea and reasons why the school will use the Baldrige criteria for school improvement. Present your ideas to the entire faculty and staff, and leave no room for ambiguity about your purpose and approach. It is non-negotiable; once everyone realizes that it is not the management flavor of the month and that you are filled with resolve, there will be more buy-in from everyone. Steel yourself for the naysayers, but set the expectation that *everyone* will get on board.

2. **Identify category team leaders.** In very small schools, the entire staff and a cadre of parents or board members might be involved with specific individuals who are given leadership responsibility for one of the categories. In general, an individual would be selected to be a category leader if he or she had interest or expertise in that aspect of the system.

3. **Hire a Baldrige consultant/coach.** Find someone who has worked with educators, is or has been a member of the Baldrige Board of Examiners, and is familiar with education to provide training for the category team leaders and employ him or her as your leadership coach. Many states have Baldrige-based programs that can provide information or recommendations regarding coaching. (For more information about how to locate state programs go to www.networkforexcellence.org.) Compatibility is a good thing, but keep in mind you are also hiring someone you can trust to give you the straight scoop. This is necessary if you plan to improve rapidly with the fewest number of missteps. As Dr. Deming said, "Any system needs guidance from the outside. . . . A system can not understand itself. An organization may require someone in the position of aide to the president to teach and facilitate profound knowledge" (*The New Economics,* p. 54). The elements of Dr. Deming's theory of profound knowledge—appreciation for systems, knowledge about variation, theory of knowledge, and psychology—are, not surprisingly, evidence of the interdependencies of the Baldrige framework.

4. **Listen and learn!** Do not be afraid of the data or drilling down through many layers of data until you've uncovered the core of the problem. Data analysis is a key to school improvement, yet some become defensive when they see it. The best advice we can offer is to remember that data are data. They tell you with precision what happened on a certain day (or week, month, or year), in certain classrooms, or in areas of the building. Data have no intrinsic value unless they are analyzed and used to improve a process. Without knowing what the data are, it is impossible to have any clues about what to change. If you have made decisions in the past about new programs without completely understanding your past results, we hope you will stop, listen, and learn about the Baldrige and how it can inform you of a better way.

Before moving forward, complete the following self-assessment to see how well you know your leadership system.

Assess Category 1 (Leadership) Efforts

To what extent do you . . . ?	I don't	Not really	Occasionally	Mostly	Always	Specifically, what do you do to support your rating?
1. Share the vision and core values with all faculty, staff, students, and stakeholders						
2. Set and share clear expectations						
3. Reflect a commitment to the school's core values by your personal actions						
4. Promote an environment that fosters and requires legal and ethical behavior						
5. Create and support a school environment conducive for performance improvement and accomplishment of the strategic objectives						
6. Promote and support employee innovation and organizational agility						
7. Create a school environment that encourages and expects faculty and staff learning and schoolwide organizational learning						
8. Engage in a process to develop future organizational leaders at this school						
9. Encourage frank, two-way communication throughout the school without fear of reprisals						
10. Communicate with, motivate, and empower faculty and staff to meet the strategic objectives						
11. Take an active role in faculty and staff reward and recognition to reinforce high performance and a focus on the school as well as on students and stakeholders						

Continued

Assess Category 1 (Leadership) Efforts

Continued

To what extent do you . . . ?	I don't	Not really	Occasionally	Mostly	Always	Specifically, what do you do to support your rating?
12. Protect stakeholder interests through fiscal accountability, transparency in operations with the Board, and internal and external audits						
13. Utilize a leadership evaluation process						
14. Allow employees to evaluate the leadership system regularly						
15. Use the leadership performance reviews to evaluate and improve your own effectiveness and that of the leadership system						
16. Identify and address adverse impacts of programs, offerings, services, and operations regularly						
17. Have key compliance processes, measures, and goals for achieving and surpassing regulatory, safety, accreditation, and legal requirements						
18. Promote and monitor ethical behavior in all interactions and have consequences for ethical breaches in place						
19. Identify, support, and strengthen your key communities						
20. Contribute to improving your key communities						
21. Allow and encourage employees and students to contribute to improving your key communities						

Summary

If you haven't examined the latest (2005 at this writing) Baldrige Education Criteria booklet, make a note to send for it and read the section on leadership. You will begin to see how it all fits together. The questions regarding leadership approach, deployment, alignment, and integration, many of which are referenced directly in this chapter, will provide you with an even deeper understanding of your role. We also suggest that you use this chapter's self-assessment as a starting point to help you prioritize the next steps in your journey. Above all, we wish for you a special mentor or friend in whom you can share your feelings and insecurities as you move forward.

4

Launching Baldrige in Your School

Conversation with the Principal

In this chapter you will gain insight and practical suggestions for launching Baldrige. Depending on your leadership style, you will introduce your vision, enlist the cooperation and enthusiasm of your faculty, and begin the journey into systems thinking and results-focused planning. This chapter also outlines the beginning steps that you need to adapt to your situation in order to demonstrate the learning process that occurs when a school adopts the Baldrige framework and embraces quality practices. There are (or will be) many what-ifs competing in your head, trying hard to delay taking action. As the school leader most responsible for setting and maintaining the learning-centered school, however, you will find the risks well worth taking.

Deal with Reality

If you are a public school principal, leading a school that is part of a district, you must be aware that there is a risk involved in going it alone. In fact, it might be political suicide to embark on a Baldrige path without the support of your superintendent. Those of you who lead charter, private, independent, or parochial schools may not face the same issues of "who's in charge." Whatever your circumstances, however, it is not in your best interests to go forward without the approval of your board.

Regardless of the situation, you, a wise principal, will read as much as possible about the Baldrige framework, previous Baldrige education winners (www.baldrige.nist .gov), and review the data from the California Center for Baldrige in Education (www.qualityineducation.org/results.html). Then collect trend data on student learning results and satisfaction rates from your school and summarize this information, along with your passion for improvement and excellence. Begin conversations with the superintendent or, in the case of large districts, the deputy or regional superintendents responsible for schools in your area. Share the student learning data and your deep desire to improve the system for the sake of current and future students. Think of yourself as a crusader for systemic improvement and bring up the topic at every opportunity. It is possible that the superintendent, other central administrators, or the board members are not familiar with the Baldrige criteria and the achievements of award winning districts. Be willing to provide them with all the information you have and offer your school as a pilot. If granted permission, agree to demonstrate transparency in all your processes and results, and invite administrators, teachers, parents, and even the board to come and observe. Share the results with the central administration and parents.

You may have the opportunity to become mentors for others in your district. Let your ego go and give credit to the superintendent and board for giving you the opportunity to become a pilot school for Baldrige and for allowing you to lead the school to performance excellence. As with most things in life, it's all about building relationships. You, of course, know your situation and the key players. We realize the constraints under which many readers work, but if you are committed to improvement, do what you can do to persuade others to let you pursue a Baldrige path. Courage and integrity are important values that will help you know the best way to persuade those in power to change course. Good luck!

Take the Plunge

Leaders Set the Vision, Values, and Expectations

If your school is part of a larger district, vision, values, and expectations are usually determined by the central administration. However, if you are a leader in a charter school, private, or parochial school, you probably work directly with a board. If the latter describes your situation, you will be leading the process to establish the vision (future, desired state of the school) and values (underpinnings upon which all future decisions will be made). Figure 4.1 shows how the leader begins the strategic planning process by setting the tone and directions.

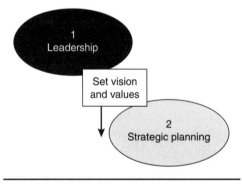

Figure 4.1 Leaders set tone and expectations.

Remember the Baldrige core values of visionary leadership, a focus on the future, learning-centered education, and managing for innovation? Think about how you view the school and consider whether your thoughts are aligned with these core values. Is it time to raise the bar on your thinking and develop a vision that everyone can embrace? A vision must be inspiring! It must be short enough to remember easily, and it must speak loudly to all who would come into the school. It is not enough to have a vision like this one: *Our graduates are good citizens.*While that vision is nice, it does not "carry" the enthusiasm, deep desire, and willingness to do whatever it takes to achieve it. What is missing? Both passion and a mental picture are missing. Consider this: *Our graduates are well-informed, educated citizens who contribute to community and world improvement.*

Decide on the core values upon which everyone will be expected to work. This is a collaborative process, and requires participation from the board (it sets policy), leadership team (they carry out policy and are key decision makers), certified and noncertified staff (they carry out day-to-day operations and make decisions along the way). You need not adopt the Baldrige core values (p. 22), but give them a close look as they are recognized as the underpinnings of performance excellence in education. They are a natural a starting point for discussion.

Does your school already have a set of core values? If it does you can ask, "Are all my decisions and actions aligned with these core values?" Ask the whole staff the same questions. You might be amazed at the responses. Ask whether all of their decisions and actions have been aligned with the values. At the very least, this is an opportunity to revisit them. If everyone is not comfortable with the current values, decisions must be made, but not before you ascertain the issues causing discomfort. Of course, if the district already has a set of core values, you must be aligned with those.

While core values are not something that should change without serious thought, they should be the guiding principles upon which all decisions are made at the school. Too often, this is where misalignment begins and frequently goes unnoticed by many until weeks, months, or years have slipped by and morale is low, results don't improve, and pride in workmanship is no longer evident.

We recommend that you post your core values prominently under your school vision and mission statements. All of these statements should be printed on any school correspondence and provided to all key stakeholders. Now is the time to start your alignment process.

Effective leaders also set expectations for all employees. This goes a long way toward getting everyone on board with your focus on performance excellence. The leader, however, must understand systems and how critical each aspect is to the performance of the whole. You'll learn more in this chapter about the necessity of aligning the strategic challenges with action plans, resources, and the use of measurement, analysis, and knowledge management. In later chapters, you will learn more about the faculty and staff focus, process improvement, and how alignment and integration can help all employees reach higher levels of performance. The goal, remember, is to improve student learning.

Strategic Planning

Your level of strategic planning will depend in part on whether you lead a school that is independent or one that is part of a larger school district. For those who lead independent schools, strategic planning will include longer-term planning—3–5 years—and short-term planning—1 year. If your school is part of a larger district, your major responsibility for strategic planning at the school level will be your school improvement plan. We have outlined a planning process that is aligned with the Baldrige categories and criteria for performance excellence. Whatever your circumstances, the essential process remains the same.

The flowchart in Figure 4.2 provides a visual of a plan for organizational performance excellence. Throughout this chapter and some others, flowchart steps are chunked with more detailed explanations. At each step you will see the appropriate Baldrige category criteria that influence that step to reach alignment and integration.

Plan for Excellence

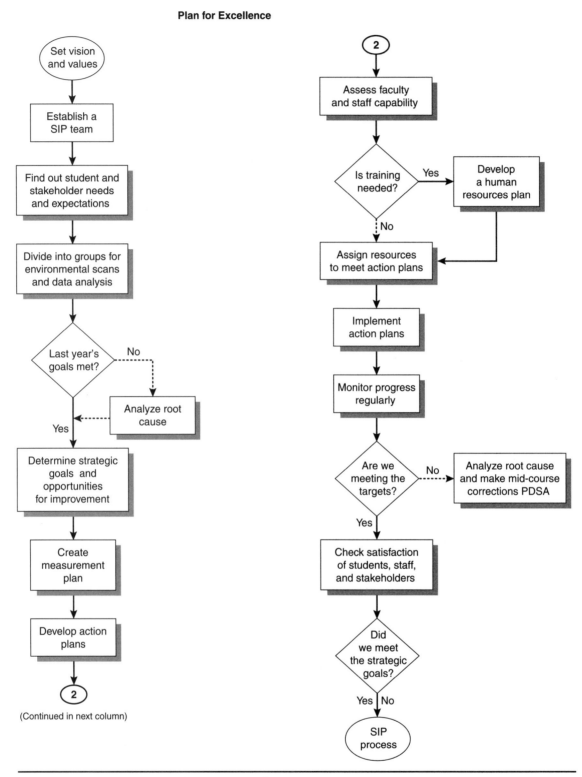

Figure 4.2 Example: Strategic planning process flow.

The significant problems we face cannot be solved at the same level of thinking we were at when we created them.

—Albert Einstein

Start at the beginning by enlisting the help of others to form a school improvement plan (SIP) team as shown in Figure 4.3. Such a team might include any members of the school leadership team, department chairs or instructional team leaders, support services personnel, and one or more students. An ideal SIP team size might be 7–11 persons, but smaller schools may have fewer. For the purposes of this book, Strategic Planning (Category 2) will focus on the SIP process.

Discover Student/Stakeholder Needs and Expectations

Leadership cannot create an adequate strategic plan without knowing what the students and stakeholders (Category 3) need and expect. It follows that the results inform students and stakeholders whether their expectations have been met, influencing satisfaction or dissatisfaction levels and market potential of the school. Needs and expectations are frequently reflected in day-to-day operations, which can be measured in-process in classrooms, through safety audits, and so forth. Obviously, a school that is outperforming others in its marketplace is more likely to gain students and increase its share of volunteerism. Review the ways in which you have tried to capture information about the needs and expectations of students and key stakeholders. Table 4.1 (on p. 51) provides some ideas about how to capture information from various groups.

It is a waste of time to prepare a strategic plan without understanding the current situation and the results from the previous plan. Fortunately, educators have come to understand that data are important, but many have not received ample instruction in data analysis. If this represents your situation, we hope these explanations are helpful. Our experience is that when a school district assigns data analysis to an "expert" in isolation of the principal and teachers, there is less ownership, less understanding, and more defensiveness. Data analysis is an activity that ought to include, at some level, every teacher in the building and the appropriate support personnel as well.

Once the SIP team is assembled and the purpose is clearly stated, you might divide the group and assign specific tasks as shown in Figure 4.4 (on p. 52). For example, you'll need a group to conduct an environmental scan, one to analyze student achievement data, and another to analyze satisfaction and complaint data and review budgets and policy or regulatory requirements. An example of what might be included in these analyses is provided in Table 4.2 (on p. 52). The degree to which a school is able and willing to analyze its current situation is the degree to which it will make better decisions about setting goals and aligning action plans to address the goals.

Analyze Current Results

When analyzing student learning results data, we cannot emphasize enough the need to provide it to the entire faculty and support staff (guidance, special education, English for speakers of other languages, and so on) in chart and graph form. Check out the Tools Selection Chart (Table 4.3) on page 53 for the most appropriate tools to use. (Many quality tools books are available. See the Recommended Reading list for suggestions.) These

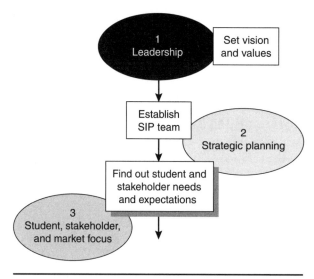

Figure 4.3   Begin the strategic planning process.

"pictures" of the current situation can be invaluable to the entire team and make it nearly impossible for anyone not to understand the significance of the results. However, it does make a difference how the charts are scaled.

Which of these charts in Figure 4.5 (on p. 54) provides a more realistic, better description of the current situation? It is quite easy to fool some of the people some of the time, but what is gained? How does that contribute to performance excellence?

While the data shown in Figure 4.6 (on p. 54) are necessary, they are not sufficient to tell the whole story. It is important to share trend data with the team in order to assess the effectiveness of previous action plans. Two data points as shown in Figure 4.6 do not make a trend, because at least three points are necessary for demonstrating the beginning of a trend.

Trends show the direction or change (positive or negative) of a school's efforts. The number of data points required depends on the cycle time of any process. For example, standardized test results yield one point per year. A statistically significant trend for these results consists of five years of data. Other processes, such as discipline referrals, yield data by the day, week, or month. A school could demonstrate a positive trend in the reduction of discipline referrals (potentially addressing a strategic goal of a safe school) by reporting monthly data for a one year period of time.

However, if you are new to data and charting, this is a good place to start. While five years of data are even better, as shown in Figure 4.7 (on p. 54), the key is to chart whatever data you have that comes from the same source. Figure 4.7 provides more information and more accurately reflects school improvement attempts that were implemented in the fall of the 2004–2005 school year.

Table 4.1 Student/Stakeholder listening and learning posts.

Group needs and expectations	Listening and learning posts
Current and future students	Focus groups
	Surveys
	Internet research on future
	News broadcasts
	Requirements from government
	Postsecondary institutions
	Businesses in your community
Parents/guardians	Focus groups
	Paper/pencil surveys
	PTA
	Breakfasts with random sample
	Telephone surveys
Community	Chamber of commerce meetings
	Social service agencies
	Juvenile justice system
	Focus groups
	Large community meetings
	Random paper/pencil surveys
	Random telephone surveys
	Workforce development offices
	Surveys of major employers
Future students	Parents planning to relocate
	Parents of pre-K students
	Workforce development offices
	Chamber of commerce meetings
	Internet research
	Meetings with next-school-in-line
	Conferences focusing on the future workforce needs
Former students	Surveys of students after leaving your school
	Focus groups of students who are at the next-school-in-line or recent graduates
	Satisfaction surveys of postsecondary institutions or next-school-in-line
	Satisfaction surveys of employers
Postsecondary or workforce	Needs assessment survey—necessary skills
	Participation on school curriculum committees
Taxpayers	Focus groups
	Large community participatory meetings
	Random surveys (phone or paper/pencil)
	Interviews with informal and formal leaders

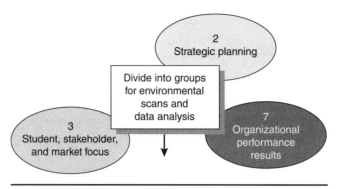

Figure 4.4 Next step in strategic planning.

Table 4.2 Example of the scope of preparations for strategic planning.

Strategic Planning Assessment of Current and Future Situation			
Environmental scan	**Student achievement data**	**Satisfaction/complaint data**	**Budget/policy/regulatory**
• New, incoming students • New, incoming students with IEPs • Current students with IEPs • New housing construction in the area, type, number of units • Planned employment growth in area • First language of new students • Needs and expectations of students • Needs and expectations of parents • Needs and expectations of community • Existing or new safety threats • Facility audit • Planned number of teachers and other personnel • New or existing environmental threats • Results of comparative and competitive schools in market area	• Normed test results analyzed by grade, class, gender, ethnicity, SPED, free/reduced lunch, limited English speakers, attendance • Item analysis of normed test results by same subgroups • Analysis of pre-post local core subject tests by same subgroups • Normed test results analyzed by teacher—trended for 3–5 years • Pre-post local core subject test analysis by teacher • Enrollment and success in more rigorous course offerings	• Satisfaction results from parents, next-school-in-line, world of work, and/or post-secondary institutions, partners, and other key stakeholder groups • Satisfaction results of graduates attending next-school-in-line, world of work, or university • Student satisfaction results • Teacher satisfaction results • Non-certified personnel satisfaction results • Other administrative personnel satisfaction results • Other measures of satisfaction such as: –Attendance –Tardiness –Participation in extracurricular activities –Volunteerism –Use of building and facilities	• Budget projections for next year • Anticipated changes in budget • Changes in regulatory requirements affecting fiscal management • Changes in policy affecting fiscal management or unfunded mandates • Review percentage of budget for "soft" money—grants, contributions, awards • Potential opportunities for "soft" money • Year-to-year budget comparison by line item

From the data in Figure 4.7, certain things are evident. One is that the interventions worked better for some subgroups than for others. But, in order to know how well it is working, you will need to get more details. The subgroups used in the figure are:

A African American
B Native American
C Caucasian
D Hispanic
E Limited-English speakers
F Free/reduced lunch

This level of detail is necessary but probably not sufficient to completely understand the current situation. We also need to look at the data by gender and individual educational plans (IEPs). Figure 4.8 shows that the approach worked better with males in both regular programs and those with IEPs. It was only marginally successful for females. The thing to do is *not* discard this approach, but continue it and analyze why the females didn't respond better. Without this information, you may have proceeded differently.

> *Avoid the temptation to compare apples with oranges. If the school has changed tests (for example, from ITBS to Stanford 9), it is not possible to place both sets of data on one chart without so noting it. Comparisons between the two are not possible, nor are these data able to be trended together.*

There are myriad ways to analyze your results. The best advice we can give you is to look at things from at least three perspectives. Then, place all the charts in a row and interpret the whole story before drawing conclusions about what changes to make.

Another way to look at student achievement data is to chart results by teacher, as shown in figures 4.9 and 4.10 (on page 55). It is also extremely important to analyze all data for trends. This is one way to help teachers see how well their students compare to students in other classes, and how well subgroups perform in each class. It is possible that teachers are unaware of special attention given to one group of students or another. Charts such as those in figures 4.9 and 4.10 can be powerful for helping leaders make decisions about professional development opportunities, teacher evaluation, and tenure decisions. Aside from the way we have presented the data, what are some other comparisons you think would be helpful?

Table 4.3 Tool selection chart.

If you want to:	Gather ideas	Group ideas	Analyze	Sequence steps	Draw a picture of the data	Collect and track data over time	Prioritize or get group consensus	Show relationships
Use this tool	Affinity diagram	Affinity diagram	Cause/effect diagram	Flow chart	Histogram	Check sheet	Multi-voting	Radar chart
	Fishbone chart	Satellite diagram	5 whys	Gantt chart	Pareto chart	Run chart	Nominal group technique	Relations digraph
	Brainstorm	Lotus diagram	Relations digraph	Systematic (tree) diagram	Run chart	Line graph	Relations digraph	Scatter diagram
	Lotus diagram	Force field analysis	Pareto chart		Scatter diagram	Pareto chart	Decision matrix	Learning and enthusiasm chart
	Force field analysis				Radar chart	Control chart		
			Plus/delta chart		Line graph			
					Control chart			
					Bar graph			
					Pie chart			

Source: This chart is modified from *Charting Your Course* by John G. Conyers and Robert Ewy, ASQ Quality Press, 2004

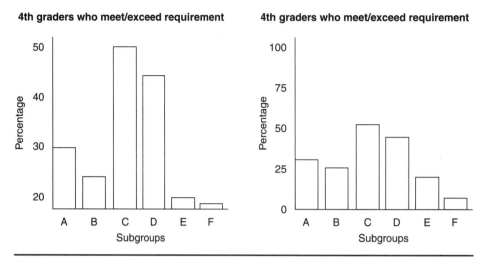

Figure 4.5   Scaling the chart makes a difference in perception.

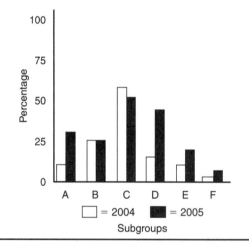

Figure 4.6   Impact of previous year's action plans.

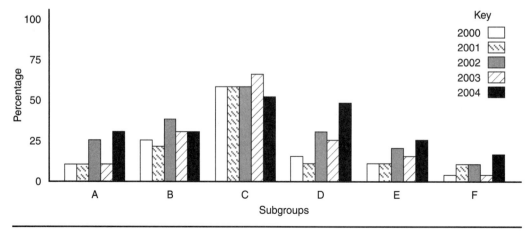

Figure 4.7   Five-year trend data by subgroup.

4th graders who meet/exceed requirement

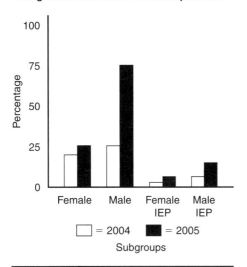

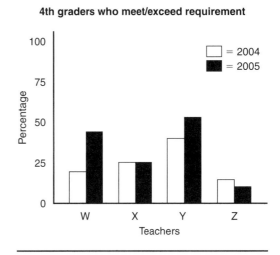

Figure 4.8 Results by gender.

Figure 4.9 Results by teacher.

Once the SIP subteams have done a thorough analysis of the data and the environmental, budgetary, and policy/regulatory scans have been completed, it is time to have the entire faculty and staff review what has been learned. Compare the results of the previous year's SIP goals to the intended action plans. If the results are less than expected, and there has been no attempt to monitor deployment of the agreed-upon strategies, it will be very difficult to assess the effectiveness of any strategy.

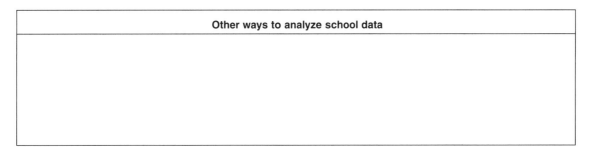

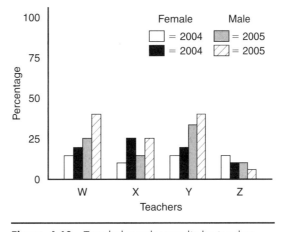

Figure 4.10 Trended gender results by teacher.

Continue to analyze the data from the past five years. Middle and high school principals will want to look at the number of students enrolled in the more challenging classes by ethnicity, gender, free/reduced lunch/pay lunch and whether the numbers are increasing or decreasing. Consider the number of students enrolled in advanced placement classes as well as the number who pass the AP exam with a 3 or higher. Do the same with algebra.

> *When levels of deployment of action plans are not monitored, conclusions about their effectiveness are rendered invalid. Alignment of action plans with a measurement system and on-the-job monitoring are essential to determine with confidence whether poor results are caused by a faulty strategy or faulty and/or spotty implementation. This is a key factor in reaching strategic goals.*

How many middle school students are participating in a challenging curriculum, or taking more advanced math and language arts courses? What have been the trends for your school? Compare the final grades (or whatever scale is used to inform parents) with any normed test results. Is there a positive relationship that gives students and parents confidence that grades are predictors of normed test results? Compare student subgroups with teachers' results.

If the strategies used during the prior year yielded the desired results, standardize the improvement. This, of course means either a train-the-trainer program, designated champions who can become mentors, or that resources are provided for training for newly hired teachers in the standardized approach. If the strategies used did not yield the desired results, the next step is to discover the problem using a root cause analysis (Figure 4.11).

While our example has addressed student learning results, you will also need to analyze satisfaction and other results of organizational performance (noninstructional) as well. Refer to page 58 for the scope of results expected in a Baldrige-based educational organization.

Root-Cause Analysis

Review all results in relation to the strategies required by the previous SIP and analyze them to determine the root cause of disconnects between process and results. If the strategies didn't work it is necessary to discover why. Some explanations might include:

- Professional development wasn't aligned with desired outcomes.

- Not everyone received the professional development training.

- Organization of the school day is not aligned to achieve the desired results.

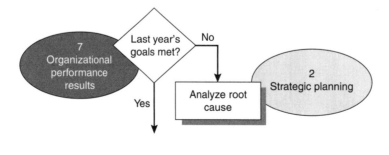

Figure 4.11 If the goals were not met.

- Teachers did not apply the approaches learned during professional development.
- Teachers did not fully integrate what was learned from professional development into daily lessons.
- Learning space is not adequate.
- Teachers' formative tests are not aligned with the state standards or district and school requirements.
- Curricula are not aligned to the standards or district and school requirements.
- Lesson plans are not aligned to the curriculum or the standards.
- Teachers lack follow-up support after professional development.
- Classroom management approaches are not aligned with desired outcomes.
- Teachers apply the school's discipline policy inconsistently.
- Teacher aides are not being used appropriately to maximize student learning.
- Pull-out programs remove students who need to learn what is being taught in class.

You can probably imagine many other reasons why a strategic goal wouldn't or couldn't be met. The important thing to glean from this is the absolute necessity of discovering the true root cause of the problem. A formal root-cause analysis should not be shortchanged as it is critical to solving the problem. See the Tools Selection table on page 53 to determine which tools to use. For example, an affinity diagram may be used to generate potential root causes. Then, taking the headers from the affinity diagram, the principal might facilitate a group in the use of a relations digraph to get to the true root cause.

One of the problems that educators have had in the past is a sense of urgency to fix problems. Unfortunately, too often educators are not disciplined enough to uncover the root cause before implementing strategies that reflect the latest craze. When the problems recur, the cycle is repeated, hence the disparaging term "management flavor of the month," which lowers morale and enthusiasm for continuous improvement and rarely solves any problems. Avoid this tendency by engaging others in a thorough root-cause analysis to eliminate problems.

Here are some key questions to ask once you've identified the root cause:

- What does the research say is the current best practice for addressing the specific problem and targeted student groups?
- Do any schools inside this district or in the area have better success with this student subgroup?

There are several ways to obtain comparative information. Inquire at the district office, if such information is not routinely provided to each school. Perform a Web search for student annual yearly progress (AYP) results from your state. Most states publish results by school, and some even categorize schools by demographics, which makes it easier to compare your school with "like schools." Go to the websites of Baldrige-winning school districts and contact them for information and results for comparative purposes. Research benchmarking websites—some are listed at the back of this book—for further opportunities. Above all, don't imagine that you cannot learn from others because your school circumstances are unique.

Analyze Previous Action Plans to Address Strategic Objectives

Figure 4.12 gives you information about where to look to see whether previous action plans were effective. Make sure you have reviewed all the results required by Category 7 of the Baldrige criteria. Table 4.4 provides a synopsis of the breadth of results required from Baldrige Category 7 (Organizational Performance Results).

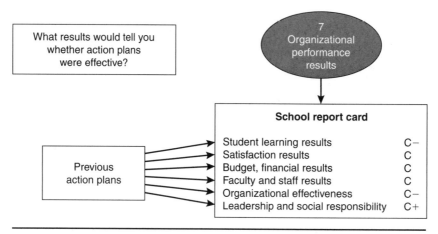

Figure 4.12 Results that demonstrate action plan effectiveness.

Table 4.4 Scope of results required by the Baldrige framework.

Item	Reporting requirements
Student learning results	Current levels and trends of: • Key learning results; comparisons with competitors and comparable schools
Student/stakeholder-focused results	Current levels and trends of: • Student and stakeholder satisfaction and dissatisfaction; comparisons with competitors and comparable schools • Student persistence, stakeholder perceived value, positive referrals, and other relationship-building approaches
Budgetary, financial, and market results	Current levels and trends of: • Results and indicators of budgetary and financial performance, including cost containment • Market performance, including market share and markets entered
Faculty and staff results	Current levels and trends of key measures or indicators of: • Work system performance and excellence • Faculty and staff learning and development • Faculty and staff well-being, satisfaction, and dissatisfaction
Organizational effectiveness results	Current levels and trends of key measures or indicators of: • Key learning-centered processes: capacity to improve student performance; student development; the education climate; indicators of responsiveness to student and stakeholder needs • Operational performance of key support processes: productivity, cycle time, supplier and partner performance, other measures of efficiency and effectiveness • Accomplishment of organizational strategy and action plans
Leadership and social responsibility results	Current levels and trends of key measures or indicators of: • Accomplishment of organizational strategy and action plans • Ethical behavior and stakeholder trust in leaders and school governance, include measures of breaches of ethical behavior • Fiscal accountability, internal and external as appropriate • Regulatory, safety, accreditation, and legal compliance • Organizational citizenship in support of your key communities

If any of the action plans included professional development, compare student learning results from classes with teachers who participated in the training and others who did not. Look for trends pre/post intervention. Measuring the value-added of staff development dollars is not easy, but it can be done. An example of this would be if you see positive trend results with targeted subgroups over time after professional development opportunities tied directly to the attribute you desired to increase. As a leader, it's important to keep track of the type of professional development provided, including when, who attended, course content, and the cost. There should always be an expectation that teachers will implement the approaches taught during the training. Classroom observations ought to provide such evidence, but you would also expect to see improved results over time.

Some action plan examples that come to mind when addressing other strategic objectives include website development as a major communication tool with parents and students, infusing technology into core subjects, project-based learning, hands-on science projects, differentiated instruction, or the use of quality tools and PDSA to improve instruction.

We recommend that expectations for implementation of strategies learned during professional development be stated up front so there is no chance for confusion on the part of faculty or staff. This is not something to be observed or evaluated once a year. Instead, if the SIP calls for a particular strategy, then there must be a means to support the expectation of on-the-job implementation. Otherwise, your system will not be aligned or integrated and the chances of goal attainment will be reduced.

Perhaps action plans revolved around the purchase of new textbooks or materials. While these are frequently decisions made at the district level, if you are the principal in an independent or charter school you and the staff may have the discretion to select these. It is hoped that you have not determined that the textbook is a problem because the fiscal investment is too high to change every year. If it is deemed to be a major problem, you would want to work with the teachers to determine how to supplement the text in ways that would support the goals.

Strategic Challenges and Objectives

After looking at the data analysis and results of the environmental scan, budgetary and policy issues, and customers' needs and expectations, make a decision about the strategic challenges associated with achieving performance excellence. With government sanctions in place for public schools not meeting the annual yearly progress requirements, student learning results are among the most important strategic challenges affecting sustainability today. Schools other than public schools have challenges related to their board policies, tuition, and obtaining competitive learning results to capture market share. Identify the strategic challenges you face.

Issue	Strategic Challenge
Education and learning	
Operational	
Human resources	
Community-related challenges	
Facility	
Technology	
Other	

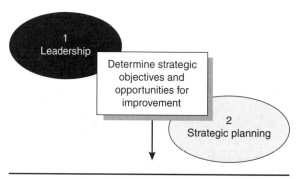

Figure 4.13 After strategic challenges are identified.

The next step, as shown in Figure 4.13, is to identify strategic objectives to address each of these challenges. In terms of accountability to your board, state or federal regulatory agencies, parents, and other key stakeholders, you must consider their expectations as you frame the strategic objectives. Student learning *always* takes priority because this is the purpose of school. Therefore, strategic objectives not focused directly on improved student learning should have some relationship to supporting learning. Strategic objectives are those things that you consider most significant in terms of school success and being competitive with other schools in your service area. The strategic objectives should guide resource allocations, so if you are an independent, charter, or site-based managed school, this has significant budgetary implications.

> *Just a reminder that if your school is part of a district, it is necessary to align with the district goals and objectives. If you work in a large district and schools are divided into areas or complexes, then your plans must also align with this level of the system.*

A partial example of a school-based alignment of strategic challenges, objectives, and strategies might look something like the example in Table 4.5.

Measurement Plan

After strategic objectives are set, and action plans have been determined, leaders will create a measurement plan (Figure 4.14) that includes leading and lagging indicators. This is a commitment to manage day-to-day operations and a way to know how much progress is being made on each of the goals in-process. In this way, you can identify when midcourse

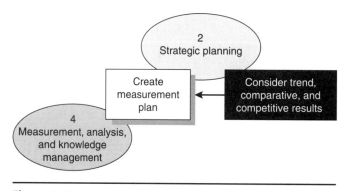

Figure 4.14 Measurement plans cross-cut categories 2 and 4.

Table 4.5   Partial example of action plan aligned with strategic objectives.

Strategic challenges	Strategic goal	Strategic objectives	Action plans—strategies	Who	When	Resources
Hiring and keeping effective teachers	High-performing staff	Improve teacher effectiveness	Professional development aligned with state test data analysis	Appropriate grade-level teachers	This summer	$3,000
		Improve work system to create more team-work and cooperation	Review way teachers are organized to work and recommend changes	Cross-grade level and cross-functional teams	This summer	$100 stipend per team member
			Provide training to accommodate changes in work systems	All affected staff	Fall in-service days	None
		Recruit and hire highly qualified teachers	Involve teachers in hiring process	Appropriate grade-level teachers	Ongoing	None
			Candidates will teach a sample lesson	All candidates	Ongoing	None
			Prepare video to promote school	Professionals	August	Up to $5,000
	Reading	Increase fluency rates	Weekly timed fluency tests.	Senior volunteers	Weekly	$100 for food during training
Large gaps in achievement levels of reading	All students will read at or above grade level	Improve reading comprehension	Grade level vocabulary lists aligned with curriculum from content areas, 1,000 most-frequently used words	Grade-level teams	This summer	$150 stipend per teacher
			Research and purchase on-line assessments	Reading committee	This summer	$250 per teacher $5,000 for assessments
			Online assessment training	Grade-level teachers	Fall in-service days	$3,000 for training
Accident rate is high:	Safe, orderly learning environment	Decrease student and staff accidents	Increase safety awareness with a schoolwide poster campaign	Art teacher	Next fall	None
			Put rubber on all stairs	Maintenance	This summer	$5,000 from district
1. Facility is in poor repair	Improve satisfaction ratings from staff, parents, and students		Review playground safety rules with students	Each teacher	Weekly	None
2. Unruly students			Safety audit of facility and grounds	Custodian and principal	Weekly	None
		Reduce student suspensions	Review the student and parent handbooks and make changes to clarify policies	Leadership team	This summer	None

corrections are necessary and provide assistance to those needing it. A brief example of a school-based measurement system might look something like Table 4.6 on the next page.

Persons required to collect the data (per the measurement plan) report it to the principal monthly and the leadership team *assesses organizational progress on each item.* Table 4.6 is not all inclusive, but it demonstrates how leading indicators help school leaders stay informed. In high-performing schools, leading indicators are routinely and systematically used to monitor the health of day-to-day operations of the school.

Develop Action Plans

Action plans (see Figure 4.15) engage faculty and staff in the strategic planning process and must be aligned, developed, and deployed to achieve the key strategic objectives. Let's take a closer look at one portion of the example from Table 4.5, the strategic challenge of hiring and keeping effective teachers. Obviously, the goal is to have a high-performing staff, and there are three strategic objectives listed to address this goal. Action plans need to be developed to address each objective and often there will be more than one action plan for each. As you can see, the school in question has a plan for teacher recruitment and hiring.

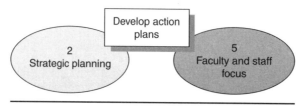

Figure 4.15   Action plans involve faculty and staff.

Assess Faculty and Staff Capability

Before establishing action plans, the leader must ask these questions: Is the current faculty capable of high-performance work and delivering the type of instruction required at this school? Is the current support staff capable of high-performance work in support of teachers and instruction? See Figure 4.16 to learn where this information would surface on a Baldrige-type school report card.

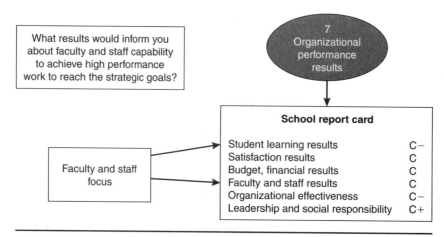

Figure 4.16   Results that demonstrate faculty and staff capability.

Table 4.6   Measurement plan with leading and lagging indicators and targets.

| SIP Goal | Success measures | Collection method | How often? | Indicator | | Current | Target | | |
				Leading	Lagging		Oct. 2005	Jan. 2006	May 2006
Reading	Fluency at or above grade level.	Volunteers	Weekly	✓		48%	60%	75%	98%
	Online assessment results	Computer tests	Quarterly	✓		n/a	55%	80%	98%
	Random vocabulary quiz	Paper/pencil quiz	Weekly	✓		n/a	37%	66%	100%
	Student enthusiasm for reading	E/L chart	Weekly	✓		n/a	80%	90%	100%
	State standards test (on grade level)	Test results	Yearly		✓	65%			85%
Math	2-minute timed math facts quiz	Paper/pencil quiz	Weekly	✓		n/a	35%	60%	95%
	Online assessment	Computer tests	Quarterly	✓		n/a	25%	50%	90%
	Math vocabulary quiz	Paper/pencil quiz	Weekly	✓		n/a	35%	75%	100%
	Student enthusiasm for math	E/L chart	Weekly	✓		n/a	70%	85%	100%
	State standards test (on grade level)	Test results	Yearly		✓	63%			88%
Safe, orderly learning environment	Student accidents	Accident reports	Monthly	✓		n/a	15	8	4
	Faculty/staff accidents with claims	Disability claims	Yearly		✓	3			0
	Student/staff perception of safety	Survey	Semester		✓	73%		90%	95%
	Discipline referrals to office	Discipline reports	Monthly	✓		n/a	20	8	5
	Facility audit	Audit checklist	Weekly	✓		n/a	95%	98%	99%
High-performing staff	Use of quality methods	Observation	Monthly	✓		12%	50%	85%	100%
	Use PDSA to improve instruction	PDSA charts	Periodically	✓		7%	35%	65%	100%
	Mentors new colleagues	Satisfaction surveys	Yearly		✓	n/a			75%
	Positive student/parent perception of teacher	Satisfaction surveys	Yearly		✓	65%			90%
	Student learning growth pre/post assessments	Paper/pencil local assessment	Yearly		✓	n/a			1.2 years

Figure 4.17 provides a high-level look at the purpose of assessing faculty/staff capability. An adequate human resources plan can provide a school leader with valuable information to approach a board or the central administration regarding resource allocation for hiring and/or professional development.

Teacher capability is a critical consideration and must be regularly reviewed and addressed by the school leaders in consultation with department and/or grade level chairs. This issue is not only one of teacher observation and evaluation, but it also takes into consideration how willing a person is to continue to learn. Some mediocre or poor teachers may be shielded by the bargaining unit, while others because of personal issues or other life and career factors are no longer enthusiastic learners themselves. A wise school leader knows what is happening with everyone on the staff and is able to make judgments about their capability.

This must not be done in isolation of a detailed analysis of student performance results *over time* in every teacher's classroom. All you need to do is think about rework and how much time is spent reteaching students without the required skills at each grade level to know that there are some teachers who are incapable of delivering the results. An effective, kind, caring school leader will identify these individuals and (1) provide them with professional development, (2) establish a mentoring or coaching program, (3) maintain optimism that each teacher can and will meet the expectations, or (4) if all else fails and after an appropriate amount of time, encourage them to consider making a change that would be win-win for everyone. A poor school leader will ignore the issues and/or claim the inability to do anything because of tenure or contract restraints, lack of time for documenting the problems, or not enough resources for full staff development, let alone individual teachers.

We remind you of the work of Dr. Robert Marzano, which we mentioned in Chapter 1. Ineffective teachers in low-performing schools are a disaster to students' learning results! There is no time to waste in making changes where they are needed *based on data—not intuition or personal feelings.* Our experience is that most teachers know when they are effective or not. It is neither humane nor right to turn a blind eye to the situation as it affects morale among all staff and greatly reduces the school's chances for reaching the learning goals and increased organizational performance levels.

Action plans are developed to address all strategic objectives. Consider the first action plan from Table 4.5 on page 61: Professional development aligned with areas of greatest need as shown from an analysis of the student learning results. Details of the action plan

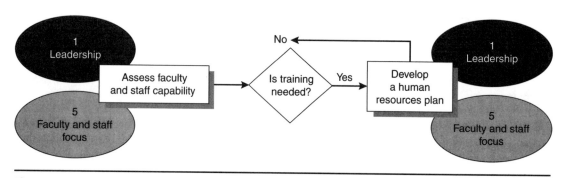

Figure 4.17 Assess faculty and staff capability.

would include researching "best practice" professional development aligned with an item analysis from the previous three years of test data. Once identified, a decision can be made about who should attend, when, how many, and what the expectations will be for implementation of newly learned strategies.

Also, note that the action plan related to improving reading comprehension has three parts. You will see a reference to online assessments. Increasingly, schools and school districts have been able to purchase reliable on-line assessments that provide nearly instant feedback to teachers about how well their students are performing in any content area. The companies who sell these assessments promote them as being aligned with the state standards. You will benefit by researching all the available assessments to ascertain the correlation with your state standards. The costs are coming down, making this a feasible alternative to teacher-made tests, and these are powerful in-process assessments that school leaders can access and review during regular organizational performance reviews. See the Interesting Websites section for more information on this topic.

You can use a decision matrix tool, described on page 66, to help decide the impact of actions on meeting the strategic goal before making final decisions.

Resource Alignment

Without resources to do the job, leaders cannot expect employees to reach high-performance levels. Therefore, it is imperative that once action plans are developed, decisions about resource allocations (Figure 4.18) based on priority strategic goals and objectives must be aligned. If instruction is the most important strategic challenge, resources—targeted directly and aligned with the action plans—must be given top priority.

Implement Action Plans and Monitor Progress

Once action plans are identified and put into place, regularly and systematically monitor progress on leading indicators (according to your measurement plan) to determine whether the school is on track to meet the goals (Figure 4.19 on p. 68). We recommend at least a monthly review of progress, but if the school is in some kind of sanction situation there is a greater need to stay on top of the day-to-day operations. This means the leader must remain vigilant and not be dissuaded by other distractions and crises. He or she must, with the leadership team, systematically monitor progress and if any indicator goes below acceptable levels mobilize a team to implement a Plan-Do-Study-Act improvement cycle. This is why targets are so necessary. Missing them is a direct signal to leaders that immediate action must be taken.

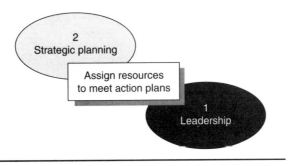

Figure 4.18   Resource alignment and strategic planning.

Decision Matrix

What: A tool that helps individuals or teams determine a course of action based on the highest degree of probability of alignment with desired result.

How: The steps to making a decision matrix are:

1. Decide on the desired result and place it as a title to the chart.

2. Create the matrix by drawing a horizontal line about 6 inches from the top of a piece of flip chart paper.

3. Starting about 8 inches from the left-hand side of the paper, draw 5 equally spaced vertical lines down. Label them as shown.

4. In the top left-hand space draw a diagonal line from the upper left corner to the lower right corner. Write *criteria and strength* in the top right hand triangle and *tasks and options* in the lower left triangle.

5. Draw equally spaced horizontal lines on the chart.

6. Copy the matrix onto individual papers and give one to each person.

7. Brainstorm all possible solutions to ensure that the desired result is achieved. Write each under task/options.

Criteria and strength / Tasks and options	Effectiveness	Feasibility	Time	Cost	Total
A					
B					
C					
D					
E					

8. Use these priority-setting symbols.

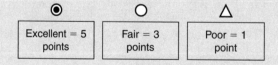

| Excellent = 5 points | Fair = 3 points | Poor = 1 point |

9. Have each member of the team score each task or option for each of the criteria.

10. Add up the total point value for each item and write it in the total column.

11. The action with the highest point value is considered the most effective and efficient approach.

Continued

Continued

When: Use this tool when you need to prioritize tasks or options for any action plan.

Example: After reviewing the results of the decision matrix, the leadership team decided to change the school day by adding more instructional minutes. They did this by adopting a modified block schedule, and therefore they did not change the length of the school day.

Need: Improve reading fluency of ESOL students.					
Criteria and strength ⟍ Tasks and options	Effectiveness	Feasibility	Time	Cost	Total points
Buy software	△	○	◉	△	10
Professional development	◉	◉	△	○	14
Ability group students	○	○	○	◉	14
Add instructional minutes	◉	○	○	◉	16
Hire teacher aides	◉	○	△	△	10
Find and train volunteers	◉	○	△	◉	14

We've already established that it is not enough, however, for leaders to know about the results. In-process data must be made available, in a timely manner, to anyone who needs the information to make decisions to improve. (See Figure 4.20 and note the dotted arrow to satisfaction results. We believe that as teachers use in-process data to make midcourse corrections in instruction, student and parental satisfaction will increase.) This is why it is vital to measure in process, regularly and consistently. If data are not made available to teachers until the end of the marking period, semester, or year, it is too late to make midcourse corrections to improve results. All certified staff ought to have access to the appropriate student information and learning data as quickly as possible. Fortunately, now that online assessments are becoming less expensive nearly instantaneous data can be made available.

When results are shared with parents or the public a leader must be careful to sanitize it for confidentiality reasons, removing names and identifiers such as ethnicity, gender, free/reduced lunch status, and so forth. Leaders also have a responsibility to ensure that all data and information are secure and that only those with a need to know have access to sensitive student information and results. In larger districts this may seem rather obvious where security measures have no doubt been in place for years, but in rural districts, independent schools, or any small school where people know everyone who attends, the leader must take extraordinary measures and remain vigilant to ensure the confidentiality and security of all data and information.

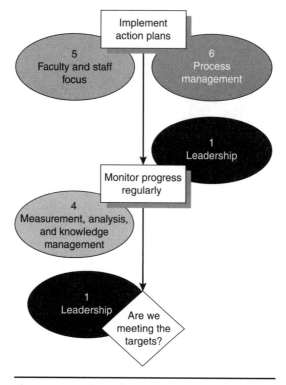

Figure 4.19 Flow of monitoring the system.

Take safeguards to ensure continuity of the school's ability to remain in business in the event of a natural or other disaster or interruption of normal school days. Create a plan to back up all data regularly and designate an off-site, highly secure storage area. Most importantly, enact the plan! Don't wait for the emergency to happen.

If there is no process in place to ensure that action will be taken on measures that drop below acceptable levels, you would want to work with the leadership team to establish one. Without a formal process that includes a timeframe for reporting back to the leader, employees may not be inclined to follow through. Instead, doing so may be considered an

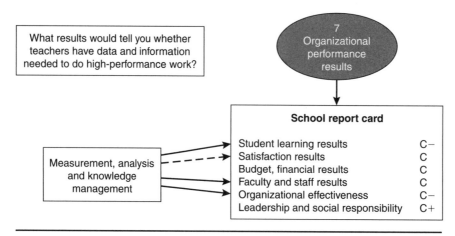

Figure 4.20 Results that demonstrate use of data for improving instruction.

option, which would not be acceptable in any school that is serious about performance excellence.

Some school leaders have established data walls to share in-process and trend results of the school's key indicators. Data walls might include the following:

- Vision, mission, school goals

- The most critical leading indicators

- Trend results from previous years that address strategic objectives and longer-term goals

- Storyboards (PDSA) from one or more school improvement goals

Care must be taken to maintain the confidentiality of the students and teachers, but adopting a culture of transparency does keep everyone's attention on the most important things on which the school is focused. How the data wall looks is not important. What is most important is *how* the data are used.

We share the following example of one approach—the flag system—modeled after a noneducation Baldrige-winning organization. It is impossible to imagine that any staff member could ignore the flags. Teachers whose classes perform below the acceptable targets would not be able to "hide" from their peers and the leadership. This isn't about shame and blame, but it is about getting everyone on board toward excellence.

The Red-Yellow-Green Flag System

This idea comes from a previous Baldrige business winner, but it is so simple and powerful that we think it is worth bringing to school leaders' attention. Check out the School Measurement Plan example, Table 4.6 on page 63, especially noting the targets for each leading indicator. If a school were to use the flag system, a decision would be made by the leadership team as to what warnings would be posted if any indicator dropped below the target. For instance, a team might decide that 1–5% below targeted results would warrant a yellow flag. Anything from 6 percent below the target would warrant a red flag. If the target is met or surpassed, a green flag is shown.

What is the purpose of such an approach and why would any organization want to use it? This is one way to ensure alignment and integration by managing day-to-day operations. It signals everyone in the organization: (1) Green flag—all the wonderful things that are happening related to the strategic goals. Green flags help improve morale, give everyone a sense of pride in workmanship, and are something to proudly point out in publications. (2) Yellow flag—what areas are falling behind and need to be given a special look before they deteriorate any further? What does the organization need to do to bring the results back to target? (3) Red flag—what areas have fallen below to the extent that unless a PDSA is implemented to discover the root cause of the problem, the strategic goal associated with this indicator will most likely not be met? Red flags mean that everyone in the organization is expected to rally around and assist in whatever way possible to bring the results back into control. (The latter thought comes from the Ritz-Carlton Hotel Company, multiple Baldrige winners. If you work at the Ritz, no matter what your job description is, when there is a problem in one area, others are expected to fill in and support the worker handling the problem. Hotel managers often clean rooms if a situation requires rapid turn-around of rooms and there isn't enough staff to do so; they cut carrots when there is an unexpected rush in the dining services; or they might handle reservations if a crowd is waiting to check in at the same time. No one is exempt from helping, ever.) In a school, this idea might translate into members of the administration or staff assisting by listening to students read, or tutoring in math, for example. Imagine what it would be like to work in a school where everyone (including custodians, food service workers, aides, secretaries and everyone else) was totally focused on doing "whatever it takes."

Where will the flags be hung? School leaders might decide to hang them in the teachers' lounge, in the office, or in the main entrance. The level of transparency you aspire to will enter into your decision about that. Of course, we recommend they be hung in the main entrance to the school because it clearly sends a message of complete focus and dedication to meet the goals. Such a system could be a motivator for teachers to discuss issues with their students if targets are not met, and engage their class(es) in PDSA to improve instruction, decrease accidents, or discipline referrals. Imagine walking into a school and seeing the flags. If nothing else, this approach will encourage discussion among parents, staff, students, and other stakeholders and lend credibility to a seriousness of purpose.

Along with the flag system, there should be a large data wall or board with the results posted each month. This should be public so that teachers and other staff, students, parents, and other stakeholders can see the progress your school is making. This represents another opportunity to approach parents and other stakeholders by inviting them into the improvement process. It is also a potential approach to use for enlisting more volunteers.

Such a system could be a motivator for faculty, staff, and students to discuss the current situation and engage in teams to analyze root causes of problems. The energy that comes from focused improvement efforts is inspirational and provides a healthier climate within which to work. Improved results are cause for celebration throughout the school.

The Improvement Process

The decision to make midcourse corrections is determined when in-process indicators don't measure up and pose a threat to meeting the strategic objectives. A root-cause analysis is the next step (see Figure 4.21) and is part of the Plan-Do-Study-Act (PDSA) process. PDSA improvement processes for any goal can be storyboarded (steps outlined with data and research attached) on the walls of the school. Parents who come to schools where the leaders are using these approaches are bound to be impressed with the leadership and commitment to excellence. Good public relations and relationship building are important steps in garnering support for current and future projects or direction. The more transparent you are with data and PDSAs, the more everyone will focus on improvement.

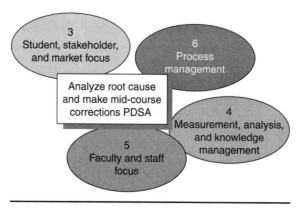

Figure 4.21 Steps to take when targets are not met.

Remember the earlier quote from Vince Lombardi: "Perfection is unattainable, but if we chase it, we can catch excellence." Many championship teams are composed of players who would not be considered the very best; but because they know how to work together, are willing to improve their own skills, and are committed to helping the team win, they are contributing to the desired result. You've known of some champion athletes who are ego driven and bent on capturing the spotlight rather than helping the team. Sometimes these teams win, but frequently they do not become champions.

In Chapter 6 we will detail a Plan-Do-Study-Act cycle for improvement of a school-wide process.

Check Satisfaction Periodically

Typically, schools survey students and stakeholders annually to discover satisfaction rates. This is necessary, but it may not be sufficient to ensure that you are on the right track to improved relationships and enthusiasm and pride in school (see Figure 4.22). Aside from paper-and-pencil surveys, review the other approaches mentioned Table 4.1 on page 51 to gain information about needs and expectations from students and key stakeholders. Some schools in the Palatine, Illinois, Community Consolidated School District 15 (2003 Baldrige education winner), in response to relatively low student survey results, instituted schoolwide plans to improve the students' respect for one another. Following a Plan-Do-Study-Act cycle, storyboards took up whole walls in the school lobbies. Students and teachers and the leadership team worked together to collect and analyze the data, discover the root cause, and come up with an improvement theory. Data was collected periodically and results posted. At the end of the year, student satisfaction results greatly improved in these schools. Had they not used a formal improvement process, the level of improvement would have been questionable.

In addition, a school leader can use focus groups or call randomly selected parents or guardians to take the pulse of this key stakeholder group. Simply talking to members of the PTA or those most involved in volunteering is anecdotal and is not terribly reliable, as these individuals are usually champions of the school. It is imperative to hear from a cross-section of parents before making changes, and then only after a root-cause analysis is performed.

Finally, it's equally important to routinely and anonymously survey all employees about quality of working conditions. We recommend a short survey perhaps every nine weeks (twice per semester). Chart the data, report it back to your employees, and seek volunteers to participate in a PDSA cycle for improving one area mentioned as having the

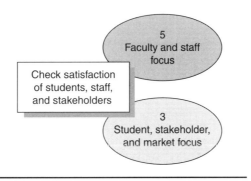

Figure 4.22 Leaders must check for satisfaction.

lowest satisfaction rating. If it is not possible to address the biggest concern (for example, you need more space but there are no resources available), an honest and forthright response is most appropriate. The worst thing to do is ignore staff concerns.

Naturally, you will resurvey everyone at the end of the year and use these data for inclusion in the next strategic planning process.

Year-End Assessment

At the end of the year, review the strategic goals and your school results (Figure 4.23). Don't forget to include all results called for in the Baldrige criteria as we discussed earlier. These results will give you valuable information about whether or not your key processes are capable of yielding the desired results and whether or not the current faculty and staff are capable of delivering the desired processes as designed.

Figure 4.23   Approach to take at the end of each year.

Last, but not least, it is important to get feedback from faculty, staff, and other key stakeholders (board or district) regarding your leadership and the leadership system. This might be part of a performance management system directed by the board or the central administration. If no such process is in place, it is wise to institute one. Left to your own devices, you might create or obtain a survey instrument for employee satisfaction with your leadership style, focus, and approaches. Again, our advice is to be very transparent with the results and use them to improve. It is a tremendous way to build trust and therefore advance the way to performance excellence.

We remind you: Dr. Deming said that your system would yield exactly the results for which you planned. Are you satisfied with the results? Use what you have learned, along with the results and plan for improvement during the next year. As shown in Figure 4.24,

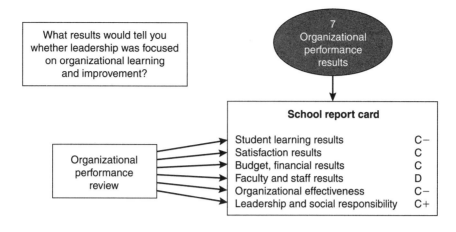

Figure 4.24 Results that demonstrate effective leadership and organizational learning.

lessons learned are going to be a key as to whether or not your school will improve and ultimately whether students receive the education they need and expect.

Complete the assessments for categories 2 (Strategic Planning) and 4 (Measurement, Analysis, and Knowledge Management) on the following pages to discover some opportunities for improvement to assure you lead the strategic planning process toward alignment with the school's vision and mission.

Assess Category 2 (Strategic Planning) Efforts

To what extent are these aligned with the desired goals?	I don't know	Not really	Somewhat aligned	Mostly aligned	Highly Aligned	What do you do to support your rating?
1. Strategic planning is regularly and systematically done; short and longer-term goals are established.						
2. Before goals are set, a complete data analysis is done.						
3. Needs and expectations of students and all key stakeholders are factored into the strategic plan.						
4. Before goals are set, the process includes an environmental scan of strengths, weaknesses, opportunities, and threats.						
5. Strategic planning takes into consideration the employee's ability to execute the plan.						
6. Strategic objectives are set to address key strategic challenges.						
7. A timetable to accomplish the strategic objectives is set.						
8. Specific, measurable goals address all strategic objectives.						
9. A measurement system is in place with targets to monitor progress toward the strategic goals.						
10. Action plans are aligned with the strategic objectives.						
11. Resources are aligned with action plans to accomplish the strategic objectives.						

Continued

Assess Category 2 (Strategic Planning) Efforts

Continued

To what extent are these aligned with the desired goals?	I don't know	Not really	Somewhat aligned	Mostly aligned	Highly Aligned	What do you do to support your rating?
12. A human resources action plan is developed after assessing faculty and staff capability to deliver the action plans.						
13. The action plan measurement system reinforces organizational alignment and covers all key aspects of the school, all students, and stakeholders.						
14. Performance measures are in place for both short and longer-term strategic goals.						
15. Projected performance is compared with comparable and competitor schools.						
16. Plans are in place to address performance gaps against comparable and competitive schools.						

Assess Category 4 (Measurement, Analysis, and Knowledge Management) Efforts

To what extent are these aligned to help you reach the desired goals?	I don't know	Not really	Somewhat aligned	Mostly aligned	Highly Aligned	What do you do that supports your rating?
1. Data and information are selected, collected, and aligned to track the school's daily operations.						
2. Data and information are selected, collected, and aligned to track the school's progress toward the strategic objectives.						
3. Data and information are selected, collected, and aligned to track progress toward the action plans.						
4. Data and information are used to support organizational decision making for planning all aspects of the school.						
5. Data and information are used to identify when a continuous improvement process is necessary and/or when benchmarking/innovation is required.						
6. Comparative data are selected and effectively used to support operational and strategic decision-making and innovation opportunities.						
7. The performance measurement system is kept current with school needs and sensitive to rapid or unexpected organizational and external changes.						
8. Organization performance and capabilities are reviewed regularly to assess school success relative to strategic objectives and action plans.						
9. Regular and frequent performance reviews help the school rapidly respond to changing needs and challenges.						
10. Organizational performance review findings are turned into priorities for continuous improvement and/or innovation.						
11. Data and information are easily accessible to teachers and staff to make timely decisions.						

Continued

Assess Category 4 (Measurement, Analysis, and Knowledge Management) Efforts

Continued

To what extent are these aligned to help you reach the desired goals?	I don't know	Not really	Somewhat aligned	Mostly aligned	Highly Aligned	What do you do that supports your rating?
12. Hardware and software are reliable, secure, and user friendly.						
13. Emergency plans are in place to ensure continued availability of data and information.						
14. Hardware and software are kept current with changing needs and directions of the school.						
15. Organizational "lessons learned" are captured and managed to transfer knowledge among faculty and staff.						
16. The school has a mechanism in place to transfer relevant knowledge to and from students and stakeholders.						
17. The school has a mechanism in place to share best practices with all faculty across the school.						
18. There is a process to ensure that data, information, and organizational knowledge is accurate, timely, and reliable.						
19. The school has a process to ensure that data and information are secure and kept confidential.						

Summary

When the steps described in this chapter are implemented, you will have taken the most critical move forward in your journey to launch a Baldrige-based quality school. If you are already a data whiz, comfortable with data analysis, graphs, charts, and trend lines, you are ahead of the game. But if you are like so many principals we know, the data part may be your biggest learning curve, and we can only assure you that your comfort level will increase over time. Don't be afraid to enlist the assistance of staff members in your school or district who "love that graphing stuff." They will be your best allies in data-driven decision making. Also, as faculty members begin to view you, their principal, as the lead learner, you will find it easier to communicate your leadership vision and set direction. They, in turn, will find it easier to bridge these systems approaches to the classroom, where the results really count.

5

Build and Manage Relationships

Conversation with the Principal

The need for good communication, especially with parents, has always been a top priority for educators. The Baldrige framework, however, may put a new spin on parent and student relationships because it asks that you take time to learn the needs and expectations of these stakeholders, taking into consideration their satisfaction as well. Also, in your school, students may not be viewed as the key customers as described in Category 3 of the Baldrige framework. By implementing a management complaint system, you will be delighted with the results over time as you are able to focus on those areas that really need to improve. These may all represent changes that you, the principal, will need to model for your staff. The payoff, however, is huge.

Build Relationships

Student and Stakeholder Relationships

An important aspect of leadership is building relationships (Figure 5.1). It's not enough to acknowledge that students, parents, and other stakeholders hold keys to the success of any school. All groups must be willing partners who are committed to the vision and core values of the school. A school leader committed to the Baldrige approach will focus on finding out what each group needs and their expectations by using one or more of the suggestions found in Table 4.1, on page 51. While it is a necessary step, it is not sufficient to build a relationship.

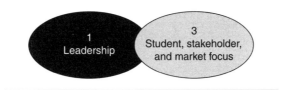

Figure 5.1 Leaders build and maintain relationships.

The Baldrige criteria ask leaders what communication strategies are in place to listen and learn about key student and stakeholder requirements, changing needs, and priorities, satisfaction, and dissatisfaction. It goes on to ask what methods the school employs to

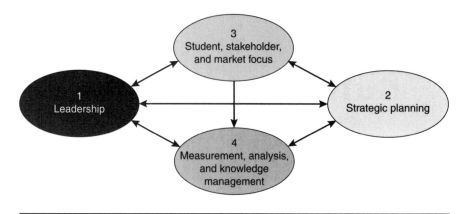

Figure 5.2 Stakeholder relationships and connections between the Baldrige categories.

enable students and stakeholders to access information, make complaints, and pursue common interests.

As Figure 5.2 shows, the two-way communication between students and stakeholders (Category 3) and leadership (Category 1) is essential for satisfying these important groups. Each provides information and data that can be captured and evaluated in Category 4, which is then fed into the strategic planning process (Category 2). Everything is aligned and integrated within the system.

The flowchart in Figure 5.3 provides an example of how a school might develop and manage relationships with students, parents, and other stakeholders, to improve satisfaction and decrease dissatisfaction.

During the strategic planning process, you've probably identified a strategic objective related to student and/or stakeholder satisfaction. This will necessitate action plans and an accompanying measurement plan. Then, along with every other aspect of the organization, these become part of the organizational performance review that triggers Plan-Do-Study-Act (PDSA) improvement projects when in-process measures (leading indicators) indicate the need.

Students as Customers

The development and commitment to positive student relationships is one of the important elements for any school of excellence. Successful school leaders can tell you they know the name of every student in their school. They take time to learn as much as they can about them in order to learn from, support, encourage, listen to, and advise them as needed. A lot is gained if someone knows the student's name—it sends the message that "You are important." More is gained when the relationship rests on trust and openness.

An example of this is an elementary school in Pennsylvania where, in response to teacher and parent complaints about the strict cafeteria policies that came from unruly student behavior, the principal and nurse/counselor developed what they called the Serendipity Lunch Program. This school of 900 students had a revolving lunch schedule that didn't seem to work for anyone. Teachers complained that they didn't have a common grade-level planning time and that students were coming back to class after lunch so riled up from incidents in the cafeteria and playground that it took upwards of 10 minutes

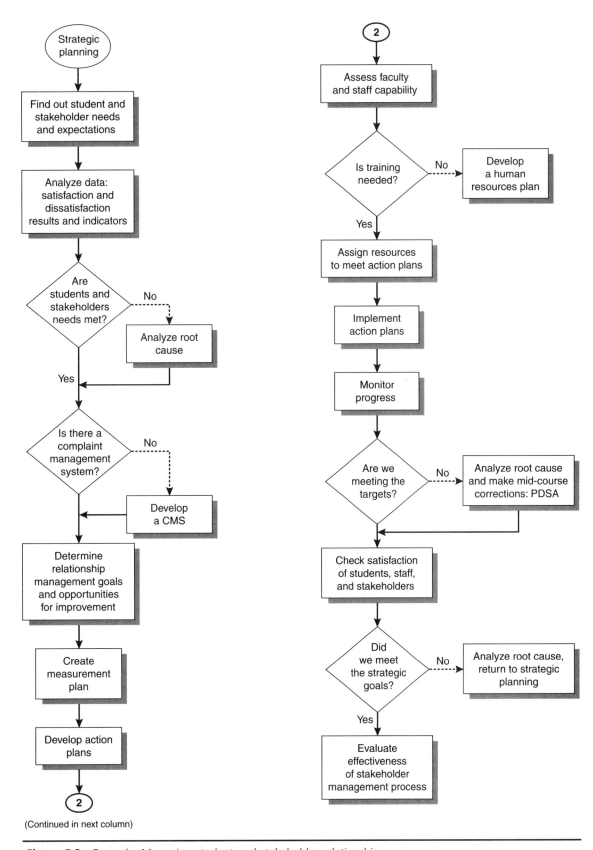

Figure 5.3 Example: Managing student and stakeholder relationships.

to settle everyone down before instruction could begin. Parents complained that the lunch-room monitors were yelling at their children so much that some children became physically ill.

After collecting data and assessing the root cause, lunch times were reorganized and students began eating with their grade level. New, child-sized tables and chairs were ordered and the long-bench tables were removed. Each month, a different grade was responsible for making placemats and table decorations in art class. Leadership responsibilities were given to a few students to go to the cafeteria a few minutes before lunch to set the tables. At the end of the lunch period, students from the last grade level to eat cleaned all the tables and put away the placemats and decorations. Lunch periods were reduced from 45 minutes to 35 minutes.

Other changes took place too. Teachers ate with their grade-level peers to discuss curricula issues and methods. The principal and nurse/counselor began eating lunch in the cafeteria with the children throughout the entire lunch period. All medicines were passed out when the children came to lunch, and the principal and nurse were able to see each child interact with his or her peers. Students were allowed to sit with their friends, even if not in their class, unless they became unruly. When this occurred, those students ate lunch with school leaders and manners were modeled and taught. The leaders were also able to counsel students and defuse problems before they got out of control. Soon parents began calling the school to inform the principal or nurse of problems their children were facing.

When the children finished eating, they would gather around the leaders, who led them in singing or in an extended educational lesson. During the first year, the nurse/counselor had the fifth-graders counting fat grams in the school lunch and lunches brought from home. They posted the data on one wall of the cafeteria. After collecting and analyzing a month's worth of data, they decided to request changes in cafeteria lunches. The students received permission to share their ideas with the superintendent and food service director, and changes were made.

The results of the Serendipity Lunch Program were incredible. A strong, caring environment became evident as these school leaders took the time to speak with and develop relationships with all the children. Students came back to class more relaxed and ready to learn; valuable instructional time was recouped. Teachers felt better because they had time to talk with their peers. Parent complaints were dramatically reduced. Most important, the lunchroom monitors stopped yelling at students and modeled the behavior set by the school leaders. Students were the big winners because these enlightened school leaders instituted a unique relationship management approach in response to a critical need.

In the early 1990s we learned of an example from an elementary school establishing the concepts of civility, kindness, and respect for one another. The students were all educated in this "Bill of Rights (Table 5.1), which was developed by teachers and the student council. It seems like a nice way to introduce the concepts of *I am responsible for my own learning* and *I am response-able to the success of the group.* (These are the two principles of a Baldrige-based quality classroom as described in the book, *There is Another Way! Launch a Baldrige-based Quality Classroom.*)

As a result of this approach, student respect increased and there were fewer incidences of student misbehavior.

Table 5.1 Example of rights and responsibilities in one school.

Our Bill of Rights
Core beliefs
Trust   Respect
Our Human Rights

I have a right to be happy and treated with compassion.

No one has a right to laugh at me or hurt my feelings.

I have a responsibility not to hurt anyone's feelings.

I have a right to be myself.

No one has a right to be unkind or unfair to me because of:

The color of my skin, eyes, or hair,

My size or shape,

My clothes,

The way I look,

Or whether I am a boy or girl.

I have a responsibility to respect people's differences.

I have a right to be safe.

No one has a right to: hit me, poke me, push me, pinch me, or hurt me.

I have a responsibility to help keep people safe.

I have a right to hear and be heard.

No one has a right to: yell, scream, shout, or make loud noises.

I have a responsibility not to make loud noises and to listen to others.

I have a right to learn about myself.

I should be able to express my feelings and opinions without being interrupted or punished.

I have a responsibility to respect other people's feelings.

I have a right to learn according to my own ability.

No one has a right to call me names because of my abilities or the way I learn.

I have a responsibility not to call people names.

Here's another example: A Texas middle school reported that each Friday, students in every class had reflection time. Part of that was spent on personal reflection and goal setting, but another ten minutes or so was spent on capturing ideas from each class about what was great about the school and what could be improved. The ideas were brainstormed then prioritized, and a final list of improvement ideas by class was given to the student council. A committee of that group met each week with a committee of teachers, and they prioritized the combined lists of all classes. The principal and teachers were committed to making improvements based on student ideas. Some of the ideas were quick and easy to implement, while others—ones that entailed resources—were sent to the leadership team for approval. Often, the children's ideas were accepted and changes were made. The students were informed when it was not feasible to implement their top ideas because of a lack of resources or district policy.

Whenever possible, engage students in schoolwide improvement projects such as the one we have described. Think about implementing a systematic approach to engage every student in school improvement. Can you imagine the pride students feel when they are empowered to make a difference in *their* school?

Parents as Key Stakeholders and Partners

How you lead the relationship building process with parents is very important. To achieve the goal effectively, a good communications system is required. This includes a combination of two-way communication opportunities such as an interactive Web page, open house, conferences, PTA meetings, and so forth. We've learned that relationships are one of the keys to future success of the leader and the school. Aside from two-way communication channels, the level to which all parents feel welcomed and comfortable in the school dramatically affects their satisfaction levels. Basically, it is wise to remember that parents send their most precious possessions (their children) to your care every day. It follows, then, that basic trust and respect are of great importance to both educators and parents. Occasionally, these obvious truths are forgotten when problems arise.

We believe that Stephen Covey's *7 Habits of Highly Effective People* are important lessons for all, and especially school leaders and other educators. We assume that the school leaders have already accepted responsibility for the current situation and realize the need to change. We also assume the school has developed and aligned its vision, mission, and goals and set priorities to improve (the first three habits). Next there is the much more difficult challenge of mastering Covey's three communication habits, which lead from independence to interdependence. These are Habit 4, Think win-win; Habit 5, Seek first to understand and then to be understood; and Habit 6, Synergize. If you are not familiar with Covey's book, run, don't walk, to get a copy and absorb the lessons. (While you're there, pick up his newest book on the 8th Habit, and practice it too.) *Interdependency* is what is meant by those who say it takes a village to raise a child. On all levels, a principal must foster interdependency to reach performance excellence. Principals, teachers, and staff must exercise open and honest two-way communication with and among teachers and students, principals, and all educators and parents, and so on with all stakeholders.

While open communication sounds easy, it does not come without first having earned trust and respect. These begin with personal interactions between the principal and each teacher, each parent, peers, and others. Interpersonal trust means that one can count on you to do what you say and stand behind your actions; that is, you have established credibility and integrity. The leader is a role model for truth, high ethical standards, and compassion. As these skills are practiced regularly, the circle of trust and respect widens to larger groups.

Within any organization, the level of trust is about equal to the amount of cooperation you will receive and willingness of others to work with you to achieve performance excellence.

Once you build up trust, you can build strong relationships. Real examples of parental or guardian relationship building from principals we've known include:

- Writing personal letters from the principal to parents of newly enrolled students welcoming them to come and visit and get a personal tour of the building, meet with the principal, their child's teachers, and the PTA officers at an informal after school coffee.

- Translating all communications into the most frequently spoken first language of families.

- Arranging for translators during all conferences or during PTA meetings.

- Inviting all parents to participate in an international cultural celebration to honor the diverse school family. Participation may include sharing native foods, music, photo exhibits, costumes, folk dance, and/or sharing traditions.

- Inviting a small, randomly selected group of parents to join the principal for school lunch each week or month

- Making home visits

- Arranging more informal group coffees at community venues, such as churches, community halls, or homes of informal leaders.

- Making phone calls to five randomly selected parents per day to inquire how their children enjoy the school and to seek any concerns. (A team consisting of the principal, assistant principal, and counselors were involved, each making five calls per day.)

- Holding quarterly focus groups with a random sample of parents representing all subgroups.

- Requiring participation of all teachers and staff at PTA/PTO meetings.

Community Agencies as Stakeholders

Seek and build relationships with social service agencies, police, and juvenile justice authorities too. These relationships will be vital to you when dealing with those families with complex situations requiring you to work with several sometimes conflicting agencies. It is not a bad idea to invite representatives from each of the agencies in your town to sit down and share information about services rendered and the chain of communication. When you include the school nurse, counselors, social workers, and assistant principals in these meetings, it demonstrates your desire for a total team approach to help all students become successful.

We never know when or even whether we will need to call upon any of these professionals, but if relationships are established you can be sure they will be more responsive than if no relationship exists. Some principals have established monthly or quarterly working lunch meetings with this group to stay abreast of recent developments and to solidify the strength of the partnerships. Of course, sharing information learned at leadership team meetings (without revealing confidential information) and with the appropriate professionals strengthens the team approach you are building.

Taxpayers as Stakeholders

It is faulty thinking to assume that you don't need a formal process to capture satisfaction data from taxpayers. Even if you lead an elementary school, there is a need to know what these people are thinking about the education you provide and also the behaviors of students. If your school is located in an area where many elderly citizens reside, or where the community is changing and young adults with no children have replaced families who have outgrown their homes, there is a definite need to systematically communicate with them. At some point, the district will seek an increase in property taxes or a bond referendum, and the relationships you have developed may be the difference in the amount of support received. If you lead a private, independent, or parochial school, the need to develop strong relationships with parents is paramount to garnering support if you need to increase tuition or raise funds.

The Next-School-in-Line and the World of Work as Stakeholders

Treat the next-school-in-line as a direct customer. If you lead an elementary school, build strong relationships with the middle and high schools to ensure their satisfaction with students coming from your school. Articulation across the content areas is a place to begin. It is vital that you find out the absolute essential skills a student must have when leaving your school to be successful at the next level. This might be easier within a district, where common in-service days are planned and when teachers representing each grade level meet with teachers of the same subject from the next-school-in-line. A seamless K–12 curriculum with specific, necessary skills learned at each grade level is the goal.

Aside from skill articulation, there is a need to survey teachers in the core subjects of math and language arts about students' abilities coming from your school. Probably, the best time to survey is about one month after school starts each fall to give the middle or high school teachers an opportunity to assess students' skills. This is valuable information for teachers and if done systematically, can greatly enhance student success and minimize the amount of reteaching required at the next level.

Business owners have a vested interest in the school too. Owners of mom-and-pop convenience stores, or other retail establishments where your students spend time and money, may have deep concerns about behavior, loitering, and theft. Also, your students may become future employees, and the business owners will want to know they have the necessary employment skills. Either informal or formal approaches can be useful to a school leader. Focus groups followed by periodic phone or short mail surveys send a message that you care about their opinion and building strong community relations. These will become stronger as you share the results and any improvement plans.

If you lead a high school, there are three very important primary customers. Besides students is the world of work. One approach that will help build relationships with employers is inviting them to become advisers to teachers who teach subjects related to their business. The purpose is to ascertain specific skills students need to know to become successful employees. The third most important customers of any high school are all postsecondary institutions, especially those in your service area who attract the most graduates. Counselors probably know where most, if not all, technical or community colleges or universities your graduates will attend are because they assist with the paperwork. If possible give them time to go out and develop relationships with the admissions people so that you can tap that resource for information on your graduates later, especially with regard to enrollment in remedial classes. This information is an important school improvement tool.

Develop Partners

Stakeholder Relationships Lead to Volunteer Partners

The complexities of education make it difficult to imagine getting the job done without additional help. This suggests tapping the community to recruit a cadre of volunteers. Perhaps in the past it wasn't as important to have volunteers help out in schools. In fact, we continue to hear from some teachers that they are not in favor of having volunteers at all, expressing the opinions "It takes too much work to get the volunteers started" or "They are more of a distraction than a help." In spite of these complaints (and some may be legitimate), there are so many tugs on a school that it is difficult to imagine a Baldrige school leader not seeking and training a cadre of volunteers.

In part, because of early retirements and longer lifespans, there are large, untapped groups of people (all stakeholders), many of whom are looking for something productive to do. This is a huge plus because there are many, many ways a volunteer could help, such as reading to a child, listening to a child read, reading stories to a class, testing fluency, tutoring in math, correcting quizzes, manning the computer labs, and helping with science experiments. It would be wise to work with the teachers and staff to create a list of volunteer opportunities available at the school, perhaps including painting the school and/or cleaning and manicuring the exterior grounds and checking and repairing playground equipment or athletic fields. The trick is to find volunteers and then train them to do important work, not busy work.

As part of relationship building with an ulterior motive, you will want to find the untapped potential in your area. Here are some groups you can mine for potential volunteers: retired educators; retired professionals; other active, vital senior citizens; and United Way volunteers. Other sources for volunteers include service clubs, postsecondary students, and high school students who are required to complete community service work to graduate. (More and more schools require service learning.) Service clubs such as Rotary, Lions, and Kiwanis often look for opportunities to do community service. Check with employers to see whether they would let their employees volunteer during working hours.

Your process might include the creation of a brochure or public-relations announcement for the local newspaper or radio or television stations to generate a list of potential volunteers and invite them to the school for coffee and dessert. Let this be a get-acquainted session, and be sure to include a tour of the building. Make sure the volunteers see (1) it is clean, (2) it is safe, (3) the teachers are friendly, and (4) the students are respectful and polite. (We assume you have already worked on all these things by creating a new climate based on the Baldrige framework.) During this session, you can present the volunteers with specifics about how they might help.

To ensure that volunteers are effective, seek out someone to become the coordinator of volunteers. This might be a school employee or even a PTA member. Get a team together to help write the curriculum for the volunteer training, give certificates or membership cards, and then build in a celebration for completion of training.

Today life is more complex because of child safety issues. Certified volunteers (this should be an honor and reported with all other data) may have to be fingerprinted (see if you can reduce the cost by asking your police department to pick up the tab) and have background checks run. Even when you think you know someone very well, make this a nonnegotiable policy. (Some states already require fingerprints and background checks for anyone working with public school children.)

Each year you will want to solicit feedback from the volunteers about what rewards and recognition they'd appreciate (managing the relationships). Prioritize their ideas and build these into your process. Often just a pat on the back, a handwritten note of thanks, or an end-of-the-year celebration is all that is expected. However, you might also consider free passes to school athletic events, plays, or concerts that typically cost money. Perhaps if a business sends a team of volunteers, you can provide them with free use of the athletic facilities once a week. Another idea is to provide some kind of lessons of interest to your volunteers such as web page design, beginning swimming, painting, ceramics, or photography. Seek suggestions from teachers (what they might be willing to offer) and parents (what they'd be interested in learning). Use the information and put a plan together that builds further win-win relationships.

Aside from the personal notes and a thank-you, which are undoubtedly the most important, see whether you can get your newspaper or television stations to come and periodically highlight the important work of the volunteers. The more you build relationships and encourage your staff to do likewise, the greater the community involvement and sense of pride everyone will have in the school. Oftentimes it is the little things that capture the hearts of volunteers, but any serious gestures will buy huge amounts of goodwill. Remember, it is a basic human desire to want to help.

Check for Satisfaction

Student Satisfaction

Surveying students is a good idea, made better when surveys are anonymous and administered by someone other than the teacher. We suggest surveying students at least twice yearly about their satisfaction with school. High among the items to survey are those related to safety and being treated fairly by adults in the building. Other things to survey include satisfaction that teachers are available to help, that student support services are easy to access, and that the services themselves are helpful. Likert scales (rankings of 1–5) are better than open-ended items, as they provide you with quantifiable data that can be charted.

If the school is large, a random sample of students can be surveyed, with close attention being paid to adequate inclusion of all subgroups, including SPED, ethnicity, free/reduced lunch, paid lunch, and gender. If your school has one or two very small subgroups, everyone in these groups should be surveyed so you can have confidence in the results.

Very young children can be surveyed using happy, straight, or sad faces. Be sure to have someone other than the teacher administer surveys to these students to help eliminate the halo effect.

With all surveys, chart the data and share it with student council and/or in the case of secondary schools all English classes. This way you will be certain to get the information to all students; there will be no secrets. As always, select a team that includes students to Plan-Do-Study-Act (PDSA is detailed in Chapter 7) the lowest scoring items for improvement.

An idea that might work in middle or high school is a postcard survey of satisfaction with services for students to fill out after receiving any support services. A receptacle could be located in a neutral place, so students would not feel intimidated by employees. The job of collating and charting the results might be given to the student council or some other student leadership group. Each week, results could be given to the principal for review along with all the other organizational performance review targets. If something is reported that needs immediate attention, the process would include a means to do so. Again, at the end of each year, ask the student committee and the leadership team to evaluate the effectiveness of the process and modify it if necessary.

These examples are not meant for you to "copycat" (see the benchmarking discussion in Chapter 7). Instead, they are shown as examples of possible systematic approaches to relationship management. You and your leadership team know what makes your school unique, and therefore any system put into place must be evaluated for effectiveness annually. It is important for you to consider how you might engage students in the process, to empower them to help improve the school, and also to recognize their importance as workers in the system that is the school—and beyond that, the classroom system. Be careful not to assume that for some reason the children are unable (too small, disabled, and so on) or would be unwilling (undisciplined, middle or high school ages) to want to be involved. Instead of having a student council that addresses only surface issues (prom, homecoming, etc.), why not consider engaging the members and their expertise to systematically help and, in the meantime, learn some important leadership skills.

A wise school leader will also ask the counselor and/or assistant principal to survey recent graduates (sixth or seventh grade, ninth grade, and those leaving high school) for their satisfaction with how prepared they feel for the new school experience. If surveys are not an option, randomly select students to participate in focus groups and be sure to take plenty of notes to share with others as part of organizational learning.

Other, more indirect measures of satisfaction/dissatisfaction include discipline referrals, tardies, unexcused absences, and involvement in extracurricular, athletics, or fine arts clubs. Data can be collected and analyzed as part of the leadership team's regular organizational performance review as described in Chapter 4.

Parent and Stakeholder Satisfaction

An important way to keep parents satisfied is to regularly and systematically survey them. While necessary, it is not sufficient to survey yearly as doing so gives you no opportunity to improve along the way. Regarding surveys, it is frequently the "how" question that trips up many school leaders. Before you start, it is important to decide on the purpose of the survey as this helps focus on the important feedback you need. Short surveys that are easy to read and understand using a 5-point Likert scale are more effective than surveys with all open-ended items. As an exercise in developing satisfaction surveys, visit several businesses in your area and collect their surveys. Analyze them and ask yourself the following:

- Does the survey address the core work of the business? (Those are the things that are most important to the business.)

- Is the survey short enough to complete within a minute or less?

- Are the survey items written to solicit actionable feedback? (Can I use the feedback and make improvements based on it?)

- Are all the survey items easy to understand without being biased toward one response or another?

- Does the survey have any room for open-ended response?

You can also access survey information from other educational institutions by visiting sites listed in the Helpful Websites at the back of this book.

Identify a group (perhaps a combination of faculty and PTA members) willing to write a survey instrument and test it on a variety of people for consistency of understanding, then make corrections where necessary. Prepare the survey and give it to parents at a significant schoolwide event (this dramatically increases response rates), send out surveys by mail, and/or conduct telephone surveys.

Once you get the responses, chart the results and share the data with everyone, including all parents. Newsletters or community forums are two ways to share information. Once the data are reported, seek volunteers to work as teams to engage in PDSA projects to improve the items with the lowest scores. (Remind staff that feedback is essential to excellence. At the same time, note what percentage of responses are received and reject the idea of making major changes based on the responses of a few. Instead, seek more information through focus groups before deciding to begin a PDSA.) Report results of all improvement efforts back through the original communication channels.

One school in New York uses a random-sample, short telephone satisfaction survey of parents each week. Using random-sample tables from a computer program, five people from the leadership team call a handful of parents seeking information on 5–7 items. The surveys take about 45 seconds and results are charted. Results are posted in the faculty lounge. Because so many parents work, the calls may have to be made in the evening. Even though this is time consuming and difficult, the benefits are untold as parents begin to realize the school really does care what they think. Several improvement cycles ought to greatly reduce complaints.

An example of a telephone survey is shown here.

This year is the first year we've done block schedules. Has your child told you about his or her schedule? (Yes or No)

- On a scale of 1–5 (5 being the highest or best)

  —How is your child adjusting to the new school schedule?

Has your child been bringing home a school communication folder each Tuesday? (Yes or No)

- On a scale of 1–5 (5 being the highest or best)

  —How do you like receiving school information this way?

As you know, we instituted a dress code policy this year. Has your child brought the details of the policy home? (Yes or No)

- On a scale of 1–5 (5 being the highest or best)

  —How do you like the dress code?

  Or

  —How well do you like the uniforms?

As you might suspect, the least effective approach is to send surveys home with students as they are not always reliable messengers. If you lead a large school, then it is more efficient and probably as effective to randomly select parents to survey. Random-number charts are available on the Internet. Keep in mind, if you have small subgroup populations, it is important to survey all in the smallest subgroups in order to have confidence in the results. Also, if you translate surveys into the first language of the parents, there is a greater chance they will respond. The higher the return rate, the greater confidence you can have in the results.

Assuming you have information from graduates about where they work, it may be possible to survey employers about these former students' employability skills as well as academic skills. If not, then we recommend holding focus groups with the larger employers in your area to seek information from them about necessary employability skills and their satisfaction with recent graduates as employees.

Another very important stakeholder group is postsecondary institutions. If you lead a high school, they are one of your direct customers and therefore, it is urgent that you seek information about satisfaction levels with your graduates. While there are some issues related to the Privacy Act, we believe it is possible to seek information about how many of your graduates have enrolled and do not require remedial courses, especially if your counselor or you have established a good relationship with the admissions personnel. Many high schools tout how many of their seniors have been accepted into a postsecondary institution, and while that information allows the counseling staff greater insight into how colleges and universities make decisions about admission, it does not give you the same information as knowing how many actually enrolled for classes and did not require remediation. This is one of the best indicators of successful high schools, and therefore one you may well want to consider pursuing.

Naturally, collecting feedback from these stakeholders is necessary, but not sufficient, if you are serious about performance excellence. You will need to review these data as part of the organizational performance review and set into motion PDSA projects when results are below acceptable levels. Whether you choose to do phone surveys, written surveys, focus groups, "donuts for Dads," or "lunch with the loonies" is irrelevant. What is important is that you regularly, systematically, and randomly select parents/guardians and other stakeholder groups to capture their satisfaction levels. This is the only way to have confidence that improvement efforts are aimed at the most important things.

Managing Complaints

Experience as a Baldrige examiner has shown that one area that is seldom sufficiently addressed by schools or districts is a formal complaint management process. Usually, a complaint management system for students does not exist, and it is basically anecdotal as parents' complaints are not captured systematically.

Few K–12 schools have a system to formally capture student complaints. Some don't even recognize dissatisfaction indicators that can be quantified, such as tardiness, skipping classes, or dropping out. There are legitimate direct complaints too, such as those related to counseling and college advising services, equality of policy enforcement, crowded halls, and a bell schedule that makes it difficult to get from one class to another on time. This is just a short list of legitimate complaints students might have. If you don't have a mechanism that allows students to register their complaints without fear of reprisal or being dismissed, you might consider working with a teacher team and student council to establish one. The time to change that is now.

Student Complaint Management Process

The idea of a formal complaint system for students may seem a bit over the edge for school leaders new to Baldrige. For others, it may be a natural extension of processes already in use, such as student advisory groups who give input to administrators. Keep in mind, the process is not about shame and blame; it is about being fair and listening to student complaints in an effort to eliminate system barriers keeping them from being successful.

Some schools put the student council in charge of taking student complaints. The approaches may vary widely, given the size of school and ages of the students. A formal process might include steps to lodge the complaint, a hearing, time to gather information and evidence, followed by a decision, with a built-in appeals process. To expedite matters, complaints can probably be segmented by type, that is, by broken equipment or facilities; by policies, rules, and procedures; by issues relating to adults; by issues relating to other students; and so forth. In the first instance (broken equipment), these complaints can be immediately passed along to the principal, who will direct the appropriate staff person to make the repairs. Other complaints may require more time. In all cases, the process should include responding to the complainant within a reasonable amount of time. As with all key processes, this one should be evaluated yearly for effectiveness and efficiency.

Parent and Stakeholder Complaint Management Process

A typical approach to dealing with parent complaints is to have a telephone conversation, perhaps a meeting, and either the parent is satisfied or takes the complaint to the next level, which is usually the district office or the board. Teachers often try to deal with complaints on their own so they don't escalate to the principal's level, and while this is not a bad approach, it is simply incomplete. Unfortunately, when the process doesn't include aggregating and charting the complaint data, there is no way to understand whether a complaint is part of a system problem or an isolated incident. If it is a system problem, there is no way to analyze the root cause, leading to dissolution of the problem. If it is an isolated incident, the leadership would not want to respond with a decision that significantly changes the system, which may or may not remove the problem.

What is missing, yet very much needed, is a means to capture each complaint, log it in, and give details about how the problem was resolved. Within 24–48 hours the one making the complaint should be contacted for satisfaction with the resolution of the matter. One person in the school could be designated to collect and manage the complaint log; however, this will probably be effective only if the leader has established a high level of trust in the building. If parental satisfaction levels are below a threshold determined by leadership, this would become one of the in-process measures reviewed monthly. Also, annually during the strategic planning process, complaint data is one aspect of the results studied.

Complaints can be categorized into common themes. Here are some examples:

- Transportation—late buses, issues with drivers, unruly students

- Food service—cafeteria line issues, menus

- Safety—student behavior, facility, grounds

- Programs—not enough honors classes, inadequate SPED services, lack of arts/music/drama/physical education/other electives

- Teachers, aides, support personnel

- Policies—tardy, unexcused absences, discipline, equity of administering policies

- Communication

Without a system to capture both satisfaction and dissatisfaction data, it is not possible to be certain how well things are going in the school. Consequently, decisions might reflect inaccurate conclusions, which might easily lead to more problems and greater dissatisfaction. Be careful not to assume that all is well unless you have hard data to support your claims. To optimize organizational and personal learning, the information would be collected in a data warehouse; the data would then be regularly placed into a Pareto chart and analyzed for root cause, followed by an improvement process.

Make certain that you also capture information about satisfaction with complaint resolution. The goal is to increase satisfaction and decrease cycle time to resolve issues. Share the results (on your intranet or in hard copy) in a notebook kept in a place where employees have easy access. It's all about lessons learned and continuous improvement, *not* shame and blame. Figure 5.4 shows you where to look to assess the effectiveness of your approach to complaint management.

If one person is the focus of many complaints, it is a signal for the leader to discover more about the problem. Occasionally, a parent or student will have a personality clash with a teacher or other employee. Usually, this results in power plays and often end up as lose-lose scenarios. How often have you heard a teacher say, "This administration does not support teachers!" It behooves you to do some personal reflection on the answer. Is it that (1) in fact, you don't support that particular teacher and/or in general, your policy is "parents are always right," or (2) you believe that in this instance the teacher's response was inappropriate; and, therefore, you cannot support him or her at this particular time? The answer to this dilemma is important. We believe that as part of your introductory statements to the staff each fall you must share your beliefs clearly so there can be no

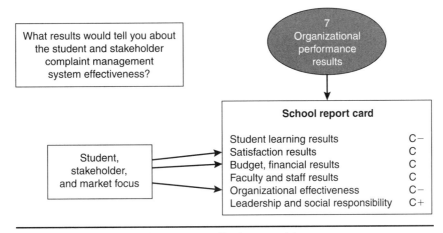

Figure 5.4 Results that demonstrate effective complaint management.

misunderstanding. It will not be a problem if you let everyone know your expectation of teachers when parents complain about their child's placement. Here are examples of such expectations:

1. Be pleasant and seek first to understand and then to be understood, using Stephen Covey's habits to arrive at win-win.

2. Be prepared—have data (and examples if necessary) to support your position.

3. Brainstorm, with the parent, ways to resolve the problem and then seek common ground and/or prioritize the interventions.

4. Communicate the results to the principal within one day.

5. Keep a log of all complaints and track them.

Within 48 hours the school leader might call or write a note to parents thanking them for bringing their concerns to the school's attention and asking them to rate their satisfaction with the outcome.

Formal or Informal Stakeholder Management Systems

Perhaps the school has an informal or a more formal system for capturing information about the satisfaction and complaints of key stakeholders. We believe that a more formal approach is better because you won't rely on anecdotal information, and when a problem arises, you have some historical data to refer to. However, if you lead a small school in a rural area, the culture may be more suited to a more relaxed, informal approach. Table 5.2 provides some ideas that differentiate an informal system from a more formal system.

A normal reaction from a school leader might be, "That's all well and good, but when will I have time to do any of that when I've got more than enough work now without this?" We agree; this is no doubt your plight if your school has not been involved with the Baldrige process long enough to deploy effective and efficient systems. Once the crises stop happening, because you have implemented a systems approach, there will be time—there must be time to engage your stakeholders. Now, you're probably thinking, "What's the payoff for me?" It's a legitimate question. Here are some of the benefits you will derive from engaging stakeholders in relationship building through a more formal satisfaction and complaint management system: (1) Trust and confidence build up that someone is listening and cares about what they think. (2) Because the channels of communication are open, you will be able to respond more quickly to complaints and resolve them without escalation. (3) There is a huge potential pool of volunteers who will be more willing to help if they feel good about the school. (4) Win-win relationships can be developed for mentoring, facilities use, tutoring, and student service learning projects. It is never too late to begin.

Figure 5.5 shows you where results of your relationship management efforts appear on the school report card. We have drawn a dotted line to budget, financial results because

Table 5.2 Examples of approaches to capture feedback from stakeholders.

Formal Satisfaction	Informal Satisfaction
Twice-yearly random sample phone call surveys to segmented stakeholders	Conversations with people after church, temple, or at other community meetings
Quarterly focus groups for randomly selected business owners, senior centers, or housing facilities	Attendance at community-related (Lions, Rotary, etc.) meetings
Semiannual paper/pencil satisfaction surveys to randomly selected taxpayers	Attendance at Chamber of Commerce meetings
Establish a citizen advisory committee for quarterly focus groups	Conversations at senior citizen centers
Annual surveys to all business owners, and random sample of taxpayers	
Focus groups held at informal leaders' homes	
Formal	**Informal**
Complaint management	Complaint management
School Internet site with a form for registering complaints	Complaints are made during any of the above meetings
Telephone or in-person complaints are logged in and directed to the appropriate person for resolution	Telephone and in-person complaints with the principal's response. There is a time frame for responding to the complaint
There is a time frame for responding to the complaints and a process for seeking satisfaction with complaint resolution	No system has been established for capturing data and reporting to leadership for evaluation, and there may not be a system for seeking satisfaction with complaint resolution
Complaints are logged into a database and regularly reported to leadership for evaluation; a PDSA process is instituted when "below the target" levels are hit	

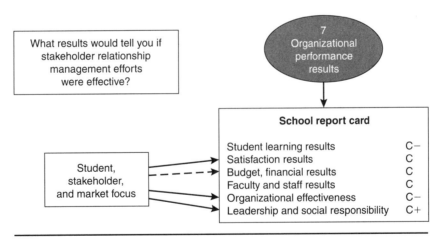

Figure 5.5 Results that demonstrate effective relationship management.

fundraising efforts and support of increases in tuition and/or taxes are related to your ability to develop and maintain positive relationships with all stakeholders.

Complete the following self-assessment to see how well you know your system before moving on.

Assess Category 3 (Student, Stakeholder, and Market focus) Efforts

To what extent do you . . .	I don't	Not really	Occasionally	Mostly	Always	What do you do and/or what results back up your rating?
1. Identify students and markets your educational programs will address						
2. Determine which student and market segments to pursue for educational offerings and services						
3. Identify future and potential students						
4. Have listening and learning posts to determine students' and stakeholders' key requirements of courses, programs, and services						
5. Use relevant feedback and information from former students related to persistence and use of facilities and services						
6. Use feedback and information from former students for the purposes of planning, process improvement, and development of other services						
7. Use complaint data for the purposes of planning, process improvement, and development of other services						
8. Use information and data to become more student and stakeholder focused and to satisfy student and stakeholder needs						
9. Evaluate and keep listening and learning posts current with needs including changes in the community and from key stakeholders						
10. Build relationships to attract and retain students and stakeholders; to meet and exceed their expectations.						

Continued

Assess Category 3 (Student, Stakeholder, and Market focus) Efforts

Continued

To what extent do you . . .	I don't	Not really	Occasionally	Mostly	Always	What do you do and/or what results back up your rating?
11. Make key access mechanisms available for *all* students and stakeholders to seek information and to pursue common interests						
12. Make key access mechanisms available for all students and stakeholders to make complaints						
13. Have a process to manage and resolve student and stakeholder complaints effectively and promptly to minimize dissatisfaction						
14. Aggregate and analyze complaints from students and stakeholders and use it to improve throughout the school						
15. Evaluate relationship management approaches and keep them current with school needs and directions						
16. Use different methods to determine student and stakeholder satisfaction and dissatisfaction according to student segments and stakeholder groups, and capture actionable feedback						
17. Use student and stakeholder satisfaction and dissatisfaction information for improvement						
18. Follow-up with students and stakeholders on programs, services, and offerings to receive prompt and actionable feedback						
19. Obtain satisfaction data and compare it relative to satisfaction with competitors or comparable schools						
20. Evaluate the approaches used to obtain student and stakeholder satisfaction determination and keep them current with school needs and directions						

Summary

This chapter emphasized the absolute importance for the leader to devote time to listening and learning. As you actually get feedback and act on that information, you are modeling the most important aspect of Baldrige for your teachers. If you think about it, many of the approaches and examples discussed in this chapter are related to practices already in place in your school, but perhaps not documented as processes that can be measured. The examples are intended to prime the pump; remember, you will need to adapt the information to your own school's situation. We would again remind you that using the Baldrige framework gets easier when you *just do it*.

6

Lead the Faculty and Staff

Conversation with the Principal

This chapter gives you the broad perspective as well as practical examples of how to lead a Baldrige-based faculty and staff. Without a doubt you can expect that staff will be uncomfortable with system change. That is the human condition. Resistance will increase when you begin to put all the data out there for everyone to see, and teachers will fear comparisons. As the school leader you will keep pressing the fact that system change and analyzing data is not about them (teachers); it is about making data-driven decisions around best practice. We're asking you to trust the process. As teachers begin to share and learn, they too will be more interested in getting results. As a consequence, they will become more self-managed with regard to their own growth.

The Challenge of Leading

The Curse of Competence

Good is the enemy of great. That good is the enemy of great is not just a business problem. It is a human problem.

—Jim Collins
Good to Great

For those who find themselves in a situation with a school that is performing competently and where students are making satisfactory, if not good, progress, the challenges to reach performance excellence or sustainable greatness are different than those in low-performing schools. The school culture here is one of a comfort level associated with "good." They have a mentality of if it isn't broken don't fix it. Educators in these schools delude themselves that current levels of performance are adequate to sustain them over time. This is the curse of competence that business has had to learn, often going out of business because they cannot sustain the impetus for excellence. When a school or a business is on the survival line, everything changes and there is an urgency and motivation to do things differently.

We have frequently encountered the truth of this firsthand. Educators who think they are okay have little or no incentive to roll up their sleeves and focus on going from good to great—for example, to performance excellence. This is a similar mentality to learned mediocrity. Unfortunately, what was good enough last year or the year before will not be good enough for the future. If you doubt this, then think about the fact that *no one knows what students will encounter* during their adult lives in terms of the job or career challenges, national and global economics, security, and environmental sustainability. Is your school, with all its employees, capable of moving from good to great to meet these unknown challenges? You must reflect on whether you and your teachers are consistently doing a great job of delivering instruction so that *all* students are learning the skills they *must* have such as fundamental literacy (reading, writing, speaking, listening, math, and technology), accessing information, analyzing data, and solving problems.

If you lead a low-performing school, the challenges you face are difficult—not only or even necessarily in terms of student demographics, or resources, but in making sure the right people are on the bus. In his best-selling book, *Good to Great,* Jim Collins says, "If you have the right people on the bus, the problem of how to motivate and manage people largely goes away. The right people don't need to be rightly managed or fired up; they will be self-motivated by the inner drive to produce the best results and to be part of creating something great. If you have the wrong people, it doesn't matter whether you discover the right direction; you still won't have a great company. Great vision without great people is irrelevant" (p. 42). At the same time, a leader who has the right people on the bus, and then micromanages them, displays a lack of trust, making it very difficult to boost morale or motivate employees to achieve high performance work.

Put Together the Right Team

Is it possible that even in good schools some of the wrong people are on the bus? Absolutely! (And the converse of that is also true.) How would you recognize them if you were the leader; more importantly, how would you go about changing the culture of the organization to turn these people around and encourage the wrong ones to get off your bus, allowing you to hire the right ones? What are the factors of the right people for your bus? This list is not complete, but it will give you a place to begin thinking:

- Demonstrates a high degree of competence in the subject matter to be taught
- Has very high ethical standards and exhibits integrity
- Is willing and eager to put forth an extraordinary effort—for the long haul
- Is not ego driven
- Engages students as partners and uses feedback from them to improve instruction
- Understands and defines oneself as a *facilitator of learning,* not a teacher
- Shows a strong desire to become part of the team that is making something extraordinary happen
- Believes in the window and mirror approach to responsibility and applies it to his or her daily work

Collins, in his leadership hierarchy, discovered that organizations move from good to great when they are led by CEOs who use a blend of personal humility with professional will to build enduring greatness. He refers to this as the window and mirror approach.

> *[Great] leaders look out the window to apportion credit to factors outside themselves when things go well. At the same time they look in the mirror to apportion responsibility, never blaming other people, external factors, or bad luck when things go badly.*
>
> —*Jim Collins*
> Good to Great, *p. 35*

The worst thing any school leader can do is ignore problems associated with ineffective, tenured teachers. One way to approach this situation is to take the following steps: (1) Read and share Robert J. Marzano's research about effective teachers versus ineffective teachers on student achievement gains with any teacher whose students have consistently not achieved at expected levels. (2) Analyze the results of normed tests over a 3–5+ year period *by teacher*, chart the results of student achievement, and prepare to give them to each teacher in the school. (3) Interview each ineffective teacher (those whose students rarely, if ever meet school or district expectations for student learning) and see whether they meet the factors on the previous page. Keep in mind, professional development can help bring people up to speed and help them reach competence in their content area, but the willingness and eagerness to put forth an extraordinary effort for the long haul must come from within. This is the straw that breaks the camel's back. Either they do have the will or they don't.

At the same time, a wise school leader must maintain an optimistic point of view that everyone (teachers, aides, and support staff) *wants to* and *is capable of* becoming part of the high-performing team. This is why it is absolutely essential to help each individual analyze his or her strengths and weaknesses, then provide them with opportunities to improve. If, after a reasonable period, any individual demonstrates through his or her behavior or rhetoric an unwillingness to improve, it is the responsibility of the leader to counsel them to seek other employment opportunities. As Marzano has shown us, you simply cannot afford the alternative!

To help you hone your leadership skills, here are some honest-to-goodness real-life examples. We encourage you to reflect on how you would respond to each one.

Example A. A veteran, award-winning advanced placement teacher, extremely knowledgeable about her subject area, decided to move from the high school where she had taught for 17 years to a small middle school four years ago. Techniques that were highly successful at the high school level were abysmal failures with middle school students. Frustrated, she wondered whether to continue teaching or make a career move. She cared deeply about the students and the fact that they were not performing as she knew they must.

Example B. A veteran elementary teacher started each day with students doing "seat work." She used this time to read the newspaper, so when the principal walked into her room, she didn't stop reading the paper nor change her normal routine. Students were not performing very well in her classes, and she "knew" it was because they were from poor families. She expressed impotence to change the situation.

Example C. A relatively new teacher, who prided herself on organization and whose students had always achieved at expected levels, was disturbed when she got a class of students who had not met the previous years' achievement requirements. Not knowing what to do first, she instituted strict classroom rules and focused on reteaching using prepared worksheets. She was puzzled when discipline problems escalated in spite of the rules.

Example D. Mr. C, the football coach with a record of 10 years of championship teams, also teaches social studies. During the spring and fall, Mr. C's classes spend most of their time on independent study and watching videos of historical events. Parents and students love Mr. C. He is a friendly man with a great sense of humor, which he frequently brings to his classes. His students consistently perform just below average on the required normed tests.

Once you get the right people on the bus, the stage is set for greatness.

Leader as Service Provider

As the leader, you are also a service provider and one of your responsibilities is to find and allocate resources to help strengthen the skills and abilities of all teachers and staff. As such, it is necessary for you to understand that the people who work in your building are your key customers. Some of the services you provide include:

- Communication links between the central administration (the board if you lead a private, parochial, or charter school) and staff

- Communication links between the parents and other stakeholders and staff

- Observation and coaching

- Technical assistance as the instructional leader

- Resource allocation (site-based schools)

- Leadership—the "climate" and tone of workplace including expectations for high-performance work

- Support—morale booster as well as materials provider

- Advocate for teachers, staff, and students to the community and district

As we have discussed throughout this book, the leader is the key figure in achieving the desired results. You need only think about faculty and staff morale to realize how important your role is and the absolute necessity of maintaining a positive, open, two-way communication approach with everyone.

Figure 6.1 reminds us again of the direct link between leadership and the work core and how the other Baldrige categories interface with Category 5, Faculty and Staff Focus. This category has three elements. They are (1) work systems (how work is organized to do the jobs and the performance appraisal system; (2) learning and motivation (how to increase capability to meet current and future needs and contribute to career development;

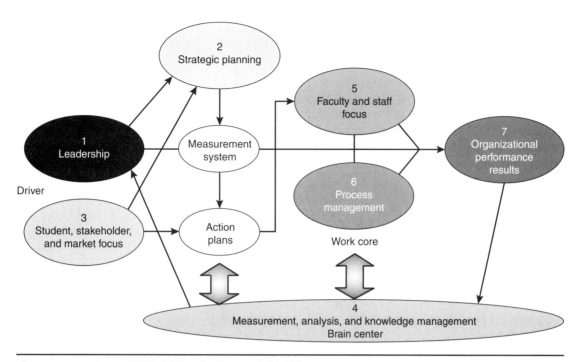

Figure 6.1 Role of leaders relative to the faculty/staff focus.

and (3) well-being and satisfaction (create a work environment that supports all employees as well as students). In the remainder of this chapter we will explore each of these in more detail.

Promote High-Performance Work

Work Systems

As Figure 6.2 shows, to reach performance excellence you must not only hire people dedicated to getting the job done, but also give careful consideration to how people will be organized to do their work.

Aspects to take into consideration include:

- The way in which certified staff are organized to do their work (for example, grade-level instructional teams, looping, multiage group classrooms, independent classrooms, subject-matter departments, and cross-functional or cross-grade level instructional teams). Think about how well-certified staff cooperate with each other across grade levels or departments, across special education (SPED), English for speakers of other languages (ESOL), and other student support services and classrooms. To be effective, faculty, and staff must be empowered to identify and solve problems. Review the data (student learning and student and staff satisfaction results) to learn whether the work system fosters high-performance work.

- How is work space determined, and how does it encourage cooperation, empowerment, and innovation among faculty? Does the current work space and facility (in general) align with the culture of the school and foster a climate of

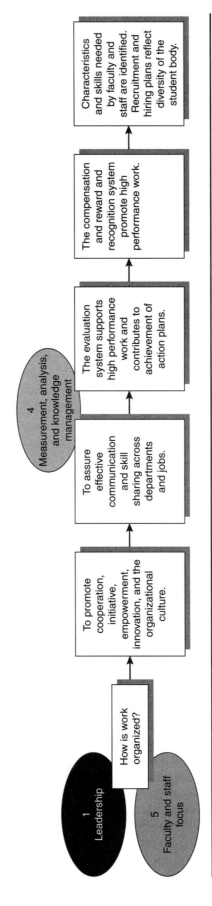

Figure 6.2 Work systems aspect of faculty/staff focus.

performance excellence? Consider ways custodial and other support staff services are aligned with the strategic goals and integrated with the faculty to provide a safe, secure environment where students and faculty can learn and where organizational performance will improve.

• How is the school day organized, and how does the school schedule flow? It is possible that you are not able to reach your objectives because there has been little or no consideration of the impact of the schedule on strategic challenges and meeting the strategic objectives. If this describes your situation, you are likely to have an alignment problem. For example, think about the action plans, the need to promote cooperation and integration among all faculty and staff before you consider the options (block, flexible block, traditional, alternating schedule, and so on). It is important to consider the schedule that offers the best opportunity for teachers to teach and students to learn, and, therefore, achieve improved learning and satisfaction results. Reflect on what drives your school schedule. Is it transportation, teacher preference, availability of "specials" teachers, athletic team practices, pressure from parents, or the budget? Does the tail wag the dog at your school? If you lead a school that is part of a district, perhaps some of these decisions are out of your hands (for example, yearly calendar and daily start and end times). Most superintendents, however, allow some flexibility in the way a school organizes its day. It is a key point and *will* make a difference in your level of success.

• Next, consider how students are grouped. Are they heterogeneously mixed; are they in ability tracks, mixed ages and grade levels; are the gifted and SPED students always segmented out for special services? This is an important philosophical issue and also one of alignment, and it should be discussed with the whole faculty. Consider the action plans and strategic objectives and research best practice with schools having similar student populations before making this important decision.

• In what ways do you assign teachers to classes or grade level? Is it on the basis of years of experience or number of preparations? How do you decide who will teach the underperforming students? What cooperative or innovative approaches have been taken to assure that students with the greatest needs receive instruction from the best teachers?

Again, we remind you of Marzano's research on effective and ineffective teachers. Some principals reassign teachers who are poor performers to other classes, to "fix" a problem, but all too frequently they are reassigned to students with lower skill levels. In defense, principals say that they feel impotent to do otherwise because of Board policy and/or bargaining unit agreements. We suggest you consider engaging bargaining unit leaders to become your partners in the achievement of strategic objectives. Work with them to consider ways to improve the work of ineffective teachers—perhaps through jointly sponsored professional development, or mentoring programs. Then, plan a joint celebration when the goals are achieved.

• What internal communication system is in place to share lessons learned, results of Plan-Do-Study-Act (PDSA) cycles, excellent lesson plans, and other skill sharing methods across the school including cross departments, grade-levels, and support services? Is there an expectation that people will share knowledge, therefore expanding the benefits across the school? Examples of skill and knowledge sharing include an intranet, demonstrations at teacher meetings, a PDSA binder with process and results from all school projects, and a special bulletin board in the faculty lounge. Without a system to capture and share organizational knowledge, pockets of excellence may appear in the building but the whole school may not reach its goals in a timely manner. This is another organizational and personal learning and integration issue.

Figure 6.3 shows where the results of your work system appear on the school report card. If you are not getting the desired results, engage the faculty and staff in a root-cause analysis of the work system to discover the extent to which it leads to the current results.

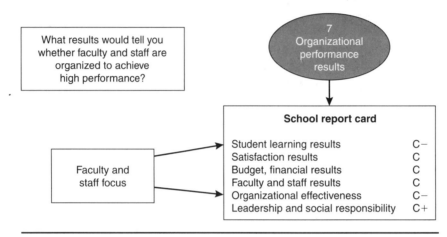

Figure 6.3   Results that demonstrate whether faculty and staff are organized to achieve high performance.

Support a Different Work System: A BBQ Classroom

Our previous book, *There Is Another Way: Launch a Baldrige-Based Quality Classroom!* (see Recommended Reading and Web sites), provides a new paradigm for how teachers work, and it works where simply adding a program doesn't. Learning about and supporting teachers who use a BBQ approach is an important role of school leaders with a desire to lead a school to performance excellence.

A Baldrige-based quality (BBQ) classroom requires a different work system and, because the paradigm shift is so great, it is vital that principals learn along with their teachers in order to understand how to provide appropriate support along the way. Attend the entire training with your staff, participate, and keep your cell phones turned off. That's the first step (and one of the most important) a leader can take. It sends a strong message about your seriousness of purpose, focus on results, and visionary leadership. As you experience the training with your teachers, you will begin to realize what is entailed in the establishment of a BBQ system.

Figure 6.4 details how the Baldrige criteria provide a framework for a classroom. Note that the only category that is any different is Category 5. Here, instead of Faculty and Staff Focus, we have Student as Worker Focus to illustrate that students are both customers and workers in the classroom. Traditionally, they have had to work in a system largely created by teachers to meet the teachers' needs and comfort zone and, as a result, learning results have been mixed. Students in classrooms using the Baldrige-based quality approach, regard-

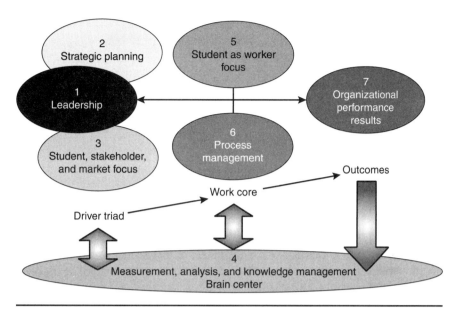

Figure 6.4 Framework adapted for a Baldrige-based quality classroom system.
Source: Modified from Blazey, Davison, and Evans. *Insights to Performance Excellence in Education,* 2003, ASQ Quality Press.

less of grade level, the curriculum, or subject area, demonstrate improved learning results, exhibit fewer discipline problems, and share increased enthusiasm for learning. This is why it is imperative that you learn all about the approach to support its use in each classroom.

The Baldrige core values of managing for innovation and focusing on the future are significant as a leader strives to break out of any box that is holding back teachers, students, and other staff members from being successful. In *Good to Great,* Collins tells us that a leader must demonstrate "ferocious resolve, an almost stoic determination to do whatever needs to be done to make the [school] great" (p. 30). When you support teacher-leaders in their classrooms by expecting alignment and dedication to the Baldrige core values, framework, and PDSA improvement process, you demonstrate this resolve.

Performance Management and Appraisal Systems

When your school and work systems are completely aligned with your vision, mission, and strategic goals, the next consideration has to be how people will be evaluated and supported to achieve high-performance work. Take another look at your strategic objectives and action plans that flow from those goals. Look at the current performance evaluation system. Is it aligned and robust enough to reach the strategic goals? Does it reflect the new culture and expectations at your school? Does the evaluation instrument require teachers and staff to reflect on their work and provide data to support their conclusions? Is there an expectation that each individual will prepare a personal professional development plan (PDP) based on areas of greatest need? Last, performance reviews should always be placed in context along with each teacher's student performance results.

We suggest you engage in a discussion of the effectiveness of the current performance management system with the faculty and staff and others with a vested interest. Bring data to support your position. If trend data show that students are not learning at expected levels, it may be evidence of a disconnect with the performance management system. In other words, those things that are assessed may not be the critical things that influence learning.

Or, the PDPs are not aligned with demonstrated needs. In Appendix B we provide an alternative performance management instrument for your perusal, and we hope it sparks discussion. To get from good to great requires innovation or outside-the-box thinking. You know that people will practice that on which they are evaluated, so if your evaluation instrument and process are not aligned with the new approach, don't assume employees will do what you expect or know they must do. This is a huge issue for educators, one that is evolving with increased demands for accountability, and one that will take courage to tackle, but one that cannot be overlooked.

Alignment of the performance management and appraisal system for teachers in BBQ classroom is necessary. You want to be assured that your observations are focused on the classroom as a system, looking at key instructional and noninstructional key processes and how students are engaged as copartners in managing their educational experience. Visible signs to look for in a BBQ classroom are shown in Table 6.1.

Reward and Recognition System

Like all other aspects of your system, the way employees are rewarded and recognized makes a huge difference in their motivation to reach the desired result. The expectation is that people within a Baldrige-based system will become risk takers and innovators, and use action research to accomplish the strategic objectives. Ways in which people are rewarded and recognized for their efforts will either encourage them to continue or to feel unappreciated, suffer burnout and give up.

Because integration (every department and individual is dedicated to helping the others succeed and working to make sure that happens) is critical, your reward and recognition system (RRS) must encourage cooperation and teamwork. We assume that you've already aligned the system (vision, mission, values, strategic objectives, measurement plan, and action plans) to address all strategic challenges.

Recognition is easily handled and relatively inexpensive, yet all too often it becomes overshadowed by daily crises. Keep in mind, if you consistently apply Collins's window/mirror approach you will gain the respect of others and the staff will beam with pride for being a part of the team. Here are a couple of inexpensive and nontraditional ideas:

- Staff team recognition ceremonies at report card time

- Balloons for uplifting service to the school

Recognition ceremonies are important motivators as everyone enjoys (and at least occasionally needs) a pat on the back. Center stage is not where the leader needs to be. Instead, drop your ego needs and give credit to those who make great things happen. It'll pay big dividends as you go through the journey to performance excellence.

Often, during workshops we ask teachers whether anyone has ever asked them for feedback on the rewards that would motivate them to do high-performance work. Their response is always the same (no), yet we believe this is simply because leaders haven't thought about it. We suggest holding an all-employee meeting and ask them to brainstorm a list of desirable yet feasible rewards. If your group can't think of any ideas for rewards, prime the pump and offer a few suggestions. Suggest such things as tickets to the movies, a gift certificate for a favorite restaurant or department store, an engraved plaque, flowers, and

Table 6.1 Observables in a BBQ classroom.

Performance review system: Teachers		
Are you . . .	**Yes**	**No**
Receiving higher quality work from your students?		
Involving students in planning?		
Involving students in decision making?		
Seeking feedback from the next-teacher-in-line about skills students need to succeed?		
Providing learning experiences dealing with real-life application?		
Using a variety of teaching strategies that address multiple intelligences and incorporates the latest brain research?		
Using differentiated instruction?		
Setting personal goals and measuring progress toward them?		
A role model for continuous improvement?		
Using quality tools to enhance your effectiveness as a teacher?		
Becoming a quality learning risk taker?		
Sharing your lessons learned with colleagues?		
Becoming more a facilitator of learning and less a "boss manager?"		
Able to analyze data to know what to change? Becoming a better problem solver?		
Seeking feedback from students regularly to eliminate barriers to their success?		
Organizational review system		
Does the classroom have . . .	**Yes**	**No**
A collaboratively established vision and mission statements? Is each signed by all and posted in the classroom?		
A climate that demonstrates the two principles of "I am responsible for my own learning" and "I am response-able to the success of the group?"		
Measurable class learning goals? Are they posted prominently in the classroom? Are there charts on the walls showing progress toward the learning goals?		
Charts and graphs posted that show evidence of improvement of key classroom processes?		
Well-defined procedures that are reviewed for alignment with the best practice and improved as needed?		
Students who are enthusiastic about learning, have few discipline problems, and have high attendance rates and low tardy rates?		
Community members and parents involved?		
Performance review system: Students		
Are the students . . .	**Yes**	**No**
Involved in planning learning activities?		
Setting personal goals?		
Measuring progress toward their goals?		
Working cooperatively in teams on projects?		
Improving the quality of their work?		
Becoming better listeners?		
Becoming learning "risk takers?"		
Making suggestions to improve classroom procedures?		
Using the PDSA process to improve?		
Familiar with, and use quality tools to improve learning?		
Becoming better problem solvers and making better choices?		

so forth. After the list is generated, have them prioritize it. In fairness, it's important to share budgetary constraints with everyone upfront before you go down this path.

None of the aforementioned rewards is very costly, yet when multiplied by the number of employees, can add up to quite a large sum. Consider approaching your corporate partners or the PTA to help offset the cost of any rewards. Both certified and noncertified staff can be rewarded for innovations or for leading a PDSA team to solve a difficult problem. In addition to teachers, food service workers or custodians who receive A+ ratings on health, safety, and environmental inspections from outside regulatory bodies deserve rewards, as do bus drivers for safety and on-time delivery of students. Rewards or recognition might also be given to support service departments who have dramatically lowered complaint levels.

There is a lot of debate about how to reward teachers for student achievement. There are several things a Baldrige-based leader needs to consider. Foremost is the absolute necessity of alignment and integration to achieve performance excellence. If you base the reward system on individual pay-for-performance based on how well students achieved on a normed test, you must consider the downside of discouraging teachers from sharing lessons learned and best practice. Then too, the fairness question becomes paramount, as some will say, "I had more students with Individual Education Plans," "I had a disproportionate number of ESOL students," or "I had too many students who didn't meet last year's requirements." These are not necessarily unsubstantiated concerns and can certainly become the cause of morale problems. Some will argue that the most effective reward system is for the entire team or school. This approach makes it okay, encouraging cooperation and teamwork to help one another improve.

A system that fosters teamwork and collaboration *and total dedication* to achievement of action plans and strategic goals will, over time, yield the greatest sustained results and best possible chance of success. Our advice is to find a balance of a combination of rewards and recognition, for individuals, teams, and the whole school. We understand that those who lead schools that are part of a larger district are not in a position to make these decisions, but we offer these ideas for everyone in the hope it will spur a dialogue:

- When student achievement targets on normed tests for the entire grade level, department, or middle school instructional team are met, reward all teachers, aides, and certified support personnel who contributed with this group of students.

- Reward everyone in the school (including support personnel) when all student learning targets are met.

- When there has been a major increase in student, parent, and stakeholder satisfaction rates reward everyone in the school (including noncertified personnel).

- When all bus drivers have achieved the target (above 95%, we hope) for on-time delivery of students to school, reward all drivers and the supervisor. (To accomplish this, the drivers will have to collect data and work closely with the scheduler to share information about road closures, potential for rerouting buses, and so on.)

Human Resource Plans

Annually, during the strategic planning or SIP process it's important to identify short-term human resource needs (to identify gaps in skills and knowledge needed among the current staff) and longer-term needs. Teacher shortages are a reality, and many rural schools and inner-city schools have difficulty recruiting the "best and brightest," not to mention those who reflect the diversity of the student body. Innovative recruitment approaches may be necessary:

- Partner with a university to pay (offset tuition costs) exceptional student teachers during their last semester internship with the proviso that they will be employed upon graduation and completion of certification requirements.

- Start a Future Teacher's Club and mentor students with a desire to become teachers. Set up a foundation (or partner with a local one) and reward students with excellent high school academic records with partial scholarships to become teachers. Promote the idea that if they teach in their hometown for five years, the foundation will provide some relief of their student loans.

- Help pay university tuition costs for aides, custodians, bus drivers, clerical, or food service employees to pursue a teaching degree, with the expectation they will teach at your school for a designated number of years. Employ them full-time and have them tutor students when they are not assigned regular work. (Example: A bus driver works about five hours a day. During the off time—usually in the middle of the day—he or she might read to children, test fluency rates, or tutor in math.)

Learning and Motivation

Figure 6.5 addresses how a Baldrige-based school would approach the issue of professional development, education, and career development. However, while professional development or staff training may be one way to help people reach the desired performance, it is not always the only way. To ascertain the most effective approach to use in your school, conduct a complete professional development and training analysis as shown in Figure 6.6 (on p. 113). Use the strategic goals and objectives, action plans, and organizational performance results to discover the gaps between the desired and actual state of workplace performance. This will disclose employee education and training needs and wants, a key to the wise use of dollars and improved worker effectiveness.

Figure 6.7 (on p. 114), a school report card, shows you where to look for results affected by professional development. If the results are not trending upward after implementation of skills learned from professional development experiences, there is a need to reexamine the cost effectiveness of the new approach. Baldrige-based leaders use this information to gain support from boards and/or central administration during the budget process to receive resource allocation for targeted professional development.

Career Progression

Perhaps you've worked to establish career ladders for teachers to become master teachers or administrators. If you've done this, we applaud you because it is one way to retain your best teachers—the biggest asset you have on this journey to performance excellence. The alternative performance appraisal instrument we've provided in Appendix B has a progression toward becoming a master teacher. At the very least it will spur discussion in your school.

As a leader, it is important to realize your role in helping mentor others to become leaders. Some principals we know have monthly brown-bag book clubs to discuss a variety

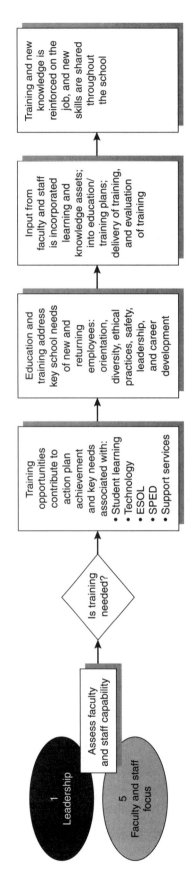

Figure 6.5 Aspects of learning and motivation.

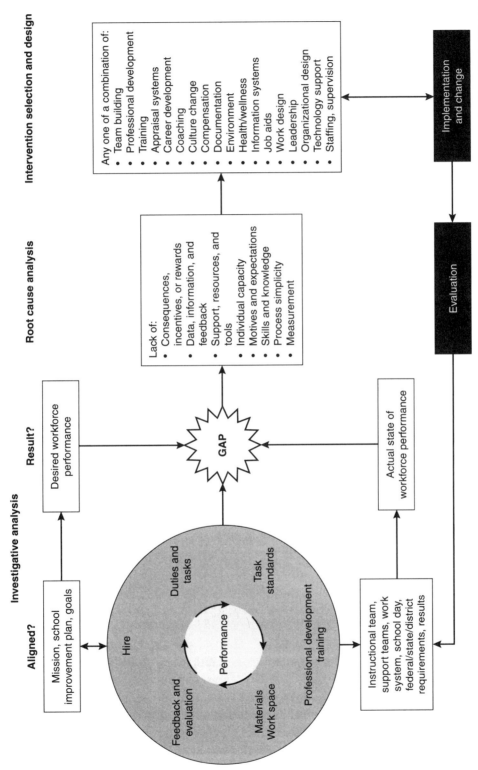

Figure 6.6 A process to analyze education/training needs.

Source: Adapted from "Performance Wheel" model, trademark Performance Technology Group, Inc., and United States Coast Guard Human Performance Technology Model.

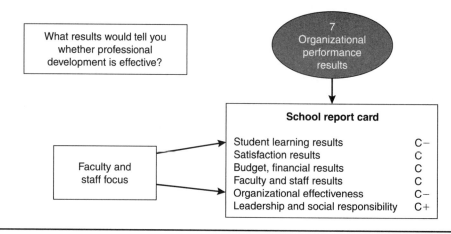

Figure 6.7 Results that demonstrate whether professional development leads to improvements.

of works from experts in leadership, pedagogy, and other topics. These discussions often lead to an interest in obtaining graduate degrees.

Another way you might promote career progression is to ask a local foundation, your school's corporate sponsors, or PTA to see whether they are willing to pay tuition for one or two graduate courses for outstanding teachers. Of course, you will need to include a selection process to make certain it is perceived as fair to all.

Leaders as Professional Development Providers

Another valuable leadership approach in closing performance gaps among teachers is to model PDSA (as described in the next chapter) or use a different quality tool during each faculty meeting. Along with the tool demonstration, provide explanations of its usefulness and then recommend classroom applications. Hands-on experience with the tools in such a setting helps alleviate skittishness among teachers about trying something new. After you provide ideas and examples, and provide opportunities to practice the tool, challenge teachers to go and use it with their students. Each faculty, department, or grade-level meeting might begin with a share session with the expectation that teachers will bring examples of classroom tools and/or PDSA use. Over time, energy will begin to develop and confidence will rise as more teachers demonstrate various tools and classroom improvement projects. Modeling what you ask teachers to do goes a long way toward helping them understand and realize the level of your commitment.

Satisfaction and Well-Being

Figure 6.8 shows all the elements considered in this aspect of Faculty and Staff Focus. Leaders who desire performance excellence work hard to ensure a healthy, safe work environment knowing that no one can do their best in unsafe conditions. Aside from the usual health and fire department inspections, consider developing a building audit instrument and ask a local contractor or inspector to take a quarterly tour of the building with you and the head of your maintenance or custodial department. Small things that contribute to accidents and loss of time on the job can often be spotted and corrected immediately. Furthermore, unsafe conditions inside or on the grounds outside the building put everyone in harm's way. One suggestion is to ask the advice of a contractor for ideas about specifics to be audited. Use the results to make immediate repairs if possible; when it is not imme-

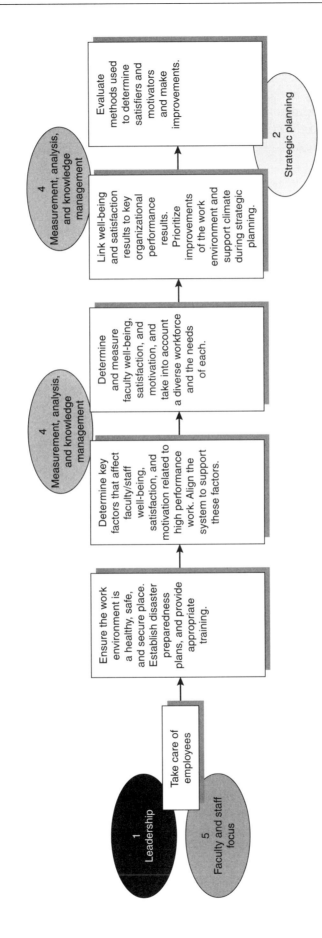

Figure 6.8 Things that contribute to well-being and satisfaction.

diately economically feasible, inform the central administration or your board that you need resources.

You'll have better luck in securing resources if you go armed with data to support your position. The audit and comments of the inspector will be very helpful, but you can also use data on accidents and the cost of worker's compensation claims, plus time lost on the job to address staff injuries.

It's always a good idea to get input from teachers and other staff regarding safety concerns. A major concern in some parts of the country is mold in the buildings. It is better to pay for an air quality inspection than to have students and teachers getting sick. One school district we know had to bring out the inspectors several times before anything was discovered. In this case, it was the persistence of a teacher that prevailed and led to improvement.

This process, along with everything related to quality and Baldrige, requires you to evaluate the results of each audit against the previous ones, and then against the health and fire departments' safety inspections. Collect the data and chart it, then post it so it is visible to all. Remember, it's all about continuous improvement.

There are many ways to determine factors that contribute to employee satisfaction and well-being. You'll want to establish several communication paths (we call these listening and learning posts) to get some understanding. Be sure to involve your teachers and staff in a discussion of these factors. Making assumptions in isolation can lead to misunderstandings and ultimately cost you in terms of low morale and lowered pride in workmanship. We'll discuss in more detail two listening and learning posts that can also be used as measurement tools: surveys and focus groups.

Understand Faculty and Staff Needs and Expectations

Surveys

At least twice yearly and more frequently when beginning your Baldrige journey, survey everyone who works in your building for satisfaction. Take precautions to ensure complete anonymity to avoid any hint of bias in the results. It's always best to personally stay out of the whole charting process unless you work in a very small school where it is not feasible to hand this task over to someone else. You need people to be honest, and if there is any hint of reprisals or fear, the respondents will give the answers they think you want, not what you need to hear.

Avoid the mistake of a principal of a large Midwestern elementary school. This well-meaning person created a satisfaction survey and included as a last item the following: *Use the back of this sheet to tell it like it is.* So, while the other survey items were structured using a 1–5 Likert scale, the last one was open-ended. The intent, of course, was that if there were important issues not included among the scaled items that everyone would feel free to express their concerns. As a result the principal ended up in tears because some of the faculty took her seriously and shared concerns about how her leadership style affected their ability to work. As word spread about how upset she was, staff members started approaching the principal to tell her that they knew who wrote the comments and, "Don't worry about it." This principal decided to take the words "don't worry about it" seriously and ignored all the comments. Lesson learned? *If you don't want to know and are not prepared to use the feedback to improve, don't ask. If you ask for feedback and don't use it, expect morale to go lower, fear to increase, and trust to fall to lower levels.*

A better way for this principal to have approached the survey results would have been to put the general comments into an affinity diagram or chunk the responses into logical groupings. Then, depending on the number of comments in each chunk—or the number under each header of the affinity diagram—turn this information into a Pareto chart. Return to the staff and ask for volunteers to form an improvement team to address one or two most significant issues. It is important to know how many responded in a certain way or about a certain topic. *You do not want to respond by making system changes if complaints come from a single source.* This is called tinkering with the system and may make matters worse over time.

Ask the team to collect more data and analyze the root cause. Once it is determined and after an improvement plan has been implemented, resurvey the staff to see whether any improvement has been made. Most of all, you need to learn to be transparent in your actions and reactions. If you allow the Baldrige core values to be your internal compass and remember the purpose of school, you should be fine. Imagine the trust that will develop when you follow through on this approach and walk the talk every day.

While accreditation organizations require schools to survey faculty, staff, and parents annually, these results are not sufficient to guide decision making about day-to-day operations. See the Recommended Reading and Interesting Websites at the end of the book for more information about surveys. This information can help you support the staff and ensure that improvement projects address their most pressing concerns. If your budget doesn't allow you to pay for surveys from an outside organization (these are best because you probably will have an option to receive comparative data with your results) but you have little experience in writing surveys, we have provided some information in Appendix D.

Focus Groups

Another good approach to finding out what employees think is to hold focus groups. We suggest at least semiannual focus groups. These, in conjunction with surveys, can give leaders a good handle on employee morale and satisfaction. It is impossible, however, to hold successful focus groups without hiring someone from outside the school who is unbiased and who has no ties to the school, preferably someone who doesn't know anyone who works at the school. Without the safety of knowing that they can trust the facilitator, it is not likely the staff will be honest in their responses.

It's a good idea to separate certified and noncertified employees, holding separate focus groups for each. This is because the issues will be somewhat different, and occasionally noncertified staff will be less open and participatory if they are with their more educated colleagues. The facilitator must be skilled at quickly building rapport with participants in order to get the maximum response to each question. *Everyone must feel confident that what they say will be shared in total with leadership, but that names of individuals making the comments will not be revealed.*

The focus group questions should come from leadership and be directly aimed at what the organization needs to learn at any given moment. About three or four open-ended, big-picture questions are sufficient, and all should be related to the strategic goals and action plans. Put a time limit on the focus groups—certainly no longer than 1 hour, but probably not less than 40 minutes—and expect a written report from the facilitator within a few days. Timing is important! Place the facilitator's unedited report on the intranet or in a binder in the teacher's lounge in order to improve trust levels. Greater trust leads to more cooperation and greater insights. Secrets are a sure-fire path to gossip, rumor, and disaster. Above all, use the results to improve. Do not let the report gather dust on a shelf.

One-on-One Conversations

Maintain an open-door policy and a high profile throughout the school. Invite people to come in and chat. Drop in on employees and ask how things are going. Be visible in the public areas of the school—hallways, cafeteria, media center, and lounge—and practice active listening. Make mental notes of what people are saying. Always be prepared to ask, "How are you doing with your action plan? How can we help? What are the positive things you're seeing or experiencing this year?"

After your conversations, jot down a few notes about issues—or potential issues—of which you need to be aware. This allows you to become more proactive, especially if you put these issues alongside the in-process data and survey and focus group results. Some school leaders we know create an affinity diagram of the issues that come to light in conversations. They do this by making a note and putting it on a board on their office. Once a month, the leadership team addresses the affinity diagram issues at faculty and staff meetings.

Other Listening and Learning Posts

Aside from surveys and focus groups, there are innumerable opportunities a leader has for learning about what's on the minds of employees as well as future trends. We've listed a few here:

- Grade-level or instructional team breakfast or lunch with the leader

- Observation—management by walking around

- Attendance at conferences

- Meet with principals from other schools (develop a consortium to learn and share best practice)

- Read professional journals

Complaint Management Systems

What motivates people to be complainers? Occasionally there are employees who are just plain contrary. Sometimes just to get a rise out of the leader, they will stir the pot and cause controversy. Others have a dark view of the world. They look for bad things to happen, often reading motivation into what people say. Then there are people who have a victim mentality, and others who thrive on gossip and innuendo. None of these individuals is easy to lead, and it may signal that you have the wrong people on your bus, as Collins (*Good to Great*) says. If this is true, you may need to reread the section about the importance of having the right people on your bus. Mostly, however, our observation is that people tend to become chronic complainers if they feel their opinions have not been valued by the system. These people can try the patience of any leader, and ultimately it is up to the leader to interview these individuals and repeat the question, "Are you willing and eager to put forth an extraordinary effort for the long haul so we can meet the strategic goals?" Negativity is poison to the school and goal achievement and, while complaints are not to be discouraged, general negativity ought not to be tolerated. It affects everyone, including students!

A process to capture employee complaints and resolve their issues in a timely fashion is an important part of the Baldrige approach. The process, while it can be more informal than structured—based mostly on the size of the school—ought to be systematic. To ensure that everyone knows the complaint management process, include it as part of the welcome-back in-service each year.

A complaint management system includes (1) a vehicle for registering complaints (for example, form, computer, and so on), (2) a method for collecting complaints, (3) a root-cause analysis, (4) the complaint resolution process, and (5) the process to survey the individual making the complaint for satisfaction. Depending on the size and complexity of the school, different approaches are more appropriate. A common pitfall is holding the belief that there is no need to have a complaint management system. Instead, leaders rely on anecdotal information, rarely collect data on types of complaints, and therefore don't see any patterns. Because an informal system is in place, complaint information is rarely captured and shared with the whole school, so lessons cannot be learned and processes cannot be improved. When data are captured, collated, and charted, patterns become evident, providing significant insight when driving quality into your system. Like all other key processes, the complaint management system needs to be reviewed annually for its effectiveness.

Measure Satisfaction and Well-Being

Aside from the use of surveys and focus groups to measure satisfaction and well-being, other indicators include absenteeism (look for patterns), grievances, loss of work because of minor accidents on the job and worker's compensation claims, willingness to participate on committees or in the PTA, complaints, and retention rates. As a rule of thumb, a good approach is to chart the data and share them with the leadership team. Trend data are very important when you want to determine whether the faculty and staff are happy with the conditions of teaching at your school. They are also useful when you want to find out whether the work systems are helping relieve teachers of some stress and at the same time compare these results with student learning results. It seems obvious that if the employees are satisfied and student learning is not high, there is a disconnect between the performance appraisal system, the reward and recognition system, and the work system.

To gain insights into whether or not faculty and staff feel appreciated and valued, see Figure 6.9. Note the dotted line to student learning results. We believe that if faculty are dissatisfied it influences their relationships with students and therefore affects learning. Conversely, if faculty are empowered through motivational approaches to solve problems using innovative strategies, this too influences how they work with students. So, learning results can improve or decline depending on faculty morale.

It is becoming more and more difficult to hire and retain outstanding teachers, yet these are the right people for your bus. This makes a compelling reason to measure the success

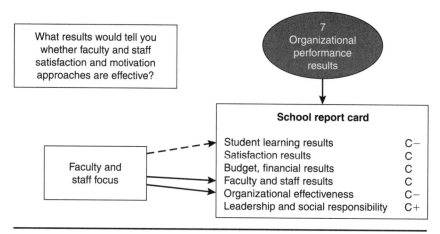

Figure 6.9 Results that demonstrate that the faculty/staff feel appreciated and that their ideas are valued.

of your action plans. Satisfied teachers and staff work differently, and sometimes harder but not always smarter, to help everyone reach the goals. Conversely, dissatisfied teachers and staff can sabotage your efforts.

Use a PDSA process when survey results are below targets, and be sure to include faculty and staff in the process to attain improvements. Remember to evaluate the effectiveness of your listening and learning posts to remain confident that you are receiving the information needed to stay the course.

Complete the following self-assessment to see how well you are doing in terms of your faculty and staff focus efforts.

Assess Category 5 (Faculty and Staff Focus) Efforts

To what extent are these aligned with the strategic goals?	I don't know	Not really	Somewhat aligned	Mostly aligned	Highly Aligned	What do you do and/or what results support your rating?
1. Work systems—how work is organized to produce excellent results						
2. Performance expectations are clearly set for all employees						
3. Performance evaluation system is aligned with desired behaviors and expectations						
4. Cooperation and integration among departments, instructional teams, and support services is evident						
5. There are several ways to regularly obtain actionable feedback from employees						
6. Skills sharing, organizational learning, and improvement based on process improvements is the way we do business						
7. Faculty and staff have rapid access to data needed to make midcourse corrections						
8. Employees are empowered to use innovative approaches to solve problems						
9. Professional development is aligned with strategic objectives						
10. Faculty and staff have input into professional development and provide feedback to improve it						
11. Faculty and staff receive on-the-job support to use newly learned skills						
12. Employee well-being, satisfaction, and motivators to support high performance work are identified and used						
13. Consideration is given to the differing needs of the diverse faculty and staff when identifying factors of well-being, satisfaction, and motivation						
14. Health and safety factors are taken into consideration to improve the workplace						
15. Diversity is valued; faculty and staff reflect the diversity of the student body						
16. Leadership and career advancement opportunities are made available for faculty and staff						

Summary

As you reflect on this chapter, you will no doubt see examples of motivation and other strategies that you are already successfully deploying. That is definitely a plus. Leading a Baldrige-based quality school is challenging in the sense that identifying key learning processes; aligning your vision, mission, measurement plan, and strategic goals; and capturing the data you must analyze in order to make good data-driven decisions may be completely new. Baldrige principals tell us that it takes great resolve on the part of the principal to initiate these systematic changes and then help everyone stay the course. Once teachers see the learning progress that takes place because they were able to identify needed midcourse changes, they become focused on improvement. The fears and difficulties experienced in the early stages begin to fade as both teachers and students become more and more self-managed. Teachers will begin identifying their own growth needs, as will their students. That's a big part of what a learning-centered school is all about.

7

Process Management

Conversation with the Principal

When a school first adopts the Baldrige framework, the language is mostly foreign to staff. As the leader, you may see some resistance on the part of teachers when they are introduced to "key learning processes" or "key support processes." How do we identify all of them, let alone measure and monitor them? That is why we suggest that the principal begin with an all-school project in which everyone can contribute and learn without fear of failure. The transition to classroom will be easier and those staff members who find it immediately comfortable can be identified and encouraged to provide support for their colleagues.

Key Processes

A significant contribution a leader can make is to provide the school with information related to the effectiveness and efficiency of key processes. Remember, a process is a series of steps taken to achieve a goal or task. A process is deemed *effective,* for example, if it meets the required specifications, and *efficient* if it does so in a timely manner, with fewer resources. In any school, there are learning-centered processes (for example, curriculum, instruction, assessment, counseling, special education) and support processes (for example, clerical, payroll, transportation, food service, technology services, purchasing, and custodial). Refer to the school-level system diagram in Chapter 2, page 19, for examples of key processes. It is up to the leadership team to identify each key process at the school.

Once key processes are identified, leaders ask those directly involved to flowchart the process. A good way to uncover some reasons why any process is not functioning effectively or efficiently is to have each individual involved in the process create his or her own chart of the flow. You will be surprised at how often none of the charts are the same. Standardization of best practice is not something that many organizations do, yet this is frequently a source of discontent between employees and leadership. Have you had one or more employees who seemingly do not pay attention to the details of accomplishing any task? If so, it probably means that not everyone understands the process exactly the same. Sometimes it may not seem to be such a big deal. Other times, it is *huge* and can cause difficulties for others because of the failure of some to stick to the process requirements. (This is something for you to think about.)

Process Capability

When the process is flowed out and everyone agrees with the steps, take a look at the results to assess whether the process is capable of yielding the desired results. Do this by looking at the trend data for at least the past five years (or as much data as you have). In order to get a clear picture of trended results, it is necessary to chart the data. (See the Recommended Reading list for books with tools and instructions.) Share the charts with all those involved and ask everyone to reflect on these questions: Are these results satisfactory? Are we going to meet the strategic goals and objectives if we continue using this process as it is? Can we improve the process by making improvements to it, or do we need to design a completely new one?

Please avoid the tendency to accept excuses for poor performance, such as "Our students are not able to do better" and "We have too many students in a class." As the leader, you must remain steadfast in your belief that everyone can do better—for example, learn more, provide better instruction, and improve school safety. At the same time, if results demonstrate the need, you have the responsibility to lead everyone in a new direction. You know the definition of insanity: doing the same thing over and over in the same way and expecting different results. Why hang on to processes that don't yield the desired results? Remember, it is important for staff morale to continue sending the message that *it's about the system and not faulty people.* No shame, no blame, but the way to performance excellence must be paved with passion, courage, persistence, and celebration. (There'll be more on that later).

Figure 7.1 shows key decisions you must make related to managing your key processes.

When Improvement Is Required

Modeling is one way leaders send a strong message to employees and students and stakeholders about a seriousness of purpose. There are essentially three ways to improve: (1) benchmarking, (2) Plan-Do-Study-Act, or (3) design a new process.

Benchmarking "Best Practice" from Organizations Inside or Outside the Educational Field

Benchmarking "best practices" is necessary when (1) the current process has not been changed in the past 7–10 years or (2) when rapid, dramatic improvement is required. In the Baldrige criteria book, *benchmark* is defined as

> processes and results that represent best practices and performance for similar activities, inside or outside the education community. Organizations engage in benchmarking as an approach to understand the current dimensions of world-class performance and to achieve non-incremental or "breakthrough" improvement. (p. 67)

As Figure 7.2 (on p. 126) shows, benchmarking is *not* copycatting someone else's approach and using it in your school if it is not aligned with your strategic objectives. Furthermore, benchmarking is not copycatting another's approach without a serious look at how it fits with your organization, and then only after it has been modified as necessary. See the Recommended Reading list for more details about benchmarking and the interesting websites for benchmarking opportunities.

Process Management in a Baldrige System

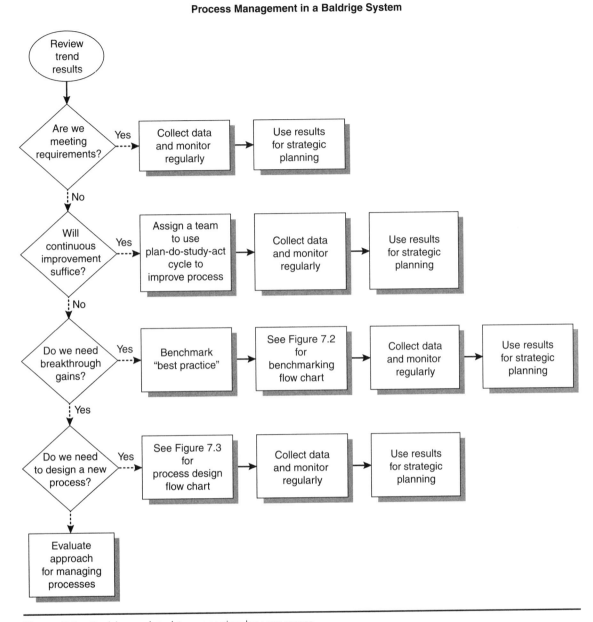

Figure 7.1 Decisions related to managing key processes.

Benchmarking others should be considered an important part of your approach to performance excellence, especially if school results show that breakthrough improvement is required. Figure 7.3 on page 127 shows what benchmarking requires of a leader. If the students at your school are not reaching the required levels of achievement and there have been no obvious, positive trend improvements in the past three years, it is time to give serious consideration to the fact that your current processes are not designed to yield the performance levels required. Before you introduce benchmarking to the teachers and staff, study the process first (see Figure 7.2) to make certain you understand the steps involved and how this approach can help.

Once it has been determined that benchmarking is required, seek volunteers (those with a vested interest in the benchmarked process) to serve on a team to take charge of the

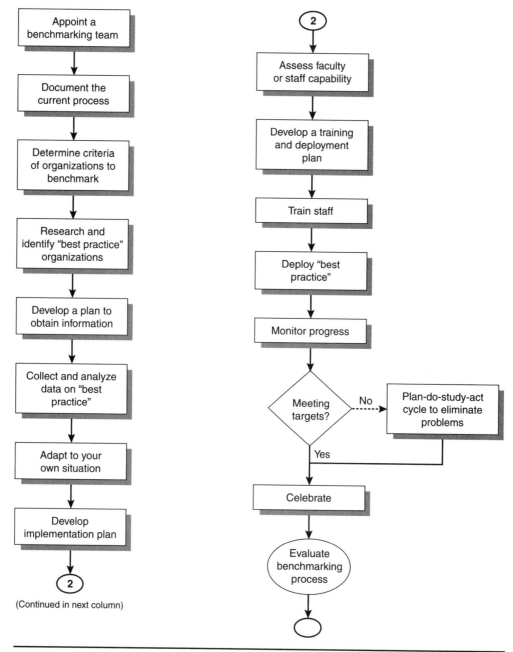

Figure 7.2   Benchmarking flow.

process and report back to the rest of the faculty before making any changes. The team will require resources to carry out their task. Be prepared to reallocate funds and don't forget the training aspect of benchmarking, as that will determine the ability of the faculty or staff to integrate the process into your system.

Plan-Do-Study-Act Improvement Cycle

The Plan-Do-Study-Act (PDSA) cycle is the improvement process developed by Dr. William Shewhart in the 1920s. It was popularized by Dr. Deming and is as important to achieving performance excellence now as it was then. This is the approach to use for

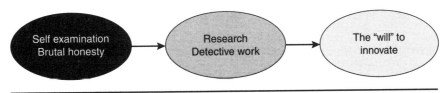

Figure 7.3 Requirements of the benchmarking process.

continuous improvement. PDSA cycles are useful if a process is yielding "okay" and incremental improvement, and there is no urgency for a dramatic, positive shift in results.

We encourage you to make PDSA a way of life in your school. Once everyone becomes familiar with the process and tools, they will see how repeated cycles of improvement can make everyone's life easier. As progress is made, teachers will begin to suggest schoolwide PDSA projects and use the PDSA in their classrooms with students. This is a principal's dream—to have everyone focused on continuous improvement and never be satisfied with the status quo.

The process steps are shown in Figure 7.4. Because this is a systematic process, using scientific principles and data analysis to drive improvements, it is a highly reliable approach. When you lead a schoolwide PDSA project and teach everyone the process, it enables large numbers of people to participate in the improvements and therefore increases buy-in into the philosophy and approach.

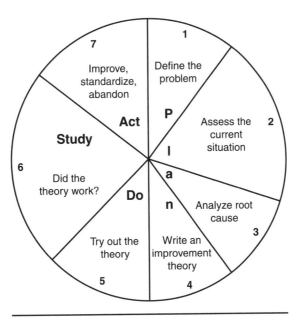

Figure 7.4 Steps of the PDSA process.

When we refer to storyboarding, we mean that each step of the PDSA process is completed and shared with others. In this way, everyone is aware of what is being done. Transparency when solving problems is very important if you desire to gain support over time. A school data wall that includes PDSA storyboards keeps everyone informed and also focuses attention and interest on improvement.

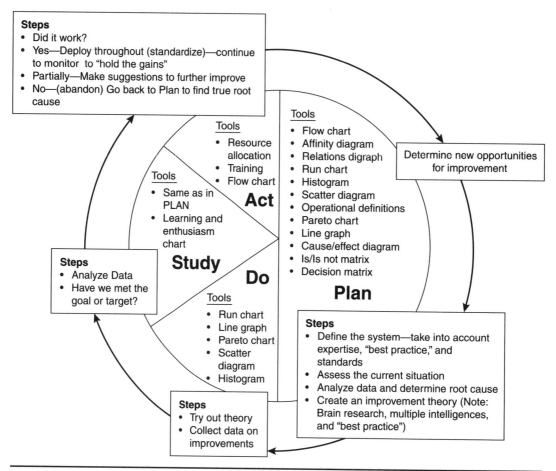

Figure 7.5 PDSA steps with tools suggestions.

The process and some tools appropriate for use at each step are shown in Figure 7.5. See the Tools Selection chart (Table 4.3) on page 53 for more information about selecting the correct tool, and then obtain a copy of one of the Recommended Reading tools books for detailed instructions. It will save you valuable time and energy.

PDSA: A Case Study to Improve School Safety

To help you learn the PDSA process, we have put together a case study for schoolwide improvement.

PLAN Step 1: Define the Problem

At a faculty meeting, Brenda Caprin, principal at XYZ School, shared the results of the most recent student satisfaction survey. It revealed that 83% of all students "mostly disagree" they feel safe at school and that more than 75% of parents felt their children were not safe at school. While Principal Caprin was aware of an increase in student suspensions because of fighting, and she had taken a weapon away from one student earlier in the year, she was dismayed at the number of students who didn't feel safe at school. When she shared the information with the faculty and staff, many nodded in agreement and shared that they no longer felt safe either. Principal Caprin knew she had a major problem on her hands.

While there had been no incidents of students suffering serious harm because of fighting or intimidation, many minor injuries had been reported: a bruise here or a scratch requiring bandaging there. None of the events seemed to warrant close scrutiny at the time. However, with the latest survey results it was clear to everyone that improvement was needed quickly. Whatever the reality, the perception of students, staff, and parents was that XYZ School was not safe. The whole staff agreed that this would be an important school improvement project. Before adding more school rules or changing policies, the decision was made to collect data to see how pervasive the problem was, when and where most of the incidents occurred, and then to engage the students and staff in any improvement efforts. At the same time she requested all staff members to become extra vigilant and be more visible in the halls and outside the building.

The improvement project was dubbed *Project Restore Safety*. The faculty lounge became the "war room," and a large PDSA wheel was constructed out of paper and put on one wall. A team of teachers and staff agreed to work with Principal Caprin on this project. Everyone agreed that the forms, charts, and committee's work would be posted for all to see.

PLAN Step 2: Assess the Current Situation

Ms. Caprin asked team members to help collect data on this year's safety problems, including where the incidents occurred, what time of day, and specifically who was involved. The school counselor created a survey for students and all employees asking for more information about the situation. This began the data collection process. See the survey in Table 7.1.

Surveys were given to all students during English classes and taken after each class to the counselor's office for collating and charting. Employees received them in their mailboxes and returned them to the counselor's mailbox within 24 hours.

Other data were also being collected by the committee, such as the past year's worth of discipline referral slips, in-school and out-of-school suspensions, and notices of bus problems. The team charted all data, and figures 7.6, 7.7, 7.8, and 7.9 (on pp. 131–132) provided samples of the results of their efforts. To gain clarity on the exact problem, it is necessary to disaggregate the data by grade level, gender, IEP and non-IEP, types of offenses, time of day, place, fear versus reality, semester suspension results, and discipline referrals (use a Pareto chart) by month, and teachers' responses.

A review of the discipline referrals revealed that four boys and two girls (all eighth-graders) had been referred for shoving, fighting, and taunting incidents a total of 100 times this school year. Ms. Caprin directed the team to investigate these students, their attendance records as well as academic records. Table 7.2 (on p. 133) shows what they found.

An investigation of the teachers who reported being taunted or shoved by students showed that four teachers were involved. All four were eighth-grade English teachers, and all four had at least one of the above named students in class. Two of the teachers required students to read out loud during class. The students in their classes included AJG, BEH, LCH, and TWS. These teachers consistently reported the incidents and referred the students for in-school suspension. None of the six students received special support services or had an IEP.

Table 7.1 School safety survey.

Please describe your current situation at school.
Student   Grade 6 ☐   Grade 7 ☐   Grade 8 ☐   Male ☐   Female ☐   Do you have an IEP? ☐   Yes ☐   No ☐
Teacher ☐   Other professional staff ☐   Teacher aide ☐   Clerical staff ☐   Custodial/Maintenance ☐   Volunteer ☐

Please check the places where you feel less safe and circle the top 2 places you feel most unsafe.
Hallway ☐   Cafeteria ☐   Near my locker ☐   Outside my classrooms ☐   Bathroom ☐   On the bus ☐
Inside my classrooms ☐   Behind the school ☐   In front of the school ☐   Gymnasium ☐   P.E. locker room ☐
Media center ☐   School lobby area ☐

Please check the time of day when you feel less safe and circle the top 2 time periods you feel most unsafe.
Immediately after school ☐   In between classes ☐   Before school starts ☐   During lunch period ☐
After activity period ☐   During class ☐   On the bus coming to school ☐   On the bus going home from school ☐

Please prioritize the things that happen that make you feel less safe at school. (1 = TOP priority—biggest fear, 7 = LOWEST priority—almost no fear about this)
_____ Verbal shouts, taunts   _____ Being shoved or pushed   _____ Slammed into walls/locker
_____ Being hit   _____ Threatened with knife   _____ Threatened with gun
_____ Other (describe) _____

Please check If you have been the victim of any of these types of incidents.
☐ Verbal shouts, taunts   ☐ Being shoved or pushed   ☐ Slammed into walls/locker
☐ Being hit   ☐ Threatened with knife   ☐ Threatened with gun
Other (describe) _____

Please check If you have seen of any of these types of incidents happen to other students or teachers.
☐ Verbal shouts, taunts   ☐ Being shoved or pushed   ☐ Slammed into walls/locker
☐ Being hit   ☐ Threatened with knife   ☐ Threatened with gun
Other (describe) _____

If there is anything else you'd like to tell us about your feelings of being unsafe at school, please write them on the back of this survey or leave a note for your counselor or adviser. All information will be kept confidential.

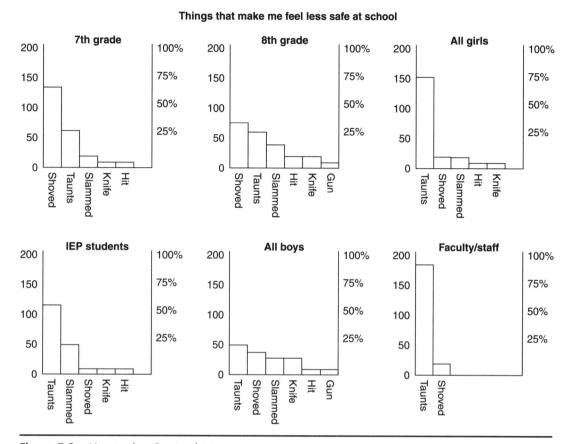

Figure 7.6 Year-to-date Pareto charts.

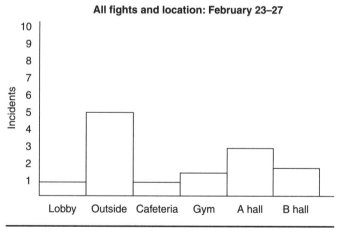

Figure 7.7 Bar chart: Fights.

The team felt that there were two issues creating the problem. First was the fact that a few teachers had sent these six students to the office for disciplinary action. These students also had poor attendance and tardy records and were reading significantly below grade level. Second was students' perception of feeling unsafe at school. The team was not sure that these six students were responsible for all the perceptions. Further investigation would be necessary.

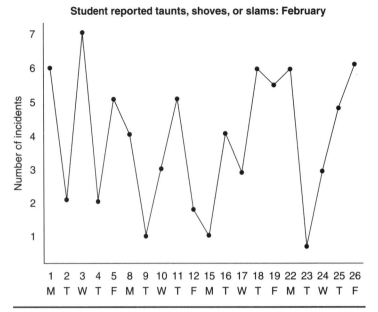

Figure 7.8 Run chart: Problems reported by month.

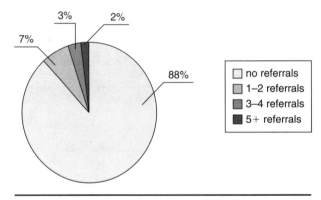

Figure 7.9 Pie chart: Year-to-date discipline referrals.

They looked at the students' class schedules in relationship to the place where fights had taken place. Surprisingly, only two of the students had classes in the A hall and, while they were not involved in any fights, their friends were. On the days the fights took place outdoors, three of the boys (LCH, JMM, and TWS) were involved. Interestingly, the fights involved student athletes as well.

The counselor was able to shed some light on the issues facing the six students. They had all experienced one family tragedy or another (for example, death of a parent, divorce, arrest of parent, or brother sent to war in Iraq) within the past 12 months.

After gathering all the information, collecting all the data, and preparing the charts, the next step was to engage the faculty and students in analyzing the root cause.

PLAN Step 3: Analyze the Root Cause

To determine the root cause of people's perceptions of an unsafe school, the counselor engaged the student council to help facilitate grade-level focus groups with randomly

Table 7.2 Students with most discipline referrals.

Name	Days absent	Tardy	Reading level	Core subjects failed previous year	Days in In-school suspension
AJG (male)	8	6	4.0	2	12
BEH (female)	5	3	5.1	1	15
LCH (male)	9	7	3.8	3	18
JMM (male)	2	2	6.8	0	10
SVM (female)	8	9	7.2	0	18
TWS (male)	8	5	6.1	1	18

selected students. Focus groups were held separately for boys and girls from each grade level, and also IEP students. Each focus group would be asked to use the affinity diagram process and then a relations digraph to discover the root cause. For the affinity diagram, the large question was "What is the cause of so much disrespectful behavior among students?" The responses were put into headers that became the central points of the relations digraph. Figure 7.10 is an example from one focus group.

The counselor took all the affinity diagrams and combined the ideas from all the focus groups and came up with five common headers that included the comments from every focus group. The two additional headers were (1) inadequate school rules and (2) kids don't know each other. A different group of students was invited to participate in the creation of a relations digraph (Figure 7.11) using the five headers from all previous focus groups.

Meanwhile, Ms. Caprin led the noncertified staff through a cause/effect diagram, asking the same question as it pertained to their areas. Certified staff used the affinity/relations digraph approach. Once results of all groups were available, Ms. Caprin and the committee shared the results with the rest of the staff and student council.

Students' lack of sensitivity

- Kids are mean
- No tolerance for difference in dress
- Those who look different are not accepted
- Big kids shove small ones
- Name calling
- Some think they're better than others

Teachers' lack of care

- Double standards
- Look the other way
- Yell at and embarrass some kids
- Too busy to notice what's happening
- No one seems to care

Building not conducive to caring environment

- Halls too crowded
- Too many kids in class
- Not enough supervision outdoors
- Graffiti on walls—not a nice place to be

Figure 7.10 Student group affinity diagram.

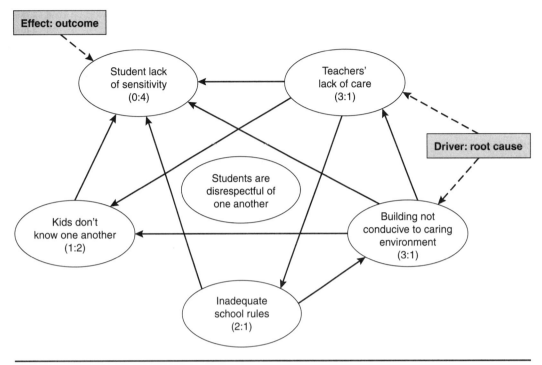

Figure 7.11 Relations digraph using headers from affinity diagrams.

PLAN Step 4: Write an Improvement Theory

Grade-level advisers, counselors, student council officers, and informal student leaders met with Ms. Caprin to review the results and came up with an improvement theory. Ms. Caprin facilitated the nominal group technique (brainstorming and prioritization) process. This is what the group came up with: (1) Host a weekend of cleaning up the school with parents, students, and teachers side by side, followed by a supper and celebration; (2) institute an adviser/advisee program using all adults in the building for 30 minutes a day; (3) send a team of teachers to an antibullying workshop with the intent that the team will institute an anti-bullying program in the school. The improvement theory read: "If we host a "clean-up our school" weekend, institute an adviser/advisee program, and start an antibullying program, more students will feel safe at school."

These efforts addressed the global concern of the school population, but not entirely the issues of the six students with the most discipline referrals. To address these, Ms. Caprin met with the students as a group and at another time, their teachers. She asked the counselor to meet with each student individually for additional insights into their issues and to provide weekly group counseling sessions for these six students for the remainder of the school year. In response to concerns about their academic achievement, the teachers agreed to have the SPED teacher observe their classes and provide suggestions for strategies that might prove helpful. A reading specialist recommended they purchase some paperback trade books at each student's reading levels, with subject matter of interest to them. The PTA was able to provide some funds for this effort and also found volunteers to help tutor these six students in reading. The leadership team agreed to evaluate the effectiveness of this approach by (1) tabulating absences, (2) the number of days tardy, and (3) the number of discipline referrals for the remainder of the school year.

DO Step 5: Carry Out the Improvement Plan

Ms. Caprin and the leadership team went right to work finding an antibullying workshop for six teachers (representing each grade level, counselors, special education, and "specials" teachers) to attend. Within a few weeks after their return the program was up and running.

At the same time, another group of volunteers researched adviser/advisee programs, and this was instituted about two months later. The challenge was rearranging the school schedule to fit the 30 minutes a day, but the teachers and Ms. Caprin were resolute in their desire to accomplish this effort.

Ms. Caprin went to the PTA and sought help from corporate sponsors to host the clean-up weekend. She was pleasantly surprised at how eager they were to help. Students received extra credit in social studies for organizing work teams, working, and helping with the celebration. Paint and other materials were donated by businesses interested in helping make the school a better place too. To gain added community support, Ms. Caprin asked the newspaper and television stations to come and publicize the event.

Ms. Caprin and the counselor trained a group of volunteer teachers, staff, and students to collect data on the number of incidents (as noted in the Pareto charts) occurring in the A and B halls between classes and outside the school for 15 minutes before and after school. In order to reduce potential variation in how the data were collected and to increase confidence in its validity, Ms. Caprin taught the volunteers how to use a check sheet (Figure 7.12), and together they wrote the operational definitions to be sure everyone knew what counted as a violation. They collected data daily for one month.

What is being studied? *The number of shoving, slamming, fighting, hitting incidents among students.*					
Who: *Anna Ortega*	Where: *Outside rooms A112–A115*	When: *8:00–8:10 am*	How: *Observation*	Dated *April 2–6*	
	Monday	Tuesday	Wednesday	Thursday	Friday
Shoving					
Slamming					
Fighting					
Hitting					
Total					

Figure 7.12 Check sheet example.

At the same time, in keeping with the improvement theory, Ms. Caprin and the counselor scheduled themselves for hall duty between classes each day to talk with students and get to know them a little better. They also began chatting with students before and after school outdoors and in the school lobby. In short, Ms. Caprin and the counselor were friendly and very visible.

STUDY Step 6: What Happened?

When the month was over, Ms. Caprin and the data committee put all the new schoolwide data onto charts. Figures 7.13, 7.14, and 7.15 (see pp. 136–137) show the results of the improvement effort.

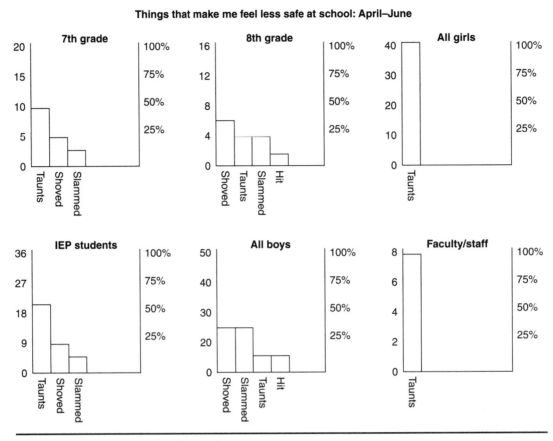

Figure 7.13 Post-intervention Pareto charts.

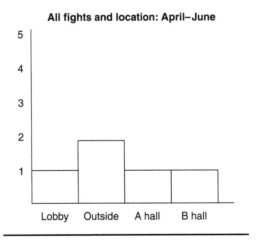

Figure 7.14 Post-intervention bar chart: Fights.

ACT Step 7: Standardize, Abandon, Improve

Principal Caprin called a joint meeting of student council and faculty and staff. She shared the pre- and post-intervention charts with them. The results were impressive, though there were still too many incidences to suit her. The group agreed to continue and standardize all the improvement efforts and to collect data weekly (albeit not on consecutive days) throughout the building for the rest of this school year and during the first semester of the

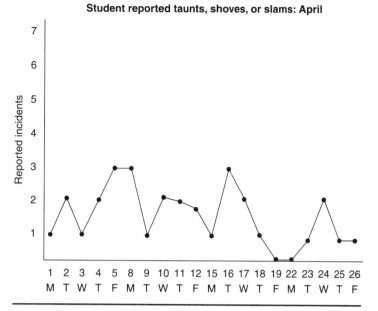

Figure 7.15 Post-intervention run chart: Reported problems.

next year to ensure they could hold the gains. These data would be charted and posted in the faculty lounge, with monthly reports going to the student council and the leadership team for review.

By the end of the school year, satisfaction survey results showed an increase in perceptions that the school is a safe school. The staff, however, agreed to survey students quarterly for the next year to make sure there was no slippage in perceptions.

The six students continued having problems with reading and their other academic classes; however, they were not sent to the office nearly as often. The group counseling sessions seemed to be working and that, combined with the advisor/advisee and antibullying programs, had a positive effect on their behavior. The student athletes also stopped taunting them as much, reducing the tensions between groups.

Ms. Caprin and the assistant principal met with the six students' teachers, the SPED teacher, counselor, and their adult advisers to brainstorm additional interventions for the next school year. Two of the students would go to high school the following year, but the rest would stay here. Plans were made to investigate learning styles and help teachers with differentiated instruction and to have student volunteers from the high school come and work with these students every week.

3. Design a New Process

Figure 7.16 shows an example of the approach to use when you have no formal process, or when the one you have is simply not working. Frequently, when an organization has to design a new process, it looks for the best practice as honored by external agencies before designing any new process. However, it is possible that an organization has determined the need for a unique process or for a process to serve a unique task. In such instances, the design process may be entirely internally developed. Factors to consider when designing a new process follow.

Design of Process

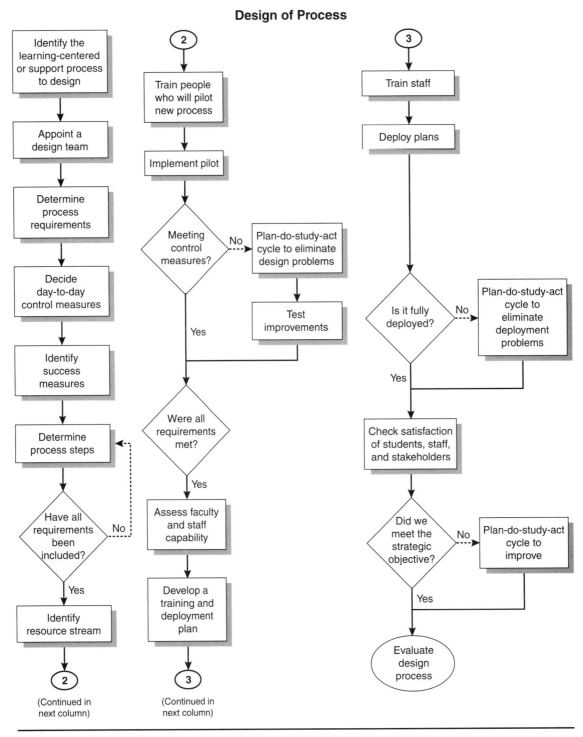

Figure 7.16 Steps to design a new process.

Table 7.3 is an example of the curriculum and custodial process designs from the 2003 Baldridge application by Community Consolidated School District 15 in Palatine, Illinois. Each of the criteria in Table 7.3 is important when designing a process, but there are more. Here are some hints to consider when embarking on a key process design or redesign:

• Determine the priorities for the process—what are the most important things to consider?

Table 7.3 CCSD-15's curriculum and custodial process design.

Process	Requirements	Measures	Expected outcome (standards)	Process control strategies
Curriculum	13 state and local requirements 3 community requirements 9 student requirements 15 teacher requirements	Degree to which student performance target measures for each subject are met or exceeded Level of student enthusiasm for learning Teacher satisfaction Principal satisfaction	Meets/exceeds state curriculum standards Meets/exceeds local, community, student, and next-teacher-in-line requirements	Flowchart checklist Communication checklist Cycle time Curriculum format templates Evaluation checklist
Custodial	Clean classrooms Clean public areas Safe school Health standards	Customer satisfaction Degree to which there are no health or safety violations Degree to which there are no accidents Cycle time from complaint to project completion	State and local fire, safety, and health codes School standards	Weekly facility audit Daily teacher checklist Random, quarterly inspections Meetings with leadership to review data

Printed with permission from CCSD-15.

- Are the appropriate people involved on the design team?

- Has the team understood all the internal and external requirements of the process?

- Have resources been allocated for (1) a pilot program and (2) full deployment if successful?

- Is there a plan to pilot the new process?

- Has a measurement system been put into place—have key success measures (KSM) for the process been determined?

- During the pilot phase, how will you monitor the success of the process—KSM?

- What if the process does not yield the required KSM? Is there a step in place to make midcourse corrections before deploying the new process throughout the school, department, or grade level?

- If the process design is successful, is there a plan to standardize the best practice and provide professional development for those involved?

- How often and how will you monitor the process midstream?

- How will you communicate the results to staff and key stakeholder groups?

Be a Role Model for Improvement and Learning

Modeling the process that Principal Caprin used with her staff and students will help increase faculty and staff confidence that the administration is committed to the PDSA process, understands the importance of continuous cycles of improvement, and that this is not a management "flavor of the month". There will probably always be a few employees who will require more persuasion to join the effort, but persistence and commitment to excellence will be strong persuaders over the long haul. Figures 7.17 and 7.18 tell you where results of effective and efficient processes would show up in your school report card.

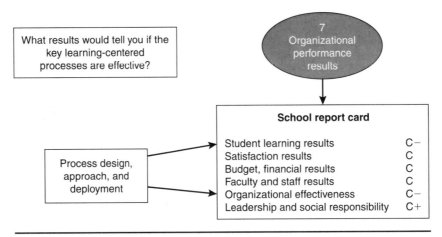

Figure 7.17 Results that demonstrate learning processes are effective.

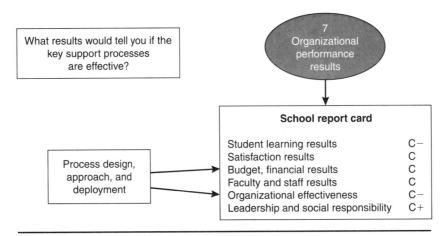

Figure 7.18 Results that demonstrate support processes are effective.

Notice that there is no reference here to having patience with people who are unwilling to learn to apply the Baldrige framework within their own work area, or to those who find reasons why "it won't work" and therefore become saboteurs. In the past, we might have suggested patience, but no longer. There is no time to waste, especially in schools that are struggling to make the grade. Instead, there is an urgency that cannot be overlooked. A school leader desirous of turning a school into one where performance excellence is proven in all areas of results will have to be strong of purpose, strong of desire, and strong of focus, never letting an opportunity to model and teach Baldrige principles or the PDSA slip by.

Individuals who are provided training opportunities and a mentor, yet who are not willing to get on board, may be candidates for other employment opportunities. It doesn't mean they are bad people, rather that they don't share the desire and level of commitment to making it work. A different employment opportunity may be a win-win for everyone.

Complete the following self-assessment to learn how much you know about your system.

Assess Category 6 (Process Management) Efforts

To what extent are these aligned with the strategic goals?	I don't	Not really	Occasionally	Mostly	Always	What do you do and/or what results support your rating?
1. Key learning-centered process requirements incorporate input from teachers, staff, students, and stakeholders						
2. Key processes are designed to meet student and stakeholder requirements						
3. Key processes are implemented to ensure they meet design requirements						
4. Key learning-centered processes are designed to anticipate and prepare for individual differences in student learning rates and styles						
5. Information and feedback from students and student segments is used to engage all students in active learning						
6. There are in-process performance measures and indicators to manage all key processes						
7. The Plan-Do-Study-Act improvement process is used when key learning or support processes do not meet requirements and midcourse corrections are made						
8. In-process measures are used to monitor day-to-day operations of key learning processes to ensure that they meet all requirements						
9. Key learning-centered processes are improved and lessons learned shared throughout the school to drive innovation and organizational learning						
10. Key support processes are identified that provide support for learning-centered processes						
11. Support process requirements incorporate input from teachers, staff, students, and stakeholders						
12. Support processes are designed to meet all key customer and stakeholder requirements						
13. Support processes are implemented to ensure they meet design requirements						
14. In-process measures are used to monitor day-to-day operations of key support services to ensure that they meet all requirements						
15. Key processes are designed and implemented to prevent errors and rework and reduce variability						
16. We regularly use PDSA to improve support services to achieve better performance and share lessons learned throughout the school						

Summary

This chapter was about identifying key processes and approaches to improvement when processes are not yielding desired results. The Plan-Do-Study-Act (PDSA) is an improvement process that is easily implemented at every level, including the classroom, grade-level teams, academic departments, and food service or maintenance groups. The school-wide project described step by step demonstrates the tools and approach one principal used with staff and students. The other effective improvement approaches discussed here were benchmarking best practices of other organizations, not necessarily related to education and steps to use when designing a new process. These approaches are your roadmap to introduce and model the process improvement to meet your strategic objectives. We know you can do it!

8
From the Trenches
Insights from Principals
in a Baldrige Award-Winning
School District

Conversation with the Principal

Among the best resources at your disposal when beginning your Baldrige journey are the principals who have gone before you and those who are doing it now. It may take some digging, but check with the Baldrige office or your state program to identify other Baldrige-based schools that have been recognized and, at the very least, strike up an email relationship. We understand that the principal's road is often full of potholes. One principal described the need to stay the course as "the loneliest road to travel because of the many stakeholders (often with conflicting expectations) converging on one leader." While a practicing colleague may not have an answer to your question, just the fact that you can share lessons learned and discuss the problems of the moment can help you gain perspective.

Over the years, we have met and worked with hundreds of principals, some more effective than others, but all of whom faced significant challenges. They felt their biggest challenge was motivating all teachers to do whatever it takes to improve student learning results, and when we spend time observing classrooms, we have to agree that this is a big problem. The real challenge, however, comes when leaders lack knowledge about systems. Many, perhaps most, university school leadership programs do not adequately prepare aspiring leaders in systems or systems thinking. This poses a distinct disadvantage for new school leaders who are overwhelmed with learning the ropes, and also for experienced principals facing challenges that come with recent federal, state, or district accountability mandates.

The Baldrige National Quality Award Program has made it easier by articulating a framework that makes up a system—the criteria categories. But, knowing about the framework categories is not enough. Excellent leaders know how to align all aspects of the system, and go way beyond to reach performance excellence. They demonstrate (1) effective, systematic approaches fully deployed throughout the school without any significant weaknesses or gap in areas or work units; (2) fact-based systematic evaluation and improvement, using this and organizational learning as key management tools; and (3) make certain the approaches used are aligned and well integrated with organizational needs identified in the profile and each category. Excellent leaders align and integrate everything, and

143

they consistently use data for evaluation and improvement, and are dedicated to personal and organizational learning. As continuous cycles of improvement progress, the school is rewarded with improved results. (See Chapter 2 for the scope of results.) If you're a visual learner, see the Baldrige framework on page 22. Note the arrows showing linkages among the categories.

As the Baldrige coach for Community Consolidated School District 15 in Palatine, Illinois, the 2003 Baldrige education award winner, the author had the honor to meet and work with the senior leadership team and school principals. These principals were, in many ways, the inspiration for this book because the leader's role is the key to school performance excellence. If you have the opportunity to visit many schools, as we have, it becomes glaringly apparent that ineffective leaders (whether at the district or school level) create systems that keep everyone from being successful. We were fortunate to interview three highly effective principals from CCSD15: Guy Hermann, Karen Hindman, and Jean Sophie. Each had a personal style and all had to work within the boundaries and mandates set forth by the superintendent and board of education. Their reflections and insights are testimony to what it takes to reach performance excellence. Each of these outstanding people is well aware of the pitfalls that await any organization before, during, or after pursuit of the Baldrige award. They, like their peers, are determined not to go back to a more traditional style no matter what happens at the central administration level.

As you read this chapter, imagine sitting together over coffee and prepare to soak up their collective wisdom, appreciate their individual differences, and reflect on their perceptions about leadership and the CCSD15's journey to excellence. We have used the interview format so you can see that individual differences in style can still lead one to performance excellence.

How would you characterize your leadership style? Did it change as you were leading the school toward the Baldrige process? In what ways?

> Guy Hermann—[My leadership style] has changed. Prior to this process I was more managerial oriented. I worked with individual teachers. I was the keeper of the big picture, and I was trying to empower everybody. I would sit down with individual teachers, help them with their goals, inspect what they had done, etc. Now I am less of a manager and more of a leader. I see myself as "holder of the vision." When people saw how Baldrige brought in systematic processes into the classroom, teachers came on board. A huge piece was when teachers got a vision for their class. Teachers began to say, "We can do this!"

> Karen Hindman—I would describe my style as collaborative and it did not change, except that it was hard for me (as a team person) to sometimes have to say, "This is the way it's going to be." Sometimes I, alone, had to make some hard decisions after looking at the data. Teachers were initially fearful of the accountability and they feared the data at first, but over time that started to change, especially when they realized how serious Superintendent Dr. John Conyers was about the Baldrige framework as the approach to reach the board goals and student performance targets.

> Jean Sophie—I'm a collaborative, hands-on leader, and I didn't change my general approach. When the board and superintendent directive came down. . . . "All second-graders will read at grade level by the end of second grade," I rolled up

my sleeves and got into the classroom and helped teachers do it. They saw major involvement from me and knew I was not going to leave them hanging out there alone. In the beginning, I needed to be more in command (although with a caring manner) and communication is the key with the Baldrige approach. Sometimes "command decisions" are necessary, and the teachers had to realize that. It was a lesson I needed to learn too.

What would you say were the biggest barriers you encountered in the beginning of the process?

GH— Without a doubt, *change* and moving away from what people were comfortable with to being very uncomfortable. They were uncomfortable having students look at data, having the central administration asking them to "teach your kids these quality tools," and, interestingly, having a strategic plan from central office that was directly linked to the classroom. "Here are the strategic goals, now do them," was the directive from the superintendent.

When two- and three-year cycles of improvement were introduced . . . [and expected] it made staff very uncomfortable. In hindsight, I think I should have started with smaller steps in linking strategic planning, although at the time it didn't seem like such a major step.

It is so important to be firm and be a strong, visionary leader; otherwise they [certified and noncertified staff] will give up. My former district started Baldrige and even brought in a Black Belt (signifying a high-level certification designation of Six Sigma) from Motorola to help. That district could not endure the beginning bumps in the road in order to reach a level of success that would allow people to look back and understand how far they had come. [Author's note: Dr. John Conyers (CCSD-15's superintendent until his retirement in 2004) and the board of education were resolute in the desire to reach performance excellence through full deployment of the Baldrige framework. There would be no turning back and no acceptable excuses. His resolve made the difference over the long haul.]

KH— Baldrige came top down from the board and superintendent, and the leadership team was expected to carry it out. The biggest barrier to overcome was the "total change" from site-based (every school and principal did their own thing). Teachers were used to the site-based approach where they were asked, "What do you want to do this year?" In the past, there was no measurement of anything we did. Scores were not improving even though more money was being spent. Letting go of the site-based model we had was difficult. Defensiveness was prevalent, for example, "We're not a business," was a common comment from teachers. There were many disgruntled employees and morale, at times, went down considerably.

We still had a modified site-based approach, but some things became standardized, such as using data analysis to make decisions about what to change and establishing key learner statements (outcomes). These were aligned with the Illinois state standards for each subject and grade level, and we began using the learner statements as the curriculum. The district mandated some professional development each year, but each building also had discretionary money to use for such things as professional development needs at the school level and hiring teacher aides. How we spent our money meant we also had to be accountable with data as to how it impacted learning results at the end of the year.

In the beginning all principals were trained on the concepts and language of Baldrige. We [principals] were all required to become Illinois Lincoln Award Program examiners [Illinois' state program modeled after the Baldrige], and every principal learned to analyze data and understand the core values of Baldrige. Tons of staff development time was focused on the principals and preparing us to lead a Baldrige-based school.

JS— I came in as an assistant principal at the time Baldrige started in the district with Bob Ewy [director of quality and planning] from Central Office doing most of the work with the expanded leadership team [superintendent's direct reports, coordinators, and principals]. The response from teachers (biggest barrier) was this [Baldrige] is a business model, and another "educational bandwagon." Some thought they could "outlive" this initiative as they had outlived previous initiatives. Other barriers included, the criteria language, deciding on the best deployment strategy, and goal setting. This was all so different from the way everyone was used to working. In my case, I took over one of the district's most diverse schools where the students were among the lowest performers on normed tests.

Teachers were defensive for good reason. Many were still loyal to the previous principal and not only did they have to adjust to a new leader, but they would now be held accountable for progress; only the data would show if we were successful. "Our kids are different" was the common response. Some teachers felt that other things besides test scores should count when assessing school effectiveness. It was hard for them to come to the realization things were different and that going back was not an option. Some teachers left because they didn't or couldn't make the required changes.

What were the most significant actions/decisions that were made either by the central administration or by you that helped turn your school around to the Baldrige framework?

GH— The former superintendent [Dr. John Conyers] felt that the community did not view the school district as a strong, vital system. He and the board made the decision to rectify this view by adopting Baldrige to get the processes in place that would lead to improved results. At the building level, as teachers experienced the discomfort of change, many were threatened when we began to examine data in a different light. As principals we were taught to look at the data from many different angles, often drilling down to the student level and looking at all the subgroups. Our job, along with professionals from the district quality office, was to teach our certified staff how to analyze our own data. Finally over the years, as we began to get trend data and study it, they could see that "data doesn't lie." A teacher may say, "I'm using the best strategies," but if the data shows otherwise, it is a powerful force in motivating the teacher to change. Especially since this was a superintendent's mandate.

KH— The 2000–2005 Strategic Plan for the district that was adopted by the board meant that we were staying the course. The principals and everyone else knew that the Baldrige framework was here to stay. The goals and accountability were not going to go away. A significant change occurred when the superintendent changed the principal's evaluation. No longer were the evaluations based on "how you feel things are going," but on the results. We were held accountable and were taught how to prepare a data-driven annual report (based on the SIP), which we were required to present to the superintendent and his cabinet. The school improvement planning process (based on PDSA), with a timeline, was put on the intranet and each school leadership team received training from the district quality office. Standardizing the SIP process was another key element in our success.

Beyond that, the senior leaders took important action to support the schools and our efforts. This was a huge relief from a principal's standpoint. Support included a unique reading intervention program, and tons of standards based instruction was given to teachers in their staff development.

JS— The most significant actions/decisions involved the board goals that said the district would be Baldrige based. For me, there was a big change in how we spent our time, especially on the expanded leadership team. [Author's note: The meetings began to focus more on Baldrige training, data analysis, and quarterly focus group reports from certified and noncertified staff.] We principals translated this to our school meetings . . . all focused on Baldrige. The teachers also knew we principals were being evaluated on student achievement. It made a huge difference to make principals accountable.

Suddenly, there was an urgency felt by all school principals, no matter how well students had performed in the past. Now, everything needed to be aligned, even the principal's evaluation. For example, one teacher had extremely low achievement and the principal made sure that was in the evaluation. The data tells all and explains a lot. This required me to counsel with the teacher, provide technical assistance through a mentor or find appropriate staff development. I also spent a lot of time in her classroom observing, assuring she was using quality tools and PDSA to improve instruction, and made certain that she reported results to me weekly. It was never an option for me to overlook what was happening in any classroom.

What were the most significant actions/decisions that were made either by the central administration or by you that helped turn your school around to the Baldrige framework?

GH— At the district level there were new pieces of curriculum developed and districtwide data collection made available. They (the superintendent with board approval) also set very high student performance levels. One example that floored everybody was, "All second graders will leave second grade able to read at or above state norms." There is a misconception about data collection. We had to learn what pieces were most important for us to understand and track and let the rest go!

At the building level we studied the ITBS [Iowa Test of Basic Skills] data together, and there was great fear of being measured against other schools in the district. We had to learn that this is not about us [leaders and certified staff]. This is about data analysis. If teacher X is doing something well and getting extraordinary results, we need to pinpoint the approach and use those strategies too.

KH— The strategic plan was the guide and the superintendent added student performance targets, which everyone was expected to achieve. This meant that everybody was on the same page. The PDSA was very visible in all schools.

The superintendent reallocated resources for development of a data warehouse, which allowed us to easily pull up information when we needed it. The number of reports available to us instantly was an enormous help. We had the ability to compare results in so many different ways and received a lot of support and training to understand how to maximize the data warehouse's usefulness. After a while it became apparent that we needed data other than year-end results, and it wasn't until much later in the journey (teachers were highly skeptical at first) that online, in-process assessments became available.

Also resources were put into the establishment of various intervention programs that made it evident that we were really doing something about the low achievers. I would also have to say that principal accountability helped drive Baldrige into the classroom.

JS—   Key factors included the following: Everybody's expectations were the same. There was alignment (same goals, same language) among board, superintendent, etc., and the fact that all were held accountable made a significant difference.

We [principals] involved all stakeholders. At my school, parents got involved by helping with our math facts goal, moving us from 65% to 93% meeting or exceeding state standards in one year. [The target was 90% of all students would meet or exceed the grade level on state or nationally normed standards tests.]

Another factor, and one that was particularly significant, was the ability to look at student data individually [as a school]. That helped a lot. With the new data warehouse we could drill down into the results to see what skills each student lacked and compare that with the rest of the class or grade level. When we looked at the data by subgroup it helped us see which student groups were most underserved. When teachers saw these results they knew they had to do something different in their classrooms. Also, when the district standardized the instruction process and required teachers to report weekly results for students at risk of not meeting the standards to us [the principals] it meant every teacher had to come on board.

What were the biggest pitfalls (issues) you encountered at the school level along the way? How did you overcome them?

GH— Resistance to change was the biggest pitfall. "Why are we doing this?" "This data isn't right." Getting past peoples' perceptions takes persistence on the part of the principal. You have to keep putting the data out there and then show everyone that we are making progress. An example is this year, first-graders will test on a "cold read," and teachers at first said, "We can't do that; they will score very low." As principal, I pointed out that this is base line data for growth. "However low, it is only our starting point. Look how far we have come in other areas. What an opportunity for improvement!" They came around and realized how significant it was to have pre and post data, not only from the teacher's point of view, but also to help students and their parents realize the extent of their academic growth.

KH— Accountability was the huge issue. Changing the way teachers were teaching and having standards that everybody knows we must meet, including the kids, was significant and it took a long time to persuade teachers how this would help. Fear of data was another. We look at the data and now must do it (teach) differently . . . no more just plugging along. In my school, which had been one of the highest-achieving schools in the district before starting the Baldrige journey, we had teachers who said, "We're already good." "It works for me." We overcame these by staying the course until teachers could see that we *were* making improvements.

JS— Pitfalls . . . hmm. Mine were different because of the stress (on staff) of teaching in the most diverse school with struggling students. It was very hard to get buy-in from parents and teachers. Honestly, it was a bit of a surprise that parents were so skeptical. A few teachers dug in their heels, but we got a big jump-start from one great teacher who started a "Quality Kids" club, grades 2 through 6. When we saw that it worked, that students were learning more and enjoying school more . . . that's when they [the rest of the teachers] "got sold." Parents began to want to learn quality tools. We ended up training them too. It was quite remarkable to see.

Overall, the accountability piece was difficult for everyone to accept. But, the process had a silver lining—as a school we learned to work together, supporting each other so that in the end, the students benefited.

How did you motivate the staff to keep improving and stay the course? How did you keep faculty and staff morale up?

GH— Like in sports, when you start winning, when test scores start going up, there is a tremendous surge of enthusiasm for the process. For us [school administration and staff], when kids learned to keep track, behavior improved. We use run charts for kids on past behavior, and they are posted all over the school. When kids see their behavior on a chart, they become reflective thinkers. When a teacher or the principal must deal with a behavior problem, it's, "Tell me about your chart. What's going on?" It could be academic, social, or emotional. We work with the student on PDSA and do a root-cause analysis, and then develop a plan with data we [administrators and students] can monitor. It works and teachers are thrilled!

We have celebrations all along the way and we problem-solve together. Just today I had a second-grade teacher come in with her ITBS scores. She wanted me to look at them because there was a 2% drop in the scores and she wanted me to help her analyze the data. I was no longer a manager. I was a leader she trusted to help her grow. She was managing herself. After she left my office, I reflected on what had just happened and realized it was a principal's dream come true. Staff who manage themselves and remain focused on the goal of improvement and better results warm the heart of any principal.

KH— For one thing, our staff meetings always were completely focused on goals. Conversations among the staff were so motivating. Teacher talk changed. There was no room or time for minutia. We used a systems approach to solve every problem. Suddenly, every problem was owned by *all* of us . . . including what was happening in lower grades and higher grades. As the level of professional dialogue changed, there was also humor amidst the stress. Recognition was of the group . . . the entire school. When the primary grades achieved something, we all celebrated. We talked about ourselves as professionals. Teachers want and need professional dialogue, and they become self-motivated under this type system.

Staff motivation comes from [the principal] being visible in the buildings and in classrooms, supporting teachers with parents, and trying to keep nonessential tasks away from teachers so they concentrate on the most important task of all . . . teaching our children. I found that teachers don't like to be singled out for praise and recognition. We benefited from being a team. We all worked toward the same goals and worked to support and compliment each other. A sense of humor was important and finding time to laugh every day was key to keeping morale high. I always was the last to leave and first to show up in the morning, was always available at any time for staff, and made sure I stopped and listened when they spoke with me . . . and followed through with requests or promises.

I also was fortunate to be sent to the Harvard Principal's Institute and from that improved my ability to "read a staff." This two- to three-week program is one I recommend for principals as a great leadership experience. [See the Interesting Websites to access information about this program.]

JS— I would add that articulation began to cross all boundaries. For example, with our second-grade reading goal, we needed kindergarten and first-grade teachers to talk with each other, but also to include the special education teachers.

Also, involvement of the principal was critical in my school. For example, for a six months period I took eight bilingual students to work on reading. I also read Terry Deal's books—all of them and used his suggestions. (See Recommended Reading.) For example, I called every teacher during the summer (when scores came in) to tell them that the scores were up.

We celebrated often and involved parents in the celebration. The principal is the cheerleader for improvement. As principal, I try to show that I value teachers' time. I try to help them and support them in using their time wisely.

Knowing everything you know now about the role of the principal in leading the Baldrige process, what would you do (actions) differently and what would you surely keep?

GH— Initially I would have liked to have taken staff members with me to visit other organizations that used the Baldrige process and use every way I could think of to get them to see the big picture of systematic process. One good thing I did was to ask teachers who became comfortable with data to share with others. Those selected must be respected teacher leaders who don't blame and who are nonthreatening to their peers. As a school, we expanded the amount of time spent discussing strategic planning and root causes of problems. A central theme was "How do you find and know what the root cause is?"

I modeled the quality tools for the staff and, to this day, I demonstrate a tool for the month and share it at faculty meeting. Teachers also share by bringing in examples of how they used the tool for the month (last month). You see teachers sharing with each other. You hear how the conversations have changed from fear and skepticism to "Can you show me how to do it?"

We have two surveys that I use to gain feedback about my leadership. They are the Conditions of Teaching and Shared Decision-Making [districtwide surveys]. I share this data with staff, regardless of what it says about me . . . and I show them how I will work on this or that. I also tell everyone how I will monitor my progress. In fact I just used a Pareto chart to do this. I can tell that teachers are impressed that I am open to growing. It has helped build trust between us.

KH— Having common goals and focusing on our processes helped us change instruction. As principals we have to be hands on, and rarely in our offices. We also needed to eliminate the mundane tasks (many of which we took on ourselves) and do the important ones. The biggest most important (two star) action we principals (in our district) did for staff was to stand in the box and deflect "the arrows." I'm referring to the fact that different parents cause stress for our teachers and we took the lead in supporting the teachers.

But, we also had to make sure our communication systems were working effectively. Principals had to make sure they shared the important things learned at leadership team meetings, so that no one felt left out of the loop. The establishment of a district intranet helped too as important documents and meeting minutes, data, and results of PDSA projects were available to everyone.

JS— Karen's points are all valid. As principal I took more time to work with colleagues and to talk things through. We worked often until 7 P.M. and on Sundays in the beginning, but it was worth it.

It appears that the principal's evaluation system changed during the district's Baldrige journey. Please describe the changes and how this impacted you and your leadership at the school. To what degree did the evaluation system affect the speed of change at your school?

GH— The principal's evaluation process *is* the successful leadership of this Baldrige-based school. It is directly linked to outcomes of student progress. As far as impact, it let me look at myself more reflectively. When we prepare for our evaluation, we list both strengths and opportunities for improvement. We use data to back up our claims. My most recent evaluation (this past week) involved a two page summary and seven charts illustrating our successes and growth areas. I could not go back. I would not want to go back to the old system.

The teachers' evaluation now looks at their growth cycle versus the old checklist. It gives the system a way to really look at staff and see whether their daily work is aligned to teaching state standards. The board expectations align with Baldrige and also all support services in our district are aligned. Now, growth [improved results] is the major point of evaluation and it has made a huge difference in how people own and manage their own professional development.

KH and JS (together)—Our evaluation system changed to "Show me the data" and "What are your goals?" Accountability for the scores drove us [principals] into the classroom. One important piece of data that is used to evaluate all principals . . . the results of the Conditions of Teaching Survey, which is a staff satisfaction survey. We joke about meeting "the firing squad" [senior leaders] and teachers know that we are accountable, so the change has brought us [as a school staff] together in supporting each other in identifying growth areas. The system is very professional and because data is data . . . we can feel proud of our achievements.

As a school leader, what was your greatest learning in the whole process?

GH— Personally, it was the change in my concept of self reflection. As a leader it was the transition to blaming processes, and *not* people. That practice frees teachers and motivates them to help every child learn and succeed.

KH— To me, it was that I could make a difference. I made an improvement!

JS— I agree with what my colleagues have said, and I also learned that leadership and communication styles go hand in hand and, that both are needed to lead the change. I also fear that "systems thinking" (which has done so much for us) will somehow go away [at CCSD-15]. We must work to keep it.

What advice would you give others "in the trenches?"

GH— My advice is from our experience. Expectations can never be too high. Make sure you have a system in place to monitor growth over time. You will be amazed at the progress and you will get closer to your goal than you ever thought you could. An example is our expectation that *all* second-graders will end that grade reading on level. Teachers were defensive and skeptical at first . . . now they, too, are believers. When you get to the top of the mountain (our mountaintop was winning the Baldrige award) you look back and say, "I love being here. It wasn't so hard after all. We realize now how much energy we wasted previously on lower expectations."

You also need a superintendent that provides Central Office marching orders. If he/she is not a firm believer [in the Baldrige framework], you will have tough going. If you are a principal, my advice is: (1) Listen carefully to someone who is doing Baldrige and learn. (2) The best way to understand Baldrige is to be an examiner. As an examiner, if you evaluate a business or health care organization it allows you to learn and practice free of your own bias about education. [Author's note: Baldrige or state examiners are trained on the criteria and then are expected to evaluate an organization's award application. Examiners read the application and write feedback to the applicant on strengths and opportunities for improvement based on how the applicant has addressed the criteria requirements. Examiners learn a lot about systems and alignment, integration, data, and cycles of improvement, which are required for all organizations using the framework.] (3) Where ever you go to learn about Baldrige, try to bring five staff members with you. They will be your cheerleaders on your return.

KH— Stay the course and never give up. It is *not* easy, but it is *so* worth it.

JS— The level of involvement by the principal is key . . . remember that you are a leader, not a boss manager. We (our district) will lose key people without continued support. Remember that Baldrige is not an award, it is a *framework*. The core values are the most important parameters and because of that they are nonnegotiable when the organization makes decisions.

Summary

As you reflect on the CCSD-15 principals' experience with Baldrige, keep in mind that at the time of their interviews, they were almost five years into their Baldrige journey. Among the most striking of their reminiscences was their unanimous feeling of, "We could never go back to the old ways." It has been our consistent observation that those schools that stay the course do indeed experience remarkable improvements in results, regardless of whether they start out as a great school or one that is struggling. Of course, we know that the principal's leadership truly counts!

9

Parting Words of Wisdom

Conversation with the Principal

At the conclusion of this book, we hope you will see the value of the Baldrige framework and make the decision to lead a Baldrige-based quality school. The learning and practice as referenced throughout the chapters are a challenge for even the most courageous of leaders. Unless you are in a district or school that has already committed to the Baldrige framework, you will first need to involve others, learn, practice the first steps, regroup from lessons learned, and move forward with continuous improvement. And it sounds so "canned" to remind you once more that the effort is worth it every step of the way. Few would argue that education today is doing its job for all of our students, and until that goal is accomplished, we must not be satisfied with the status quo.

Common Pitfalls of Low-Performing Schools

Here are some observations of common pitfalls that are almost always evident in low-performing schools. If you are not leading a low-performing school but believe that there is lots of room for improvement and you feel the pressures to become more effective and efficient, you might find some of these pitfalls in your organization. We focus on leadership pitfalls, as leaders drive the system, and set the tone and climate for the school. It is expected that the leader will role model the highest ethical behaviors, have unfailing passion, focus, and optimism about the goals and the organization's ability to reach them. Check the list (figures 9.1 and 9.2) to assess your own progress. This might be a good activity with which to engage your leadership team.

Remember, before improvement happens, the facts (data)—the good and, yes, the bad and ugly ones too—must be faced (see Figure 9.1). Part of the journey is learning about how to improve personally and then to improve the system.

Once you've checked your pulse and given yourself a quick checkup, study the common pitfalls of leaders in relation to specific criteria categories in Figure 9.2 on page 155.

Time

Yes. It takes time to learn about the Baldrige framework and to go through the self-assessment. Yes. It takes time to understand your system and identify the gaps leading to results. Yes. It takes time to dig into your results and link them back to missing links, which could

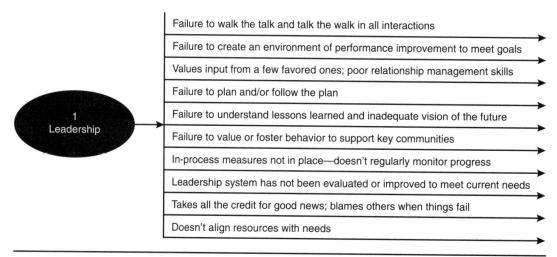

Figure 9.1 Pitfalls of leadership.

be faulty process designs, insufficient processes, nonalignment of processes to strategic goals, or the lack of a measurement system that allows you to monitor progress regularly and systematically. It could be that those who need the information do not have access to it on a timely basis. Yes. It takes time to align all systems within a school and have unfailing focus on the desired results. Yes. It takes time to energize the faculty and staff, find ways to motivate them, reorganize the way they are organized to do their work, and provide them with the right training to carry out action plans to meet the goals. Yes. It takes time to listen and learn from students, parents, and other key stakeholders. Yes, it takes time to do an environmental scan each year and go through a rigorous planning process to make certain that strategic challenges are addressed and resources aligned with the most pressing needs. But, what is the alternative? Remember the definition of insanity—doing things the same way and expecting different results.

There are no magic pills! You need only ask yourself, "Am I satisfied with the current organizational results? Am I satisfied that students who leave our school have all the skills, knowledge, abilities, and wisdom to enjoy success at the next level or world of work?" If your answer is "no" or "I'm not sure," you can benefit from the Baldrige approach. Before you answer, "Yes, I'm satisfied," be sure you evaluate your school's trend results.

Time spent learning about Baldrige and deploying a systematic fact-based evaluation and improvement approach throughout the school (at all levels, across all departments) *will* yield greater results. It will definitely yield improved results faster than a shotgun approach or putting all your efforts into one part of the system, only to discover, too late, how that affected the results of the entire system.

As the leader, you hold the future of every student and all employees. The challenge is to put aside your ego needs and learn, learn, learn with a laser-beam focus on the desired results. The Baldrige criteria and framework are available to you. This is a proven approach that works for any organization willing to undertake the journey. Is it easy? No! (Learning the criteria and framework takes time.) Is it always going to be fun? No! (But there will be many opportunities to celebrate as you progress.) Will there be times when you are informed that leadership poses a barrier to improvement? Yes! Will this hurt? Maybe it will sting for a little bit, but if you let go of your ego needs and listen and learn, the benefits will far outweigh whatever pain you momentarily feel.

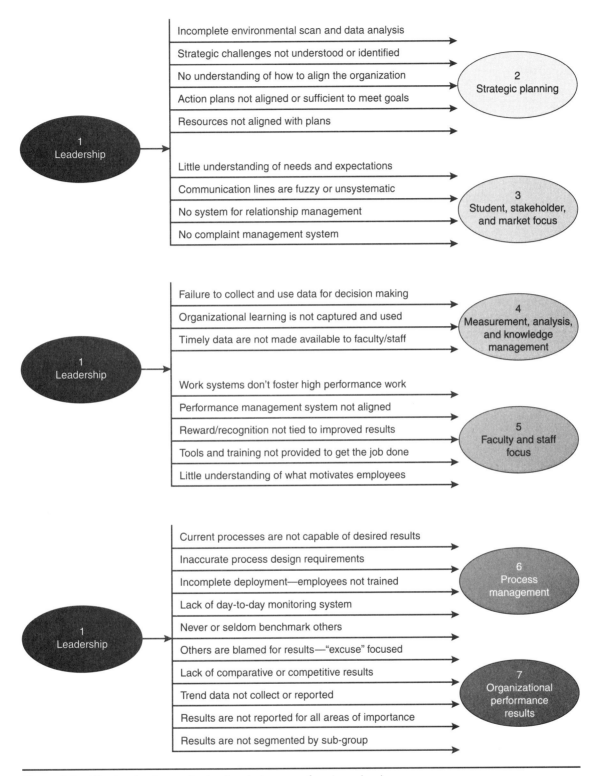

Figure 9.2 Mistakes leaders make leading to lower-performing schools.

Above our desks are three quotations that remind us that nothing is impossible and that the important things *are* necessary *and* possible (Figure 9.3).

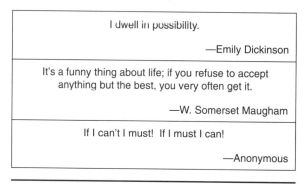

I dwell in possibility.

—Emily Dickinson

It's a funny thing about life; if you refuse to accept anything but the best, you very often get it.

—W. Somerset Maugham

If I can't I must! If I must I can!

—Anonymous

Figure 9.3 Food for thought.

In the words of principals from Baldrige-winning schools, "We were afraid at first, but now we will never go back to old ways. The benefits far outweigh the time and difficulty involved." Just about every school leader we know wants to do the *right* things *right,* but this is possible only if you learn what the right things are. Good luck on your journey, and don't let anyone deter you from the goal of performance excellence. It is not impossible.

Appendix A

Thumbnail Sketch:
Quality Tools

There are many excellent quality tools books on the market, and we have listed several in the Recommended Reading section. However, it is important to note that one book, *There Is Another Way! Launch a Baldrige-Based Quality Classroom,* written by the authors of this book, also contains tools and instructions and has an accompanying CD with templates on it. If you are leading your school to Baldrige and intend to include teachers and deploy the framework and process in the classroom, copies of that book will negate your need to purchase other books on quality tools.

The thumbnail sketches of common quality tools are presented here to give you some ideas about what each tool does and what it looks like. We find that it is helpful for educators to have a quick reference such as these sketches provide.

Stacked Cups

The stacked cups are not described in any tools book. These are simple to use and provide instant feedback from any group. We use them all the time in training to gain an understanding of how well the participants are comprehending and coping with the new materials and skills presented. Generally, the cups are brightly colored and stacked with blue or green on top, yellow in the middle, and red on the bottom. As a group's understanding changes, they change the order in which cups are stacked. If a group puts the yellow cup on top, the facilitator, who is constantly scanning the room, goes to that group to clarify any points. The class is not stopped for a yellow cup. A red cup goes to the top when no one in the group understands what is being discussed or asked. When the facilitator sees a red cup, he or she regains the attention of the entire class and addresses the issue causing a red cup signal. We have found that getting instant feedback from participants is invaluable. It certainly has led us to improve the way we deliver instruction. You might find them useful during any training you facilitate and certainly on your Baldrige journey.

Tools of Quality

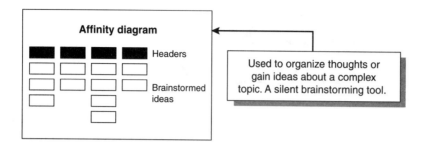

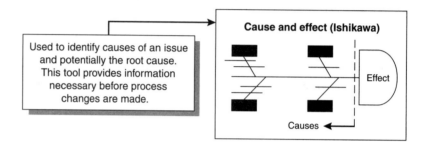

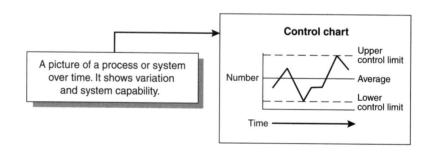

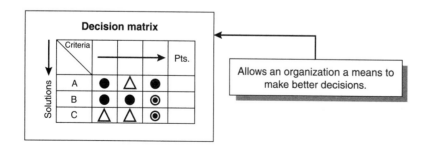

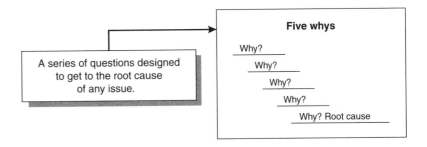

A series of questions designed to get to the root cause of any issue.

Five whys

Why? _____
  Why? _____
    Why? _____
      Why? _____
        Why? Root cause

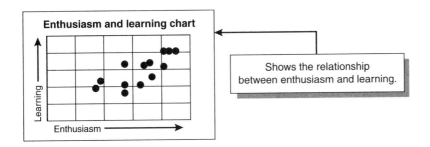

Enthusiasm and learning chart

Learning
Enthusiasm →

Shows the relationship between enthusiasm and learning.

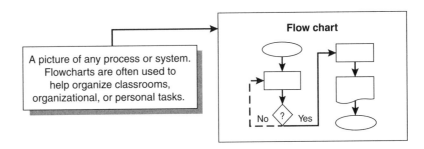

A picture of any process or system. Flowcharts are often used to help organize classrooms, organizational, or personal tasks.

Flow chart

No ? Yes

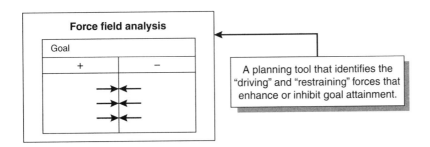

Force field analysis

Goal

+	−

A planning tool that identifies the "driving" and "restraining" forces that enhance or inhibit goal attainment.

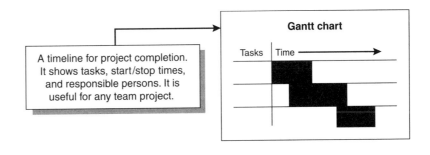

A timeline for project completion. It shows tasks, start/stop times, and responsible persons. It is useful for any team project.

Gantt chart

Tasks | Time →

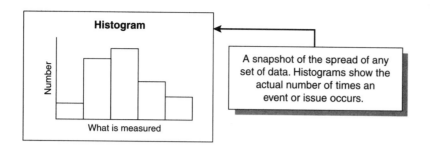

Histogram

Number / What is measured

A snapshot of the spread of any set of data. Histograms show the actual number of times an event or issue occurs.

Helps determine cause and effect and is used when there is confusion.

Is/Is not matrix

	Is	Is not	Distinction
What?			
Where?			
When?			
Extent?			
Who?			

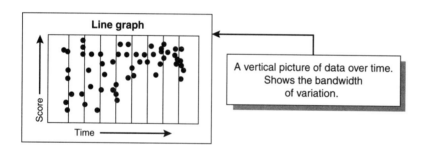

Line graph

Score / Time

A vertical picture of data over time. Shows the bandwidth of variation.

Used to organize thoughts or develop themes around a complex process or topic. A brainstorming and graphic organizing tool.

Lotus diagram

	Main idea	

Multivoting

	Votes				Total points
Idea A	3	1	1	3	8
Idea B	1	1	3		5
Idea C	1	3	3		7

A prioritization tool. Each person gets 2 or more weighted votes (1st choice = 3 points, etc.). It allows everyone an equal voice in decision making.

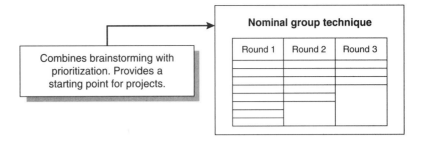

Combines brainstorming with prioritization. Provides a starting point for projects.

Nominal group technique

Round 1	Round 2	Round 3

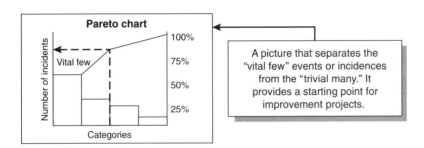

Pareto chart

A picture that separates the "vital few" events or incidences from the "trivial many." It provides a starting point for improvement projects.

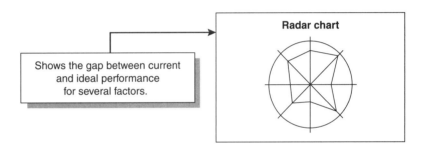

Shows the gap between current and ideal performance for several factors.

Radar chart

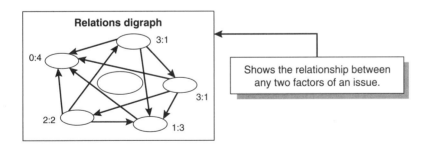

Relations digraph

Shows the relationship between any two factors of an issue.

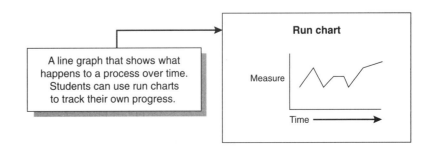

A line graph that shows what happens to a process over time. Students can use run charts to track their own progress.

Run chart

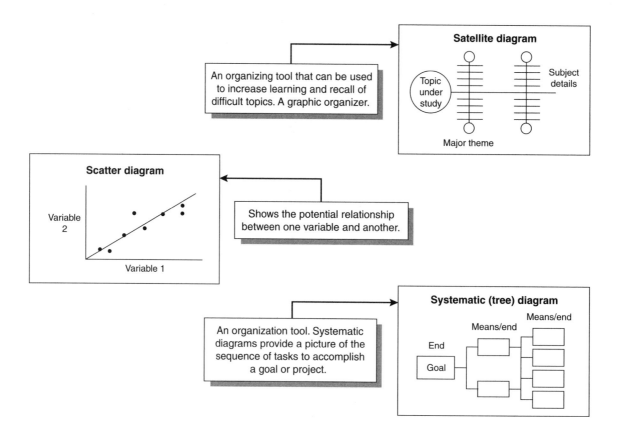

Informal Tools of Quality

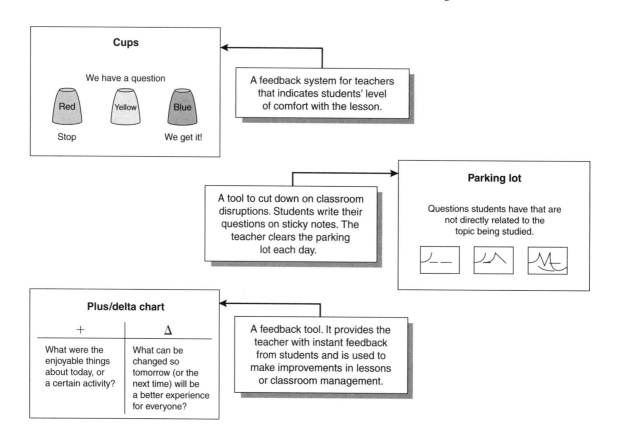

Appendix B

An Alternative Teacher Appraisal Instrument

There has been much discussion over the course of our careers (and probably long before that) about how to evaluate teacher effectiveness. For years, there was (and in some school districts probably still is) a category related to "interesting bulletin boards," yet without attention to the more critical elements of being a facilitator of learning. Some districts now expect teachers to align their daily lessons with state standards and district expectations in a more meaningful way, and they expect teachers to collect data on improvement. The importance of aligning a performance appraisal instrument to the Baldrige framework for excellence you've instituted at your school cannot be understated. It is vital! It is a given that people will do that on which they are evaluated in order to save their jobs. You cannot expect different behavior from teachers if you proceed with a traditional evaluation instrument. Life in a Baldrige-based quality classroom (as described in *There Is Another Way!*) is very different from what it is in a more traditional classroom, or even one where cooperative learning activities take place.

We offer a different model for you to reflect on and hope that it spurs discussion among teachers, the union, your board, and other stakeholders. If any part of it makes sense, feel free to use it or adopt it with some revisions. We'd certainly like to hear your experiences and have you share your appraisal instruments with us.

What follows are some reflections we have on this instrument and offer this as guidance for any school leader and/or district administrator before using such an instrument.

1. Train anyone administering this instrument on both the instrument itself and the training described in *There Is Another Way! Launch a Baldrige-Based Quality Classroom* in order to fully understand the requirements and observables.

2. Any teacher at the "needs improvement" or "novice" level would be expected to complete a professional development plan (PDP).

3. Consider giving special recognition to teachers attaining the master teacher level. It need not be monetary, but it should be creative, perhaps a press conference to recognize these individuals.

4. Master teacher status ought to be a prerequisite to leading staff development programs. This gives credence to the staff development providers and ensures that anyone who is certified has a track record of success with students.

5. Only those who attain master teacher status ought to be eligible for train-the-trainer status for Baldrige-based quality (BBQ) classrooms.

Teacher Performance Appraisal Instrument: A Model

Major function A: Curriculum, instructional strategies, and programs are in place to promote the optimum achievement of academic potential.	In what ways might a teacher demonstrate the item has been met?
1. Plans lessons that are innovative and interactive and have real-world application and problem solving as centerpieces and require critical thinking skills at all levels.	Unit and daily lesson plans and observations
2. Uses feedback from students, parents, and resource personnel to improve instruction and help design learning experiences.	The instrument used, results in chart form, lesson plans, and observations
3. Uses the teaching styles that students have given from feedback and have identified as necessary to achieve success in the classroom.	Lesson plans and observations
4. Uses a combination of individual activities, small and large groups, and teams to encourage students to complete work independently, to work as team members, and to achieve higher levels of learning and critical thinking skills.	Lesson plans and observations
5. Regularly uses action research in the form of the Plan-Do-Study-Act cycle to ensure that the instructional program addresses all students' needs.	Charts, graphs, PDSA storyboard, lesson plans, and observations
6. Uses community resources to support the instructional program.	Lesson plans and field trips
7. Provides learning experiences that are directly aligned with district or state content standards.	Unit/lesson plans, observations
8. Uses a variety of materials and learning activities with a cross-cultural focus to embed cultural diversity into the curriculum.	Unit/lesson plans, observations
9. Student success plans are collaboratively written for any student in danger of failing the class or grade as part of the early intervention strategy.	List of those involved in writing SSPs, examples of plans and student improvement results
10. Student and stakeholder feedback is gained through data collection, and results are used to improve instruction.	Examples of feedback instruments, charted data with lesson plans showing specific improvements
11. Collaboratively writes a classroom vision, mission, and class goals with the students to ensure a common focus on learning.	Observation
12. Engages in staff development related to areas of student need in order to improve instruction and learning results.	List of staff development courses completed, lesson plans including newly learned skills, student learning results
13. Assigns homework that is relevant, anchors learning, and encourages critical thinking skills.	Examples of homework assignments, lesson plans, scatter diagram— homework and unit test results
14. Engages students in hands-on learning and encourages conversations focused toward problem solving and learning.	Observations, lesson plans
15. Assumes the role of facilitator of learning. Provides coaching and mentoring to students and encourages them to seek greater levels of learning.	Observation
16. Employs quality tools as an integral part of learning content and related processes.	Lesson plans, observations, student work
Major function B: Accepts responsibility for student performance results.	
1. Aligns lessons with the state standards and district expectations— teaches the right things.	Unit and lesson plans
2. Lesson plans show where students have the opportunity to give feedback to improve instruction as an integral part of the class.	Lesson plans, classroom observations
3. Seeks input from students about their understanding throughout the learning process using quality tools.	Observations, lesson plans
4. Lesson objectives are clearly communicated for student comprehension.	Observation
5. Uses a reflective process throughout the school year for self-evaluation and improvement of instruction and classroom climate.	Discussion, notes

Continued

6. Routinely collects data and engages the class in PDSA to improve learning results.	Observation, charts/graphs of pre/post intervention learning results
7. Uses authentic assessments that directly assess what was taught.	Assessment instruments, examples
Major function C: Uses professional expertise to plan and meet instructional needs of every student.	
1. Seeks assistance from others (professionals, parents, and other stakeholders) by way of surveys or other means to continuously improve all aspects of the teaching/learning process.	Samples of surveys, charted results, and lesson and unit plans with highlighted improvements linked to surveys or information garnered
2. Is active in personal professional development to gain knowledge, seek out latest technology, brain research, and real-world applications to the curriculum, as well as continuing to learn about students, parents, and the classroom and using this knowledge.	List of professional conferences attended; journals or books read; unit/lesson plans showing how knowledge is applied; list and document any ways knowledge is gained about students, parents, and the classroom system
3. Demonstrate professional growth through planning to meet student needs.	Student success plans, lesson plans, resources used to change the classroom system and/or instructional approaches, student learning results of those with an SSP
Major function D: Is a role model for good citizenship, ethics, social skills, tolerance, and equity and establishes caring relationships with all students and stakeholders.	
1. Maintains timely communication with all stakeholders in a variety of ways, focusing on parent involvement as reciprocal partners.	Phone logs, examples of communication sent home, parent involvement numbers, and an explanation of volunteer tasks
2. Engages parents as partners by seeking formal feedback on their child's education and provides regular information about their child's progress and schedules conferences at mutually agreeable times.	Communication sent home regarding conferences and progress, examples of feedback tools and how information is used
3. Views learning as a collaborative effort and establishes an environment based on mutual trust and respect.	Survey results, observations
4. Creates an environment that appreciates and celebrates diversity routinely.	Observations, unit/lesson plans, assignments, learning activities, materials used
5. Routinely uses action research in the form of PDSA cycle to gather data to improve classroom management processes.	PDSA storyboards, data showing improvements
6. Has taken professional development courses related to diversity and successful approaches for working with a diverse group of students.	Professional development logs
Major function E: Safety of students and staff is of primary concern in order to advance learning.	
1. Collaborates with students to create classroom climate and procedures focused on creating a safe and respectful environment in which everyone can learn.	Observation, collaboratively written class mission, charts showing factors that contribute to a quality student
2. Instructs students in safe practices. Ensures that the classroom is free of obstacles and exercises care to keep potentially dangerous objects in a safe place except when they are being used by students. Collaboratively establishes procedures for accountability by all students.	Observation, written or flow charts of procedures for student accountability
3. Sets the climate for proper care, handling, and maintenance of all materials in the classroom and school. Collaboratively establishes procedures for accountability by all students.	Observation, written or flow charts of procedures for student accountability

Continued

Continued

Major function F: Demonstrates professional practices consistent with school and system policies in accordance with the conditions of employment.	
1. Maintains open communication with and works cooperatively with administrators, support personnel, parents, and colleagues.	Responds rapidly to telephone, email, and written communication; committee assignments; serves on school-wide PDSA projects as requested
2. Maintains appropriate records and provides adequate plans and materials for substitute teachers.	Records completed on time, lesson plans for substitutes on file
3. Demonstrates accurate and current best practice content knowledge.	List and dates of conferences attended, professional books and journal articles or Web research completed
4. Safeguards student records and maintains confidentiality when communicating with others about students.	Observation, uses the approved Internet user protocol
5. Conducts oneself in a highest professional manner in all interactions with students, parents, and the community.	Observations and no complaints
6. Follows all district and/or school policies.	Observation and no instances of non-compliance

Rubric

Unsatisfactory (Does not perform any major functions at acceptable levels. Forty percent or fewer of the criteria in Major Functions A–E have been met. Demonstrates less than 100 percent of Function F.)

- Has not solicited formal feedback from students or parents about needs, classroom climate, or satisfaction.

- No PDSA cycles have been attempted.

- No evidence that the teacher has communicated with the next teacher-in-line to gain information about student needs.

- Not enrolled in any university or professional development courses to improve knowledge of his/her own content area.

- Not enrolled in any professional development courses in areas where student learning results are below the district expectation.

- No evidence that student feedback or process measures are used to improve delivery of instruction, selection of materials, and types of assignments given.

- Does not implement effective classroom procedures or instruction when there is evidence that not all students are successful.

- Lesson plans and observations indicate that instruction is primarily whole group, teacher-directed with lecture as the primary methodology used.

- What is taught is not aligned with district/school expectations.

- Quality tools are not in evidence either for classroom procedures or as a means to advance or to assess student learning.

- Communicates with parents only when reminded or mandated by school officials to do so.

- Learning about and appreciating diversity is not evidenced in lesson plans or supported by observations.

- Student safety issues are addressed only when incidents occur.

Needs improvement (Does not perform major functions at acceptable levels. Improvement is needed across all major functions. Completes 66 percent or fewer of Functions A–E; less than 100 percent of Function F.)

- Has not solicited formal feedback from students or parents about needs, classroom climate, or satisfaction.

- A formal PDSA cycle on classroom procedural issues has not been completed even though observations suggest a need for improvement.

- No formal system exists for obtaining feedback on student needs from the next teacher-in-line, postsecondary institutions, or employers (depending on situation).

- Has not shown or actively demonstrated continued learning in his/her own content area.

- Has not enrolled in professional development courses to improve in areas where student learning results are below the district expectation, or has taken courses but student learning results have not measurably improved.

- Little evidence exists that students have participated in decision making to improve the classroom.

- Little evidence exists to show that student feedback (minimally from grades 1 up) or process measures (for all grades) are used to improve delivery of instruction, materials, and types of assignments given. There is no evidence to support that this is done regularly.

- Does not employ data to make decisions for change regarding classroom procedural issues or instruction.

- Lesson plans and observations indicate that instruction is mainly delivered from the teacher to a large group.

- What is taught is not consistently aligned with district/school expectations.

- Neither lesson plans nor observations indicate that quality tools are used to encourage critical thinking or assess student learning.

- Communicates with parents only when their children are experiencing academic or behavioral difficulty.

- Learning about and appreciating diversity is rarely evidenced in lesson plans or supported by observations.

- Student safety issues are addressed as incidences occur.

Novice (Meets the expectation of most major functions but still requires improvement in the deployment. Student learning results may or may not improve. Completes 67–84 percent of Functions A–E, 100 percent of Function F.)

- Has solicited feedback from students or parents about at least two of the following areas—needs, classroom climate, or satisfaction—once during the school year.

- At least one formal PDSA cycle on classroom procedural issues has been completed and data show improvement has occurred.

- There is an informal system for gaining feedback on student needs from the next-teacher-in-line, postsecondary institutions, or employers (depending on situation).

- Can document and demonstrate continued learning in his/her own content area.

- Has enrolled in professional development courses to improve in areas where student learning results are below the district expectation, but student learning results have not measurably improved.

- There is some evidence (for example, cause/effect diagram, affinity diagram, Pareto chart, brainstorming, multivote, plus/delta, fast feedback, how helpful were these resources, and so on) that students have participated in decision making to improve the classroom.

- There is some evidence to show that occasionally student feedback (grades 1 and up) and process measures (pre-K–12) are used to improve delivery of instruction, materials used, and types of assignments given. Lesson plans do not reflect changes made based on feedback or data.

- Occasionally employs data to make decisions for change regarding classroom procedural issues or instruction.

- Lesson plans and observations indicate that instruction is often delivered from the teacher to a large group but occasionally students work in small groups.

- What is taught is directly aligned with district expectations. Assessment is aligned with what is taught.

- Lesson plans show and observations indicate that quality tools are sometimes used as a means of encouraging critical thinking or to assess student learning.

- Communicates with parents when their children are experiencing academic or behavioral difficulty, and through a class newsletter or the class Web page or other formal informational system.

- Learning about and appreciating diversity is documented in unit/lesson plans, supported by observations, and through word/deed in relationships with staff, students, and/or parents but mostly during holidays or special events.

- Student discipline expectations are addressed during the first week of school. When students' safety is at stake, the issue is immediately addressed.

Advancing (Meets the expectations of all major functions and students show improved learning results. Completes 85–93 percent of Functions A–E; 100 percent of Function F.)

- Has solicited formal feedback from students or parents about needs, classroom climate, and satisfaction more than once during the school year.

- A formal PDSA cycle has been completed on at least two key classroom procedural issues and data show improvement has occurred.

- There is a formal system for gaining feedback on student needs from the next-teacher-in-line, postsecondary institutions, or employers (depending on situation) once each year but the results are not noted and there is no evidence that suggestions for change are implemented.

- Documents continued learning in his/her own content area through reading the latest research, attending conferences, participating in staff development, accessing the Internet, reading current popular literature, or other means as documented and evidenced in observations.

- Has enrolled in professional development courses to improve in areas where student learning results are below the district expectation and student learning results have improved.

- There is evidence (for example, cause/effect diagram, affinity diagram, Pareto chart, brainstorming, multivote, plus/delta, fast feedback, how helpful were these resources, and so on) that students have participated in decision making to improve the classroom climate and instruction

- There is evidence to show that the teacher regularly solicits formal feedback from students and analyzes process measures to improve delivery of instruction, materials used, and types of assignments given.

- Regularly employs data to make decisions for change regarding classroom procedural issues and instruction.

- Lesson plans and observations indicate that there is a comfortable mix of instructional approaches, some teacher-led, some discovery learning, with a mix of large, small, and individual instruction. Knowledge of the latest brain research and multiple intelligences are evident in lesson plans, assignments, and observations.

- What is taught is directly aligned with school, district, state, or federal expectations. Process measures are understood and used regularly to ensure learning has occurred. Assessment is aligned with what is taught.

- Lesson plans show and observations indicate that quality tools are used as a means of encouraging critical thinking and/or to assess student learning.

- Communicates with parents frequently throughout the school year, not only when their children are experiencing academic or behavioral difficulty, and through a class newsletter or the class Web page or other formal informational system.

- Learning about and appreciating diversity is expected. Unit/lesson plans, observations, and relationships with staff, students, and/or parents support this.

- Student discipline expectations are addressed the first week of school as part of the collaborative development of a class vision, mission, and the definition of a quality student. Procedures are drafted collaboratively with students to obtain student buy-in. Safety is always the primary concern, and students are taught and expected to treat everyone with respect. The teacher has assessed the safety issues in his/her classroom and eliminated all hazards or instructed the students in safe handling of all materials and equipment.

Master teacher (Consistently exceeds expected performance in accomplishing all major functions and students demonstrate improved learning results and/or a very high level of learning. Completes 94 percent-plus of all Functions A–E, 100 percent of Function F.)

- During this year, this teacher has solicited formal feedback from students or parents about needs, classroom climate, and satisfaction more than once during the school year. Results are reported to parents, students, and the administration. This teacher formally engages these stakeholders in determining improvement plans. Formal feedback on teacher effectiveness is solicited at least once each year; results are charted and improvements have been made.

- Students have assisted the teacher in identifying classroom procedural issues that require improvement. Priorities have been established, and evidence from PDSA storyboards (charts, graphs, showing the completed PDSA steps) demonstrate that improvement has occurred. (Grades 2 and up)

- Students, paraprofessionals, administration, or peers have assisted the teacher in identifying classroom procedural issues that require improvement. Priorities have been established and evidence from PDSA storyboards (see above) demonstrate that improvement has occurred. (Grades pre-K–1)

- There is a formal, systematic articulation between this teacher and the next-teacher(s)-in-line, postsecondary institutions, or employers (depending on situation) to improve instruction and chart data on key process measures determined through collaboration with these entities. The changes in instruction the teacher makes are documented, implemented in the classroom, and measured. Data shows improvement in student learning has occurred, and satisfaction has increased with the aforementioned customers.

- Demonstrates continued learning in his/her own content area through a variety of means and contributes to the professional body of knowledge via participation in professional conferences and formally shares what was learned with colleagues. Classroom observations, student assignments, and lesson plans demonstrate that the most current research and knowledge are part of this teacher's base knowledge.

- Actively seeks professional development opportunities to improve in areas where student learning results are below the school or district expectations. Determines the key process measures and can document that student learning as measured by both process and results measures have improved. Action research is ongoing, and lessons learned are shared with others throughout the school or district.

- Students are regularly engaged and there is evidence (for example, cause/effect diagram, affinity diagram, Pareto chart, brainstorming, multivote, plus/delta, fast feedback, how helpful were these resources, and so on) they participate in decision making to improve the classroom climate and instruction. Observations support this.

- Lesson plans show regular, formal feedback from students (grades 1–12) and process measures (pre-K–12) are used to improve delivery of instruction, materials used, and types of assignments given.

- Regularly employs data to make decisions for change regarding classroom procedural issues and instruction. This teacher continuously seeks ways to collaboratively improve the system so each student can learn to his/her optimum. This teacher is always aware of how students are doing academically, and consistently seeks ways to improve the instructional system for each.

- Lesson plans show and observations indicate that students are regularly engaged in a mixture of large group, team, and individual approaches to learning. Team activities emphasize real-life application and problem solving. The Secretary's Commission on Necessary Skills (SCANS) skills and content skills are emphasized.

- Knowledge of the latest brain research and multiple intelligences are evident in lesson plans, assignments, and observations.

- What is taught is directly aligned with school, district, state, or federal expectations. Process measures are understood and used regularly to ensure learning has occurred. Assessment is aligned with what is taught. The teacher and class routinely analyze assessment results to form an action plan for improvement.

- Lesson plans show and observations indicate that quality tools are used as a means of encouraging critical thinking or to assess student learning.

- Communicates with parents frequently throughout the school year. There are several communication portals for parents such as websites, newsletters, and conferences. The teacher has established a partnership with them built on trust and mutual respect. This is demonstrated by parent involvement, support for the instructional program, and cooperation in returning surveys, communications, and so forth. Survey results also support this claim.

- This teacher "walks the talk" of appreciating diversity through materials, lessons, assignments, and relationships with staff, students, and parents. When others are observed or overheard expressing racial, ethnic, or other biases against any group, this teacher speaks out in support of the need to dispense with this type of comment.

- Student discipline expectations are addressed the first week of school as part of the collaborative development of a class vision, mission, and the definition of a quality student and continuous improvement of the classroom system. Students' safety is always the primary concern, and students, with the teacher address ways each can ensure the safety of their classmates. The teacher has assessed the safety issues in his/her classroom and eliminated all hazards or instructed the students in safe handling of all materials and equipment.

Overall Instructions

Function F is to be viewed independently from the other functions. Anything less than 100 percent of this function signifies the teacher will be in the Needs Improvement category regardless of how many other criteria from the other functions are met.

The number of criteria met for any function is considered minimal. The rubric provides specific guidance for the school leader as to specific criteria that must be met and the level of deployment of each. The rubric is the guide for the overall rankings. This speaks to the intent of the appraisal instrument. It is not enough for teachers to do it once; rather, your concern should be for the overall deployment and consistency with which each teacher meets each criteria. The table provides a bird's-eye view of the rubric.

Major function	Unsatisfactory	Needs improvement	Novice	Advancing	Master
A: 16 criteria	8 or fewer	9–10	11–12	13–14	14–16
B: 7 criteria	2 or fewer	3	4	5	7
C: 3 criteria	0–1	1	2	3	3
D: 5 criteria	1	2–3	3	4	5
E: 3 criteria	0–1	1	2	3	3
F: 6 criteria	Fewer than 6	Fewer than 6	All	All	All

Master teachers will all have increased or high student performance results, strong student and stakeholder satisfaction levels, will work together with others to improve the instructional process, and will continuously learn and improve. He or she will be a role model for peers throughout the school, district, and state.

Appendix C

Balanced Scorecard Example

In the middle of the 1990s we did quite a bit of work with a large southern school district. Several years into our journey together, the board president and superintendent indicated a strong desire to improve the way yearly student performance data was reported to parents and other stakeholders. The compelling reason was that data analysis revealed a stable system with no significant progress over a five-year period in meeting the board goals and the existing school report cards gave equal weight to attendance (student and staff) and learning results. Everyone agreed a change was needed. Throughout this process we worked collaboratively and in partnership with the district director of quality.

The proposed change was intended to push principals and teachers to focus on improvement in student learning results, to report to the public a balanced approach to accountability that would provide a clearer description of what was happening in each school, and to report on the condition of each facility. To reach the goals, we also knew that the central administration team would have to change the way they worked, and focus their efforts on schools with the most need. If this happened, it would signal a major shift in work responsibilities for the Division of Curriculum and Instruction, area superintendents, and the resource allocation process.

We also theorized that there were certain key predictors (leading indicators) of future student success that would provide additional information to parents and other families considering moving into the district.

The collaborative process shown below came out of meetings with the board, and central administration. Everyone was sensitive to the need to involve principals in the process. The entire process as it is laid out here took a period of about eight months. During the first part of the process, the board determined what would be reported to the public.

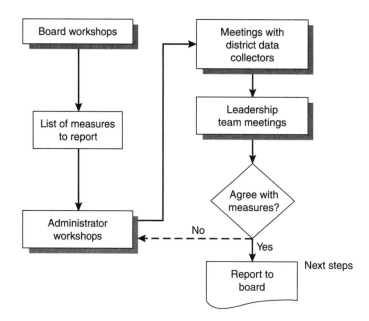

Once everyone agreed on what would be reported, and we received information about what data were available and/or feasible to collect, it became time to go to the principals about how they wanted to see the data reported. Fairness was the most frequently discussed issue. Principals were concerned about how the district would take into consideration their school's uniqueness, such as ethnicity, enrollment in special education, free/reduced lunch, and student mobility rates caused especially by the high number of military families in some school boundaries. This part of the process involved all the school principals.

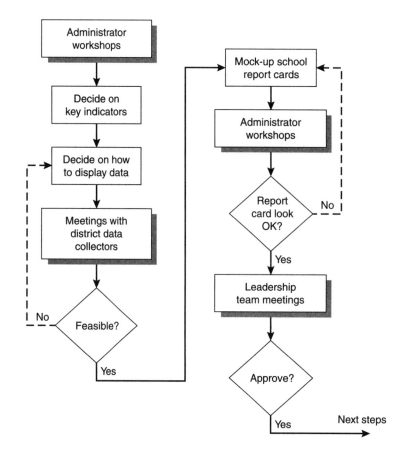

The last part of the process had to do with going back to the school board for final approval with a mock-up of the report cards. Once we got approval, the district shifted onto a different path.

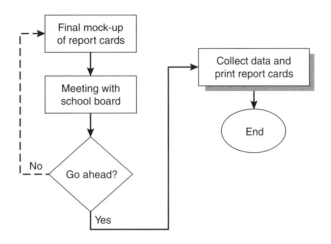

Each school report card provided information related to student learning results, which were used to yield a rating. The purpose of the rating was not to compare one school to another, but to indicate to the Division of Curriculum and Instruction and the area superintendents which schools needed immediate assistance. It also was used as a barometer of leadership effectiveness, and principals of schools ranked "needs improvement" were given two years to improve student learning results. Additional resources and technical assistance was provided to these schools, whereas in the past, there was no process for resource allocation tied to learning results. We worked hard to maintain a "no shame, no blame" attitude and approach, believing then as we do now, that the paradigm shift is huge and the focus needs to remain on continuous improvement and fact-based decision making. It certainly helped the principals address their teachers and meet them with renewed and higher expectations. This approach works only as long as resources and assistance are provided to get the job done. It helps align and integrate the whole system.

The high schools were expected to show the data on graduates attending postsecondary institutions without having to enroll in remedial courses, and the number of students jointly enrolled in a local postsecondary institution. Any data you see on these sample report cards without trends indicate that it was the first year of reporting that particular information. The expectation was that each year, the school would begin to report trended data, up to five years' worth.

The key indicators were not viewed in the same manner as student learning results, but schools did receive commendations for all they met. The key indicators agreed upon by the principals were: student and staff attendance; safe, orderly schools; facility audit; partnership activity (volunteer hours); extracurricular involvement; and satisfaction results. At the high schools, additional commendations were given for scholarships received and high school completion rates.

All data shared on the sample reports cards is fictitious and presented solely for the purpose of example.

Example: High School

Student enrollment: Grades 9-12 = 2007
Teachers: 106
Teachers with advanced degrees: 85

Enrolled 100+ days: 1878
Student/Classroom Teacher Ratio = 27:1

Academic Rank
Holding the gains
Commendations 5 of 6

Partnerships
Parent/community volunteers
347
Total volunteer hours
3,000
Students with parents who
attended at least one
teacher conference
85%

Scholarships
Offered $300,000
Accepted $221,000
Number of students
accepting scholarships
100

Drop-outs 257
GED/OPT program
50 enrolled
Eligible for exam 45/75%
Passed GED 37/82%

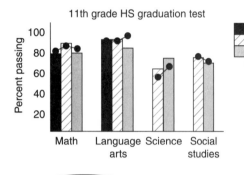
11th grade HS graduation test

Legend:
- 1996
- 1997
- 1998
- ● State average

Safe, orderly school
Students never referred to the
administration for any disciplinary action
95%
Students expelled
5
Incidents resulting in expulsion
2

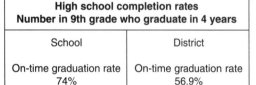

Staff attendance 93%   Student attendance 89%   Facility audit good

| High school completion rates
Number in 9th grade who graduate in 4 years	
School	District
On-time graduation rate
74%	On-time graduation rate
56.9%

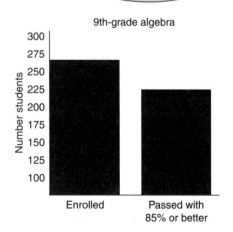
9th-grade algebra

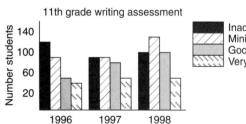
11th grade writing assessment

Legend:
- Inadequate
- Minimal
- Good
- Very good

Extracurricular activities
857 or 78% students participate

Preparation for state post-secondary institutions

Graduates attending technical schools or community college not enrolled in remedial courses
75%

Graduates attending a 4 year college or university not enrolled in remedial courses
70%

SAT scores

V = Verbal
M = Math

National average

V M   V M   V M   V M
1995   1996   1997   1998
n = 43 n = 62 n = 161 n = 168

(n = number who took the test)

10th-grade PSAT

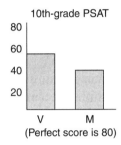

V   M
(Perfect score is 80)

AP classes

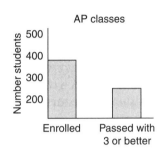

Number students

Enrolled   Passed with 3 or better

Joint enrollment with post-secondary institutions

Students jointly enrolled in technical schools
28

In 4-year college or university
19

Parent satisfaction

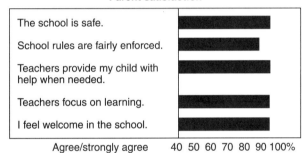

The school is safe.

School rules are fairly enforced.

Teachers provide my child with help when needed.

Teachers focus on learning.

I feel welcome in the school.

Agree/strongly agree   40 50 60 70 80 90 100%

Student satisfaction

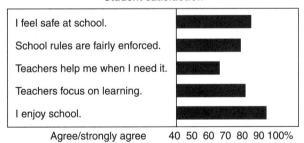

I feel safe at school.

School rules are fairly enforced.

Teachers help me when I need it.

Teachers focus on learning.

I enjoy school.

Agree/strongly agree   40 50 60 70 80 90 100%

Graduate satisfaction

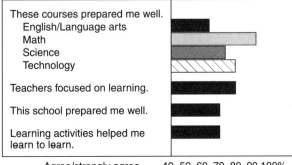

These courses prepared me well.
   English/Language arts
   Math
   Science
   Technology

Teachers focused on learning.

This school prepared me well.

Learning activities helped me learn to learn.

Agree/strongly agree   40 50 60 70 80 90 100%

The format for all levels of schools was essentially the same. Middle school measures included the following:

- ITBS—sixth and seventh grades (reading, math, and problem solving)

- ITBS—eighth grade (reading, math, language arts, science, social studies, and problem solving)

- Sixth grade—Pre-algebra (enrollment/pass with 85 percent or better)

- Seventh and eighth grades—Algebra (enrollment/pass with 85 percent or better)

- Eighth grade—state writing assessment

- ITBS cohort data for reading and math

Note that this work predates the No Child Left Behind (NCLB) Act, and the state writing assessment was the only statewide assessment available. Now, of course if you lead a public school, state standards tests would probably make up the bulk of reported student learning results. If you give achievement tests at the beginning of the school year and again at the end, you would certainly want to include the pre/post learning gains. This gives parents and other stakeholders the value-added for their tax dollars and also lets parents know that their children are making gains even if the school doesn't make its annual yearly progress (AYP) required by the NCLB.

Key indicators for the middle school were the same as those for all the other schools.

The elementary school example is shown on the next page. You can see that this district was on the leading edge with accountability and standards as the board approved a reading guarantee at the third grade, and also the central administration instituted kindergarten standards the first year to be followed by first and second grade reading standards (required to report) in the succeeding years.

This district agreed on a set of ratings for their schools based on a formula taking into consideration the student learning results. The categories were Advancing, Holding the Gains, and Needs Improvement. For schools that fell into the Needs Improvement category, which essentially meant they were significantly below expectations, the district established three subsets. These were Progressing (showing improvement, but still not meeting expectations), Maintaining (making neither significant progress nor declines), and Regressing (significant drops in learning results from the previous year and/or three or more years of negative trend data). Resource allocation followed all the schools in Needs Improvement Category, with those in the regressing subset receiving the most help. The area superintendents led teams from the Division of Curriculum and Instruction to work with principals to identify staff development needs and other technical assistance.

Example: Elementary School

Student enrollment: Grades pre-K–5th grade = 800
Teachers: 56
Teachers with advanced degrees: 37

Enrolled 100+ days: 690
Student/Classroom Teacher Ratio = 21:1

Academic Rank
Needs improvment
(Maintaining)
Commendations 6 of 6

Partnerships
Parent/community volunteers 250
Total volunteer hours 10,500
Students with parents who attended at least one teacher conference 95%

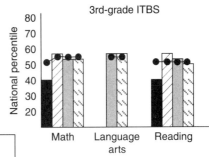
3rd-grade ITBS

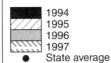
ITBS key
1994
1995
1996
1997
● State average

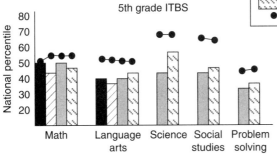
5th grade ITBS

Safe, orderly school
Students never referred to the administration for any disciplinary action 93%
Students expelled 0 Incidents resulting in expulsion 0

Kindergarteners
Number meeting district language arts/reading standards 90%
Number entering school prescreened "ready to learn" 85%
Number completing a federal or state funded pre-K program 57%

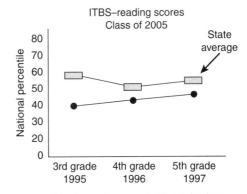
ITBS–reading scores
Class of 2005

This shows the current 5th-grade class results in 3rd, 4th, and 5th grades.

Continued

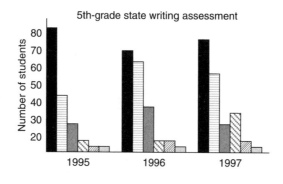

5th-grade state writing assessment

Staff attendance 95%

Student attendance 94%

Facility audit good

Parent satisfaction

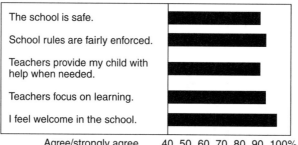

The school is safe.

School rules are fairly enforced.

Teachers provide my child with help when needed.

Teachers focus on learning.

I feel welcome in the school.

Agree/strongly agree   40 50 60 70 80 90 100%

Student satisfaction

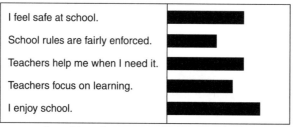

I feel safe at school.

School rules are fairly enforced.

Teachers help me when I need it.

Teachers focus on learning.

I enjoy school.

Agree/strongly agree   40 50 60 70 80 90 100%

Appendix D
Survey Writing

Survey writing requires some thought. Here are some tips to consider before writing a survey.

- Decide on the goal of the survey. What do you hope to learn?

- Make certain each item is concise and without ambiguity. Keep educational jargon out of survey items. Test the survey items out with a few people (not those you will survey) to make certain the intent of each item is clear and easy to understand.

- *Do not bias the survey* by wording items in a way that will give you *what you want to hear.* The purpose of surveys is to give you information *you need to hear.*

- Construct the survey to be able to quantify the results. Use a Likert scale (that is, rank items 1–5; 1 = strongly agree, 2 = agree, 3 = not sure, 4 = disagree and 5 = strongly disagree *or* 1 = poor, 2 = okay, 3 = pretty good, 4 = good, 5 = excellent) to force a choice.

- Make certain all items are worded positively *or* all are worded negatively. Be careful not to interchange the wording as it confuses people about how to respond and will impact the validity of the data.

- Keep survey items to a minimum—probably no more than 10, and keep the items focused on the goal.

Survey Process Suggestions

- Administer the survey in as anonymous a fashion as possible by putting the survey on a computer in the media center.

- Give employees 2–3 days to complete the survey. Too much time means they will forget about it. Too little time may be difficult for very busy people. Set the expectation in the fall that you will be periodically surveying all employees and that their cooperation is vital to achieving the action plans and getting improved results.

- Assign the task of collecting the surveys and charting the data to someone else outside of your office. This helps employees maintain confidence in the validity of results.

- After the results are charted, call a meeting to share the results with those surveyed. Anything that can be done quickly should be, and it should be reported to everyone. Those things that are not within the purview of the principal (that is, district, federal, state, or board policy) must be explained to everyone.

- Ask for volunteers (an expectation in a Baldrige-based school is to participate in improvement projects) and charter an improvement team to work on issues that are more complex and require resources.

  —Use the PDSA process and openly share the data and each step with everyone.

  —Report pre/post improvement findings to all employees.

Evaluate the survey process annually. While it is important to evaluate the process used to survey faculty and staff, parents, students, or other stakeholders remember that trend data are important too. If you continue to change the items surveyed, be very careful about how you report the results.

Sample Surveys

This survey was designed by a principal to assess faculty satisfaction with the leadership and the leadership system.

As part of our school's continuous improvement efforts I am asking for your input regarding my leadership and the school leadership system. Please put a check in the box that best represents your feelings for each item on this survey. Use the following scale: 5 = Always; 4 = Mostly; 3 = Sometimes; 2 = Seldom; 1 = Never.
Please return the survey in the sealed envelope and place it in the box in the media center before the end of the school day, next Friday, January 27.
Your responses are highly appreciated and valued. Look for the results by February 8. Thank you!

1. There are clear expectations of me at this school.	1	2	3	4	5
2. The school leader and leadership team members help with data analysis.	1	2	3	4	5
3. I know our school improvement goals and my role in the action plans.	1	2	3	4	5
4. The school has an atmosphere of optimism and leadership encourages and supports me.	1	2	3	4	5
5. I respect the principal as the instructional leader at this school.	1	2	3	4	5
6. The principal is open to suggestions for how to resolve problems.	1	2	3	4	5
7. There is a feeling of collaboration among faculty, staff, and administration at this school.	1	2	3	4	5

Continued

Continued

8. I believe that whenever I have a serious issue with instructional approaches, students, parents, or peers I can go to the principal or the leadership team and we will work together to achieve a win-win resolution.	1	2	3	4	5
9. Faculty meetings are well organized and effective with a focus on important matters.	1	2	3	4	5
10. I believe that I have the tools necessary to do the job I'm being asked to do.	1	2	3	4	5

This survey was designed by a principal to assess community perception about the school.

As part of our school's continuous improvement efforts I am asking for your feedback regarding our school. Please put a check in the box that best represents your feelings for each item on this survey. Use the following scale: 5 = Always; 4 = Mostly; 3 = Sometimes; 2 = Seldom; 1 = Never.
Please return the survey in the self-addressed, stamped envelope on or before April 15. Your responses are highly appreciated and valued. We will share the results on our school website and in the May newsletter. If you have any other comments, please feel free to include them on the back of this form.
Thank you!

1. There are clear expectations of me at this school.	1	2	3	4	5	N/A
2. My interactions with students from this school have been respectful.	1	2	3	4	5	N/A
3. When I contact the school, those answering the phones are friendly and helpful.	1	2	3	4	5	N/A
4. School grounds are clean.	1	2	3	4	5	N/A
5. The school building appears clean and well cared for.	1	2	3	4	5	N/A
6. The principal is available to discuss issues with me	1	2	3	4	5	N/A
7. I feel the school is a safe place.	1	2	3	4	5	N/A

Glossary

action plans—refer to specific actions that respond to short- and longer-term strategic objectives. Action plans include details of resource commitments and time horizons for accomplishment; they are a critical stage in planning after strategic objectives and goals are made specific. Classroom action plans are initially determined by teachers to align activities with the class strategic goals. They are set at the same time as targets are determined.

alignment—consistency of focus of every aspect of the system (school or classroom) beginning with purpose, vision, mission, and goals. Work systems, key processes, and a measurement system must be in alignment (not conflicting or deviating from the purpose) with the (school and classroom) culture. This is important for ensuring that everyone and everything is aimed toward achieving the (school and class) goals. For the leader, the term *alignment* refers to consistency of plans, processes, information, resource decisions, actions, results, and analysis to support key organizationwide goals. Effective alignment requires a common understanding of purposes and goals. It also requires the use of complementary measures and information for planning, analysis, and improvement at three levels: the organizational level, the key process level, and the program (school, class, or individual) level.

active learning—a way in which students work. Active learning engages students in higher-order thinking tasks such as analysis, synthesis, and evaluation and includes the multiple intelligences. It promotes interdependence and individual accountability to accomplish a common goal. Students involved in active learning often organize their work, research information, discuss and explain ideas, observe demonstrations or phenomena, solve problems, and formulate questions of their own. This term can also relate to leadership, faculty, and staff learning through the use of PDSA cycles.

anecdotal versus systematic—anecdotal evidence to support one's point of view relies on one or two observations, or gaining feedback from one or two sources. The danger is that you cannot generalize about success or failure of any process or program based on anecdotal information. Systematic, however, refers to periodic (regular) collection of data from a random sample or the whole group to understand the effectiveness of a process or approach.

approach—methods used address the requirements of each of the first six categories of the Baldrige criteria. The approach answers the "what" question—what do you do about this or that. (The self-assessments at the end of most chapters provide clues about the criteria requirements.) For details about the exact criteria requirements, refer to the Baldrige National Quality Program: Education Criteria for Performance Excellence. Check the Baldrige website for how to order a free copy.

Baldrige Criteria for Performance Excellence—program signed into U.S. law in 1987 by President Ronald Reagan and named after deceased Secretary of Commerce Malcolm Baldrige for his managerial excellence. A framework for excellence includes seven interdependent categories of criteria that when aligned and integrated yield excellent results. The framework and criteria are now recognized as the best approach to system improvement in the world. The Baldrige award is given to role model organizations with proven effective and efficient processes and excellent results in all aspects important to the organization. Awards can be given for large or small business, manufacturing, healthcare, and education. In 2001, the first education winners were announced. They were: Chugach School District in Alaska, Pearl River School District in New York, and the University of Wisconsin-Stout. In 2003, Community Consolidated School District 15 in Palatine, Illinois, a K–8 district of more than 13,000 students won. In 2005, Jenks Public Schools in Jenks, Oklahoma won this prestigious award. Jenks, a K–12 district of nearly 9,300 students, is located near Tulsa. For more information see the website information provided.

bandwidth of variation—every process has variation. The bandwidth is understood as the top and bottom score—or range of data points for any series of data. For example: In any class, five students score 100 percent, and three students score 5 percent, while all others are in between. We would say the bandwidth of variation on that test was 95 percent. In a Baldrige-based quality organization (school or classroom), the goal is to continuously work to reduce the bandwidth of variation for every process—pushing the mean higher for instruction and other things you wish to improve and pushing the mean lower to extinguish negative behaviors. For more information, see *variation*.

bell curve—a normal distribution of data points more or less evenly split on each side of the average (mean). Generally, we speak about data falling about plus or minus three standard deviations from the mean. A bell curve represents a traditional model of "winners and losers." Many educators and policy makers, who embrace traditional school models, consider the bell curve to be about how the data will be distributed from any group of students.

benchmark process—processes and results that represent "best practices and performance" for similar activities, inside or outside the education community. Organizations engage in benchmarking as an approach to understand the current dimensions of world-class performance and to achieve breakthrough improvement. Benchmarking is always a good approach to use if it becomes evident that current processes are not capable of yielding the desired results, and/or the process has not been changed for a period of seven or more years.

brainstorm—an active process for gaining many ideas around a topic from a group of people. Formal brainstorming requires systematically asking team members for ideas. Brainstorming rules include (1) all ideas are included, (2) no discussion until all ideas are on the table, (3) everyone is given equal opportunity to provide suggestions, and (4) no "yeah-buts" are allowed. (A yeah-but is a naysaying comment referring to a perception that a particular idea had been tried and failed in the past.)

cohort group—a single group of students who started in the same grade, and who are still together; used to compare how well a particular group of students performs over the course of time. For example, you want to compare the performance of a specific group of students in third grade in 2000 through fourth, fifth, or sixth grades on a normed test, to measure value added each year of enrollment. This constitutes a cohort group from 2000–2003. True cohort groups identify students by name and follow only those students over the years.

constancy of purpose—focus on the aim of the organization. What is it designed to do?

continuous process improvement—the quality improvement process is known as PDSA or Plan-Do-Study-Act. It is a systematic approach to problem solving and design of new processes.

customer—the primary customers of a school are students; parents; next-school-in-line; districts; for high schools, postsecondary institutions; the world of work; and the community. The primary customers of a classroom system are the students and the next-teacher-in-line. Other customers of a classroom system are the school, district, postsecondary institutions, and world of work for those leaving high school.

cycle time—the amount of time required to complete a task. For newly designed programs it is the amount of time from the planning phase until the roll-out of any new program or process. Examples include time required to repair computers and time to align curriculum with standards. The ideal is to reduce cycle time without a loss of effectiveness.

data—hard data are things that can be counted or measured; factual data. Soft data are satisfaction and perceptual data. Both types are important to collect and chart. Data are the basis for decision-making in a Baldrige-based quality school and classroom.

data-driven decision making—decisions about what to change in any process are based on data collection and a root-cause analysis.

data collection plan—a systematic approach to the collection of data to inform the organization. The decision about what data to collect is important and must be aligned with all schoolwide and districtwide strategic goals. The data collection plan addresses questions of what, how, where, when, and an explanation of how the data are to be used to improve.

deployment—answers the "how and when" question. It refers to how often, how many, where, and when something is done, for example, how widely applied the approach is. Full deployment means that an approach is used widely throughout the school with no groups, or grade levels not participating. For example, a fully deployed antibullying program would mean that all students in all grades receive the instruction and activities. A fully deployed process for sharing the vision and values may mean that the information is affixed to all communication sent to faculty, staff, parents, and other stakeholders, and that the leader and leadership team refer to it at all faculty and staff meetings, PTA meetings, and when addressing outside groups.

differentiated instruction—an approach that requires teachers to use different modalities and resources to meet the needs of a diverse student body within any class.

Dr. W. Edwards Deming—the father of modern quality. A statistician (1900–1993) who taught the Japanese his quality management theory that focused on involving the workers to improve processes and systems. Born in Iowa, he lived most of his adult life in Washington, DC. He received an MS degree from the University of Colorado and a Ph.D. from Yale University. Deming believed that 95 percent of all problems within organizations were caused by faulty systems and not people. His teachings and theory kept many U.S. businesses profitable and are the basis for the Malcolm Baldrige National Quality Criteria for Performance Excellence.

effectiveness measures—measures such as learning gains, improved attendance, student joy of learning, and graduation rates are measures of an educational system's effectiveness. It answers the question of whether a process yields the desired results. (Quality by fact.)

efficiency measures—refers to the resources required for a process to achieve its goal. The fewer resources (time, materials, personnel) required, the more efficient the process. Examples of efficiency measures of an educational system include reteaching, time away from learning, dropout rates, timeliness of data made available to teachers for making midcourse corrections, and time to make repairs.

feedback—information about the system or any process provided by faculty and staff, customers, stakeholders, and partners. Systematic feedback implies collecting data on a regular basis either using a random sample or by surveying the whole group. Informal feedback is usually anecdotal and consequently one should not have a lot of confidence in its reliability, therefore making changes based on anecdotal feedback carries some risks to avoid.

feedback instruments— tools such as satisfaction surveys, needs assessments, focus groups, affinity process, plus/delta charts, fast feedback, how helpful were these resources, enthusiasm for learning chart, stacked cups, and many others.

feedback plan—a feedback plan is a well thought-out approach that uses a variety of feedback tools and approaches on a regular and systematic basis so that the information can be analyzed and midcourse improvements made to improve the chances for achieving the goals and ultimately to delight the customer.

focus on innovation—innovation refers to making meaningful change to improve instruction, services, and create new value for customers, students, and all stakeholders. Innovation is a multistep process that involves development and knowledge sharing, a decision to implement, implementation, evaluation, and learning. Leaders of Baldrige-based quality schools seek knowledge from a variety of sources and encourage teachers to use innovative approaches that result in greater student learning and performance excellence throughout the school.

formative assessment—frequent or ongoing evaluation in-process that informs the teacher of what students are learning, and their strengths and weaknesses. Formative assessment is used to help teachers make in-process improvements in instructional methods, activities, or approaches.

goals—address a future performance level. The term *goals* refers to a future condition or performance level that one intends to attain. Goals can be both short term (marking period, semester, or year) and longer term (2–4 years); they are the ends that guide the actions. Targets (a numerical point) make the goals quantitative goals. Targets might be projections based on comparative and/or competitive data. The term *stretch goals,* refers to desired major or breakthrough improvements. Longer-term goals for the classroom would be year-end or semester-end if you teach a semester-long course. Short-term goals would be marking periods.

governance—the organizational reporting structure. Schools that are part of a larger district are governed by a superintendent and board of education. Independent, private, parochial, and charter schools often report to a board. Governance also refers to outside organizations with laws, policies that the school must adhere to, such as the health, fire, and other state or federal requirements.

hard data—factual data that can be counted or measured. Examples for leaders might include student achievement results, student or staff accidents, number of grievances, absences, tardies, discipline referrals, or books taken out of the library.

high-performance work—expectations of excellence; forever-increasing levels of individual performance as well as overall organizational performance. For example, instituting a new work system for faculty, designed to improve work performance would show up in the student learning results and also in the organizational effectiveness results. You expect greater results from individuals and groups engaged in high-performance work and the processes associated with improving those areas.

hold the gains—each process demonstrates normal variation and over time, unless specific process checks are made, will deteriorate. To hold the gains means a decision has been made to periodically and systematically gather data and analyze it at specific key process points after an improvement project has been completed. In this way, if the data start to exhibit a downward trend, targeted interventions can be implemented.

if/then improvement theory—a theory the team comes up with after identifying the root cause of any problem. The theory is written after a brainstorm session to determine actions to eliminate the root cause of a problem. It is the last step in the Plan phase of PDSA.

inputs—people, policies, and resources that flow into the system and influence it in some way.

innovation—taking an "out of the box" approach to solve a persistent system problem, sometimes this involves benchmarking an organization in or outside of education. Other times an innovation can be suggested as a result of a brainstorming process by faculty, staff, students, or other stakeholders. Innovation leads to breakthrough performance results.

integration—how all aspects of the organization work in concert with each other to support the aim of the organization and the strategic objectives. Throughout this book, you see "bubbles" attached to parts of flow charts that demonstrate how different aspects of the organization must work together to achieve the goals.

key value-creation processes—processes that produce benefit for students and for the organization (school or classroom). These are the processes most important to running the school or classroom and those that produce positive organizational results for students and next-teacher-in-line. School examples include (1) curriculum, (2) assessment, and (3) counseling.

knowledge assets—current knowledge and skills, as well as new learning that individuals within the organization possess. To optimize the capability of the school, leaders who provide an avenue for capturing the knowledge assets and ongoing learning to share skills and knowledge, and historical information about PDSAs, will increase the overall effectiveness and efficiency of the entire school. This is a key part of the Baldrige approach.

learning-centered education—one of the Baldrige core values that demands constant sensitivity to changing and emerging student, stakeholder, and market needs and expectations and to the factors that drive student learning, satisfaction, and persistence.

measures and indicators—numerical information that quantifies input, output, and performance dimensions of programs and processes; they might be simple (derived from one measurement) or composite. A measure is the direct result of the performance of any process. The term indicator is used when (1) the measurement relates to performance, but is not a direct measure of such performance, and (2) when the measurement is a predictor or leading indicator of some more significant performance. For example, a gain in student performance or satisfaction might be a leading indicator of student persistence, while student performance results are measures of the success of the instructed process.

measurement system—a systematic approach to collecting data with vision, mission, and strategic objective specificity. The system includes measures for mission and school goals and is used to inform the leadership, teachers, students, and stakeholders about progress.

multiple intelligences—Howard Gardner has identified eight ways people learn. They are logical/mathematical, verbal/linguistic, visual/spatial, body/kinesthetic, musical/rhythmic, interpersonal, intrapersonal, and naturalistic. Too often, educators rely heavily on verbal/linguistic and logical/mathematical and do not provide enough opportunities for students to learn through the other intelligences. It is the responsibility of the teacher to discover how students learn (by asking and observing) and then provide learning activities that utilize more of the intelligences. It is the combination of verbal/linguistic, body/kinesthetic, and musical/rhythmic that advances literacy skills rapidly.

operational definitions—short, precise, detailed definition of a specification. A good operational definition yields either a "yes" or "no" response. Operational definitions provide clear communication to everyone about how something is to be measured. Operational definitions allow people to understand their jobs with less confusion.

outputs—the results of value-added and non-value-added processes. In education, the outputs include student learning results, student, stakeholder, and partner satisfaction and dissatisfaction results, student enthusiasm for learning results, and results of fiscal and regulatory requirements.

output measures—measures of results. They inform policy makers and administrators about how well students achieve and measure satisfaction at the end of the year. Results measures must be considered by the leadership team during strategic planning in terms of making system improvements for the following year.

performance excellence—an integrated approach to organizational performance management that results in (1) delivery of ever-improving value to students and stakeholders, contributing to improved education quality; (2) improvement of overall organizational effectiveness and capabilities; and (3) organizational and personal learning. The Baldrige Education Criteria for Peformance Excellence provide a framework and an assessment tool for understanding organizational strengths and opportunities for improvement and thus for guiding planning efforts.

PDSA cycle—the seven-step quality improvement process that eliminates problems provided the true root cause is understood. P = Plan (four steps—identify the opportunity for improvement, assess the current situation, analyze root cause, write an improvement theiory), D = Do (put the improvement theory into practice), S = Study (analyze the results from the improvement theory), A = Act (make decisions about expanding the improvement to the whole system; go back and understand the root cause, or move to a new improvement opportunity).

process—a series of steps taken to achieve a task.

process measures—predictors of future success and allow the educator to make midcourse corrections leading to improved success at the end of the year. Data collected in-process ought to be the most critical predictors. These data, collected and analyzed regularly throughout the year, provide insight for leaders, teachers, and staff to make adjustments in all key processes to improve the chances of achieving the strategic objectives. For example, at the classroom level, collecting data in-process allows a teacher to make midcourse corrections to instruction and/or classroom management.

process measures for literacy—the five in-process measures and best predictors of future success in reading, writing, and speaking are phonemic awareness, phonics, vocabulary, fluency, and comprehension. These are the important things on which teachers ought to regularly and systematically collect data.

quality by fact—the product of the system actually functions as promised. An example in education is that students leave the grade or school with the required skills and have the ability to apply them to other situations.

quality by process—this measures effectiveness and efficiency of the processes making up the system. On-time graduation rates would be an example of the effectiveness and efficiency of the instructional process.

quality by perception—perception is reality in the eyes of the customer and stakeholders. This measures whether or not customers believe the product is of high quality. When newspapers report the results of state standards tests, perception about the quality of instruction and education at each school is formed.

quality factors—the absolute essential characteristics or elements that must be present to meet any standard and for someone to say "Wow. That was excellent." Quality factors set expectations. The customer determines quality factors and constantly raises the bar on expectations.

quality features—quality features are additional elements that delight the customer. These are not essential to the overall working of any product, but make it nicer, brighter, more alive, and so forth. Quality features often become quality factors over time. An example may be the expectation that students are required to use word processors to write essays.

segment—segmentation of data refers to disaggregating by subgroup. In education, for example, there are numerous ways to segment the data on faculty and staff. You might look at the groups by education levels attained, years of service, grade level, or courses taught. Segmenting data generally provides the leaders with a better perspective of the situation. Another example is parent satisfaction, which can be segmented by their child's grade level, special education, English for speakers of other languages, gifted, free/reduced lunch, or by those who volunteer, are active in PTA, and so on.

soft data—perceptual data that reflect a person's feelings about something. Examples include satisfaction and enthusiasm.

strategic goals and/or strategic objectives—these address the most important challenges to success that the organization faces. During the strategic planning process, after the environmental scan is conducted, strategic challenges are identified. For each one of these, one or more corresponding strategic goals or objectives is identified. Action plans are developed and resource allocation follows according to the priority of each.

student as customer—students are the direct customer of teachers. They receive instruction, instructional support, and climate for learning from teachers.

student as worker—students are workers in a system traditionally created by the teacher. Students are expected to fit into the system and if they won't or can't, they are viewed as difficult students and often cause disruptions to the instructional process. Students are frequently in the best position to identify the barriers to their success, and it is up to the teacher to change the system. Unless teachers empower students to provide feedback and make suggestions for improvement, the barriers will remain and the results will be the same.

summative assessment—the term refers to longitudinal analysis of the learning and performance of students. Summative assessments are formal and comprehensive, and they often cover global subject matter. These assessments are conducted at the conclusion of a course or program and when a pretest has been administered, can demonstrate value added of the instructional process.

system—a series of processes linked together to achieve the aim, vision, and mission of an organization.

system alignment—consistency of action plans, processes, information, resource decisions, measurement plans, results, analysis, and learning to support the organization's key goals. For example, the classroom is a subsystem of the school; therefore, its mission must align with the school and district vision and mission. Class goals will be aligned with the school and district goals and expectations.

system integration—effective integration is achieved when the individual components of a system operate as a fully interconnected unit. That is, all departments support the key organizationwide goals.

teacher as leader—teachers are leaders in the classroom, and as such they are responsible for removing barriers to student success. Most barriers are caused by faulty systems and ineffective or inefficient processes. A teacher-leader empowers students to help identify system and process barriers and participate in finding solutions. Teacher-leaders are competent, of high character, value all students, seek and engage in partnerships with students and parents, and view data as a friend that allows them to learn and to engage in continuous improvement of self and the system.

teacher as service provider—teachers provide instruction, support, and create the learning climate. These are all services. Students provide feedback in terms of achievement, satisfaction and dissatisfaction manifest by behaviors, attendance, and attitudes. Teachers need to be customer-focused to make changes based on student and stakeholder needs and expectations.

team projects—total quality education-based team projects use all the SCANS skills and engage students in problem-solving and self-directed teams. The systematic approach to organizing students in teams, and the responsibilities they each assume, allows everyone to gain important social, academic, and workforce skills. Effective teams are the result of stage 4 in team development and also demonstrate interdependence illustrated by Covey's Maturity Continuum.

trends—a minimum of three cycles of data points comprise the beginnings a trend. The number of data points is dependent on the length of the cycle to accomplish any task. For example, the results of any normed test happen annually. Therefore, a beginning trend would cover at least three years. Absenteeism might be trended by month, yielding 9–12 data points for the school year, depending on the length of the school year.

work system—how teachers and staff are organized to achieve high-performance work. In the classroom, this refers to how students are organized to get work done and to accomplish the vision, mission, and goals. An effective work system aligns the components with the vision, mission, and strategic goals and enables and encourages all employees and students to contribute effectively and to the best of their ability.

value—a perception of what anything is worth. For example, in each year a student is enrolled he or she will learn more as measured by some instrument (preferably a normed one). If this happens, we can say that each class or grade was value-added to the education of that child. Another example might be about a particular professional development program. In this case, pre/post learning results would indicate the value added by the program. If students in classrooms where the approach was fully deployed did better than previously, we could say the professional development program was value added.

variation—every process exhibits some variation whether in manufacturing or education. The idea of a quality organization is to narrow the bandwidth of variation and move the average higher for things such as learning, attendance, and enthusiasm and lower for things such as tardy, absenteeism, failure, and acting-out behavior. The way to reduce variation is to provide precise operational definitions and expectations, then measure effectiveness and follow the PDSA cycle for improvement.

Recommended Reading and Websites

Armstrong, Thomas. *The Multiple Intelligences of Reading and Writing: Making the Words Come Alive.* Alexandria, VA: ASCD, 2003.

Blazey, Mark, et al. *Insights to Performance Excellence in Education 2003: An Inside Look at the 2003 Baldrige Award Criteria for Education,* Milwaukee, WI: ASQ Quality Press, 2004.

Bolman, Lee G., and Terrence E. Deal. *Reframing Organizations: Artistry, Choice and Leadership.* San Francisco: Jossey-Bass, 1997.

Burgard, Jeffrey J. *Continuous Improvement in the Science Classroom (Grades 6–8).* Milwaukee, WI: ASQ Quality Press, 2000.

Byrnes, Margaret A., with Jeanne C. Baxter. *There Is Another Way! Launch a Baldrige-Based Quality Classroom.* Milwaukee, WI: ASQ Quality Press, 2005.

Campbell, Linda, Bruce Campbell, and Dee Dickinson. *Teaching and Learning through Multiple Intelligences,* 2nd edition. Boston: Allyn and Bacon, 1999.

Carr, Judy F., and Douglas E. Harris. *Succeeding with Standards: Linking Curriculum, Assessment, and Action Planning.* Alexandria, VA: ASCD, 2001.

Collins, Jim. *Good to Great.* New York: HarperCollins, 2001.

Conyers, John G., and Robert Ewy. *Charting Your Course: Lessons Learned during the Journey toward Performance Excellence.* Milwaukee, WI: ASQ Quality Press, 2004.

Covey, Stephen R. *The Seven Habits of Highly Effective People.* New York: Simon & Schuster, 1989.

Davenport, Patricia, and Gerald Anderson. *Closing the Achievement Gap: No Excuses.* Houston, TX: American Productivity and Quality Center, 2002.

Deal, Terrence E., and Kent D. Peterson. *Shaping School Culture: The Heart of Leadership.* San Francisco: Jossey-Bass, 1999.

Deming, W. Edwards. *The New Economics: For Industry, Government, Education,* 2nd edition. Cambridge: Massachusetts Institute of Technology Center for Advanced Engineering Study, 1994.

Fauss, Karen R. *Continuous Improvement in the Primary Classroom: Language Arts (Grades K–3).* Milwaukee, WI: ASQ Quality Press, 2000.

Gardner, Howard. *Multiple Intelligences: The Theory in Practice.* New York: Basic Books, 1993.

Glasser, Dr. William. *The Quality School Teacher.* Revised edition. New York: HarperCollins, 1998.

Jenkins, Lee. *Improving Student Learning: Applying Deming's Quality Principles in Classrooms,* 2nd edition. Milwaukee, WI: ASQ Quality Press, 2003.

———. *Permission to Forget.* Milwaukee, WI: ASQ Quality Press, 2004.

Marzano, Robert J. *What Works in Schools: Translating Research into Action.* Alexandria, VA: ASCD, 2003.

Mauer, Rickard E., and Sandra Cokeley Pederson. *Malcolm and Me: How to Use the Baldrige Process to Improve Your School.* Lanham, MD: Scarecrow Education, 2004.

Senge, Peter. *The Fifth Discipline: The Art and Practice of the Learning Organization Field Book.* New York: Doubleday Dell, 1994.

Senge, Peter, et al. *Schools That Learn: A Fifth Discipline Fieldbook for Educators, Parents, and Everyone Who Cares about Education.* New York: Doubleday Dell, 2000.

Schargel, Franklin P., and Jay Smink. *Strategies to Help Solve Our School Dropout Problem.* Larchmont, NY: Eye on Education, 2001.

Schmoker, Mike. *The Results Fieldbook: Practical Strategies from Dramatically Improved Schools.* Alexandria, VA: ASCD, 2001.

Takaki, Ronald. *A Different Mirror: A History of Multicultural America.* Boston: Little, Brown, 1993.

Tomlinson, Carol Ann. *How to Differentiate Instruction in Mixed Ability Classrooms,* 2nd edition. Alexandria, VA: ASCD, 2001.

Quality Tools Books

Arthur, Jay. *Six Sigma Simplified: Quantum Improvement Made Easy.* Denver: LifeStar, 2000.

GOAL/QPC and Joiner Associates. *The Team Memory Jogger: A Pocket Guide for Team Members.* Salem, NH: GOAL/QPC, 1995.

Kingery, Cathy. Editor. *The Six Sigma Memory Jogger II.* Salem, NH: GOAL/QPC, 2002.

McManus, Ann (adapted by). *The Memory Jogger for Education: A Pocket Guide of Tools for Continuous Improvement in Schools.* Salem, NH: GOAL/QPC, 1992.

Oddo, Francine. Editor. *The Memory Jogger II.* Salem, NH: GOAL/QPC, 1994.

Ritter, Diane, and Michael Brassard. *The Creativity Tools Memory Jogger.* Salem, NH: GOAL/QPC, 1998.

Tague, Nancy. *The Quality Toolbox,* 2nd Edition. Milwaukee: ASQ Quality Press, 2005.

Helpful Websites for More Information

American Civil Liberties Union (ACLU)   Information about the cost of incarcerating youth   *www.aclu.org*

Aldine ISD, Texas   Benchmark the support services in an independent school district of more than 54,000 students: 56.5% Hispanic, 33.4% African American, and 7.3% Anglo.

This district was one of five finalists in 2004 and 2005 for the Broad Prize for Urban Education. The award honors urban school districts making the greatest improvements in student achievement and narrowing the gaps between subgroups. *www.aldine.k12.tx.us*

Baldrige Award-Winning K–12 School Districts

Chugach School District, Anchorage, Alaska   *www.chugachschools.com*

Community Consolidated School District 15, Palatine, Illinois   *www.ccsd15.k12.il.us*

Jenks Public Schools, Jenks, Oklahoma   *www.jenksps.org*

Pearl River School District, Pearl River, New York   *www.pearlriver.k12.ny.us*

Baldrige in Education collaboration project   *www.baldrigeineducation.org*
  Sponsored by the Illinois Business Roundtable and North Central Regional Educational Laboratory

Benchmarking Network   *www.benchmarkingnetwork.com*
  Sign up for a free newsletter.

Brainchild   *www.brainchild.com*
  Online assessments aligned with state standards in math and reading

Educational Testing Service, Policy Information Center   *www.ets.org/research*
  One-Third of a Nation: Rising Dropout Rates and Declining Opportunities is available for free download at this site.

Geneseo Migrant Center   *www.migrant.net*
  Information on migrant workers and school completion rates for teens of migrant families

Harvard Graduate School of Education: The Principals' Center   *www.gse.harvard.edu/ppe/principals*
  Information on the Harvard Principal Institutes

International Center for Leadership in Education   *www.daggett.com/about_matrix.html*
  To learn about the curriculum matrix developed by Dr. Willard Daggett and his associates and alignment to your state standards

Malcolm Baldrige National Quality Award Program   *www.baldrige.nist.gov*
  To obtain a free copy of the Education Criteria Booklet   *www.baldrige.nist.gov*
  To obtain multiple copies of the criteria   www.asq.org

Minuteman Science and Technology Regional High School, Lexington, MA
www.minuteman.org
  This school was a pioneer in quality in education.

Office of Juvenile Justice & Delinquency Prevention   *ojjdp.ncjrs.org*
  For statistics and information

Pinellas County Public Schools, FL   *www.pinellas.k12.fl.us*
  District has used a Baldrige approach in a large school system to improve learning.

Southwest Educational Development Laboratory   *www.sedl.org/reading/rad*
  Information and reading assessments for pre-K–third grade in multiple languages

SurveyShare   *www.surveyshare.com/resources*
   For information about how to write surveys, survey templates that can be adapted for your use. Free membership.

U.S. Government Office of the Budget   *www.gpoaccess.gov/usbudget*
   For details about costs of welfare and other assistance programs

U.S. Department of Labor   *wdr.doleta.gov/SCANS*
   SCANS Skills

Index